Exploring the Range of Theology

Exploring the Range of Theology

THEODORE RUNYON

WIPF & STOCK · Eugene, Oregon

EXPLORING THE RANGE OF THEOLOGY

Copyright © 2012 Theodore Runyon. All rights reserved. Except for brief quotations in critical publications or reviews, no part of this book may be reproduced in any manner without prior written permission from the publisher. Write: Permissions, Wipf and Stock Publishers, 199 W. 8th Ave., Suite 3, Eugene, OR 97401.

Scripture quotations, unless otherwise indicated, are from the New Revised Standard Version of the Bible, copyright © 1989 by the Division of Christian Education of the National Council of the Churches of Christ in the USA. All rights reserved. Used by permission.

Scripture quotations marked RSV are from the Revised Standard Version of the Bible, copyright 1952 [2nd edition, 1971] by the Division of Christian Education of the National Council of the Churches of Christ in the United States of America. Used by permission. All rights reserved.

Scripture quotations marked KJV are from the King James or Authorized Version of the Bible.

Wipf & Stock
An Imprint of Wipf and Stock Publishers
199 W. 8th Ave., Suite 3
Eugene, OR 97401

www.wipfandstock.com

ISBN 13: 978-1-61097-066-2

Manufactured in the U.S.A.

To my wife, Cindy, a gift of grace and love

Contents

Acknowledgments / ix
Introduction / xi

PART I: Theology and Theologians
1 Competing Theological Models for God / 3
2 Introduction to Paul Tillich / 28
3 Paul Tillich, the Conservative Revolutionary / 41
4 Friedrich Gogarten: Consistent Twentieth-century Pioneer / 55
5 Parallels between Jürgen Moltmann and John Wesley / 71

PART II: Biblical Foundations for Theology
6 The Human Being as a Theological Animal: The Biblical Argument against Creationism / 91
7 Creation, Covenant, and Kingdom: The Human Condition in Biblical and Theological Perspective / 102
8 The Earth as the First Sacrament / 118
9 A Contemporary Understanding of the Sacraments / 125

PART III: Religious Experience
10 Orthopathy and Criteria for Religious Experience / 141
11 What the Spirit Is Saying to the Churches / 156
12 Testing the Spirits / 160

PART IV: What Can Wesleyan Theology Contribute Today?
13 The Wesleyan Distinctive: The New Creation / 173
14 Wesleyan Roots of Pastoral Care and Counseling / 188
15 German Pietism, Wesley, and English and American Protestantism / 201
16 Wesley and Liberation Theologies / 213

Acknowledgments

THIS BOOK COMES IN response to requests that have come from former students, now mostly pastors and teachers serving throughout the nation and world, to have access to my thoughts as they developed during a fifty-year teaching career. The best way to do this was to gather together articles and chapters contributed to books, some for the laity, some for pastors, and some for theologians.

Putting this together would not have been possible without my amazingly adept editor, Barbara Dick, my tech helper, John Peterson, my editor at Wipf and Stock, Christian Amondson, and my wife, Cindy, the expert proofreader. To all of them my profound thanks!

Theodore Runyon
Candler School of Theology
Emory University

Introduction

EVERY HUMAN BEING IS a theologian, as I demonstrate in chapter 6. We all have an explicit or implicit interest in theology, in the ultimate context in which we live and move and have our being. This interest needs to be aroused, encouraged and cultivated. Looking back over a career of teaching and theological reflection, I was surprised by the variety of subjects and practical issues I sought to address, hence the title, *Exploring the Range of Theology*. In the chapters that follow is a sampling of those subjects.

Theology is carried out for the sake of the church, not for its members only but for the sake of the larger world, to inform and clarify what Christian faith is all about. The first chapter, "Competing Theological Models for God," seeks to do just that, to show what is distinctive in the Hebrew-Christian heritage and to show what is shared with other religions in a pluralistic world.

My own doctoral dissertation was written at the University of Göttingen on Paul Tillich, and so it is not surprising that he has continued to influence my thinking in spite of my criticisms in chapter 1. Friedrich Gogarten, although less well known in this country, was one of the founders with Karl Barth of dialectical theology, known in this country as neo-orthodoxy, and one of the pioneers, with Dietrich Bonhoeffer, of the theology of secularity. After he received invitations to lecture in this country, he engaged me to converse with him weekly in English on theological topics he anticipated he would need to cover. Jürgen Moltmann has been a more recent dialogue partner, and I was impressed by how many of his concerns parallel the concerns of John Wesley, the founder of Methodism, two centuries earlier.

One of the challenges Christianity faces is its relation to the natural sciences and especially to theories of evolution. In chapter 6 I show there is precedent in Scripture for taking seriously the "science" of its time. Taking science seriously, however, does not mean neglecting Christianity's insights into the basic human condition, found not just in the Genesis stories of creation and fall, but anticipating the kingdom of God that was so central to Jesus' own message. His message was rooted in the covenant with God as portrayed in the Hebrew Scriptures. Jesus brings that covenant into the present and links it to the power of the kingdom where it can shape our future.

The sacraments are central to Christian worship, but often what they imply for the world in which we live is not obvious. If we understand the earth itself is the very first sacrament, the material means used by God to bind humanity to the Creator and the Creator to humanity—in the words of Genesis 2, to "till it and keep it"—then our care of the earth becomes of primary significance not just to honor this sacrament but for the future of humanity.

Because Karl Barth, the theological giant of the twentieth century, was reacting against Friedrich Schleiermacher, the chief figure of the nineteenth century, who saw religious experience as a legitimate route to the knowledge of God, Barth ruled out religious experience as too subjective and individualistic. His opposition was justified because he was fighting Nazism, which championed German experience and the Aryan race. With Nazism no longer a threat, it seems appropriate to raise again the question of religious experience because, if the reality of God is to get through to human beings, how can it happen apart from human experience? Yet there have to be criteria to set forth what is legitimate and what is not, and that is what chapter 10 attempts to do. The Spirit was the neglected member of the Trinity during the Barthian era, but the Spirit is what gives rise to faith. How this happens is what chapter 11 seeks to show, and chapter 12 explores the criteria for genuine faith.

The last four chapters spell out some of the unexpected benefits to be found by re-examining the heritage stemming from John Wesley. My intention is to point to contributions that will enrich ecumenical theology because Wesley has often been written off as important only as an eighteenth-century reformer of Anglicanism and founder of a movement that soon spread around the world. Yet when examined more closely, his theology expands Reformation insights in ways that can prove helpful to ecumenism in the future.

My contention throughout is that theology is an exciting discipline, whether pursued by the layperson or the theologian. But if you find yourself getting bogged down in theological terminology, do not hesitate, on the basis of the above overview, to press on to later chapters that to you sound more enticing.

Part I
Theology and Theologians

1

Competing Theological Models for God[1]

ORIGINALLY PRESENTED AT THE fourth Oxford Institute of Methodist Theological Studies at Lincoln College, Oxford University, 1969, which brought British and American faculties in theological education together around the theme, "The Living God."

In *The Act of Creation*, Arthur Koestler suggests that the creative imagination operates in science, art, and literature in ways that are not dissimilar. A frequent source of stimulation to the imagination in these disciplines, he says, arises from the tension produced by the comparison of two distinct and even contradictory conceptual frameworks or models, which cover the same general range of experience but express it in seemingly contrary manners. The tension introduced by such a "bisociation" presses toward resolution in a new synthesis or a whole achieved by reordering the old elements in a new configuration.[2]

Without guaranteeing that I shall be able to achieve either an adequate synthesis or a viable new configuration, if indeed one is desirable, I should like nonetheless to call attention to what seems to me to be a similar tension faced by the discipline of theology. In any attempt to arrive at new and more satisfying conceptual models for presenting the reality of God to our time, an internal contradiction that stems from the fact that we are the inheritors of not one but *two* models of the nature of

---

1. Originally published as "Conflicting Theological Models for God," in *The Living God*, ed. Dow Kirkpatrick (Nashville, Abingdon Press, 1971), 22–47. Used by permission of the estate of Dow Kirkpatrick.

2. Arthur Koestler, *The Act of Creation* (New York: Macmillan, 1964), 95–96, 229, 320.

divine reality must be recognized. Both models can claim considerable historical precedence, as we shall see. Both have served well in the past to illumine the Christian message. And both can justly claim adherents among those who stand in every shade of opinion along the contemporary theological spectrum. Yet they would appear to be almost mutually exclusive. And it is difficult to see how, if one is judged to be an adequate representation of the Christian message, the other would not by that very fact be rejected as a false and misleading rendering of the reality Christian thought seeks to explicate.

MODELS FOR GOD

The type of model for God that is by far the older and more universal, dating from the origins of religion itself, and that could therefore lay claim to the title of the religious model *per se*, can be described as *cosmic monism*. It views the divine as that which both empowers and comes to expression in the cosmos. The most universal of the primitive religions, animism, is perhaps the clearest example of this model. Animism is the belief that the world is permeated by spirits and powers, that nature is alive with divine *energeia* that can at times be friendly, at times hostile and threatening, to humanity's fragile existence. The cosmos is understood as constituting one overarching and divine whole within which everything has its being. The animist would find largely meaningless, therefore, modern distinctions between the sacred and the secular. How could one conceive of what "secular" means when one can scarcely conceive of a non-sacred world? Anything that is, exists because of the sacred energy that empowers it. Every act of normal life—hunting, fishing, fire-building, planting, and tending crops—takes place in a religious context and is assisted and validated by the proper gestures and formulas that please and appease the appropriate gods. Ancient man's "constant endeavor is to establish communion with the elemental powers."[3] What we term the secular world is able to exist only because of its participation in the indwelling spiritual presence.[4]

Needless to say, the world of the animist has cohesion. "Pluralism" is no problem, for the cosmos is a seamless garment that encompasses

---

3. G. Rachel Levy, *Religious Conceptions of the Stone Age* (New York: Harper, 1963), 214.

4. Mircea Eliade, *The Sacred and the Profane* (New York: Harper, 1959), 17.

all reality in one self-contained, spiritually completed monism. Nothing can be imagined as existing outside this cosmic womb. Even the gods have their existence within it, as is seen, for example, in a highly sophisticated version of the same basic pattern, Hinduism, where the gods usually are viewed as subordinate to the divine principle embodied in the cosmos itself. According to Hindu speculation, "311 billion years constitute the life cycle of Brahma [the highest god]. But even this duration does not exhaust time, for the gods are not eternal, and the cosmic creations and destructions succeed one another forever."[5] Only the cosmos itself is eternal, and its spiritual power provides the ultimate category beyond which nothing can be imagined.

A similar pattern emerged with the pre-Socratics in the West. Speculation was born of the desire, says G. Rachel Levy, to discover the one divine principle lying behind all nature, "the ever present and pervading dynamic force."[6] By isolating theoretically this divine principle of *animism* the pre-Socratic philosopher, Thales, "interpreted the world as a unified psycho-physical whole, governed ... by natural laws that man could hope to understand."[7] *Thus the very origins not only of philosophy but of science as well are to be found in the rationalization of the theological world view of animism.* And this was accomplished without fundamentally disrupting theological monism. Both disciplines appropriated largely without question the animistic assumptions about the nature of the unity of the world. Even Plato, in spite of his dialectical modifications, can be described by Mircea Eliade as "the outstanding philosopher of 'primitive mentality,' ... the thinker who succeeded in giving philosophical currency and validity to the modes of life and behavior of archaic humanity [through the means that] the spirituality of his age made available to him."[8] To be sure, Plato represents a formidable reworking of the monistic model. He emphasizes the transcendence of the divine ideas that lie behind the visible world, and thus introduces a distinction between reality as apprehended by the senses and reality as it actually is. Yet what really is, is in the final analysis but a more sophisticated and rationalized form of the spiritual power that animism knew to

---

5. Ibid., 108.
6. Levy, *Religious Conceptions of the Stone Age*, 301.
7. Henry B. Parkes, *Gods and Men* (New York: Alfred A. Knopf, 1959), 80.
8. Mircea Eliade, *Cosmos and History (The Myth of the Eternal Return)* (New York: Harper, 1959), 34–35.

be operative behind all appearances. Hence it would be difficult to claim that Plato broke with his religious past. Rather, he gave divine powers rational and therefore comprehensible form. He dissolved the mystery on one level while driving it deeper on another. Yet the final mystery is still conceived on the animistic-monistic model as a mystery that is coextensive with the being of the cosmos.

What is generally characterized as the Greek heritage in the West ought, therefore, to be recognized as part and parcel of a larger, more universal religious heritage that, even in the dialectical complexity of some of its developed forms, might be said to rest finally on the assumption that *the cosmos is God*. That is, divinity is the ultimate principle of the cosmos and is in the end inseparable from it.

THE HEBREW DIFFERENCE

At one point in the ancient world, however there was a variation in the otherwise almost universal pattern, a variation that would eventually prove to be of considerable significance, namely, the religion of the Hebrews. For the Hebrews provided an alternative model for describing the relation of the divine to the world. To be sure, there are indications that the remote origins of Hebrew faith may also lie in animism. And it is undeniable that animism in both its primitive and more developed forms was a constant temptation to the Hebrew peoples, especially after they settled in agricultural surroundings where identification with the local guarantors of fertility seemed a matter of economic necessity. Yet Israel's development away from whatever animism may have characterized the primeval origins of the Semitic peoples was distinctive enough to constitute a quite new type, a fundamentally different understanding of the relation of the sacred to the cosmos. In the prevailing Hebrew notion of God, as reflected in those literary sources that have been preserved, the ultimate sacred authority has an existence conceived as independent from the world. The relation is that of Creator to creation. Were this to be expressed ontologically, reality for the Hebrew would be finally dual: the reality of the world is different from the reality of the Creator. Yet such a definition would be misleading, for it is not that the Hebrews think in degrees of reality; they do not speculate about a hierarchy of being. For them the world and humanity are no less "real" than is God; they do not suffer from a deficient mode of existence.[9] The term "dual" must be restricted therefore to designating the discreteness between God's existence and that of the universe, a discreteness that does not exclude the possibility of unity but understands any such unity on the model of interpersonal relations in which the meeting of minds and wills does not mean the dissolving of independent personhood but rather its preservation and enhancement. It is especially important that Hebrew "duality" not be confused with Persian "dualism" or the mind-versus-matter dualism of idealism. The latter refer to conflicts that take place essentially within the cosmos between competing cosmic forces and thus represent variations on the basic monistic model.

The Hebrew break with cosmic monism was one of those great "leaps in being," as Eric Voegelin terms it, which was to portend a whole new direction of development in the history of humankind.[10] Hitherto unimaginable possibilities were opened up. By distinguishing God from the world the Hebrews prepared the way for the "secularization" of the animistic cosmos. Holiness was understood to reside in God alone, and any human attempts to gain control over this holiness by fashioning earthly images of it were forbidden. Nothing in the creation was to be allowed to supplant the claim upon human life that belonged to Yahweh alone. Devotion to cosmic spirits was prohibited: "Behold, they are all a delusion; their works are nothing; their molten images are empty wind" (Isa 41:29 RSV). This is not to deny that the god of the Hebrews, Yahweh, functioned as a nature god insuring the seasons and the crops, the fertility, and the rain. Nevertheless Yahweh remained distinct from the world whose existence God undergirded and guaranteed. No immanental principle of divinity was necessary to enable the world to operate, and humans were freed from the necessity of regarding the world as a divine body. Whereas previously humans had understood themselves and their society as an integral part of the cosmos and constructed the patterns of life and institutions in such a way as to imitate the sacred law of the cosmos, they now understood themselves as standing over against the world by virtue of their relationship to the Creator. Thus "man is not simply a piece of nature, however firmly interwoven his life is in the

---

9. Cf. Edmond Cherbonnier, "Is there a Biblical Metaphysic?" *Theology Today*, January 1959, 459.

10. Cf. Eric Voegelin, *Israel and Revelation*, vol. I of *Order and History* (Baton Rouge: Louisiana State University Press, 1956), 10, 50, 123.

order of nature," but is called, as it were, to the side of the Creator and confronts the rest of creation from that vantage point.[11] The discreteness of God from the world was therefore a chief means by which humans gained independence from a religiously venerated cosmos to which their religious consciousness had previously been held in bondage.

How did this variant in the religious consciousness arise that was destined to open up such significant possibilities by providing an alternative model for the relationship of the divine to humanity and the world? Those who stand in the Hebrew-Christian tradition will be inclined to speak of "revelation" and "grace," but an empirically oriented age seeks a translation of theological explanations into a more public language. Is such a translation possible, and if so, can it do justice to the distinctive Hebrew-Christian contribution? It is to questions such as these that we now must turn.

Most of the peoples with whom the Hebrews came into contact during their crucial formative period had already developed agricultural economies. Animistic religion served within such communities not only as a way of coming to terms with the forces of nature upon which the survival of the community depended but as a means of giving a people identity with reference to the sacred place they occupied in the cosmos. The Hebrews, however, at the stage in which they came to their sense of tribal identity, were a nomadic people. As nomads who occupied no one place in terms of which they could identify themselves but were constantly on the move, an alternative source of group consciousness had to be found. Nature was not so much their problem, but history. That is, if one natural environment did not suit them they could shift to another; yet they sought some kind of continuity in the midst of change, and this they found not in the recurrent cycles of nature but in the tribal memory of the unique events of their origins and development. The reality of Yahweh was to be seen through acts in the life of the people. The god of the nomads was also a nomad who was tied to no place but moved with this people, sharing their destiny with them while at the same time transcending it. To be sure, the Hebrews also had their sacred places, but these derived their authority not because they epitomized the spiritual powers of the cosmos but because they were where hierophanies of Yahweh had occurred, encounters that had made a difference to Israel's history and were remembered as occasions of judgment and faithfulness.

---

11. Walter Eichrodt, *Man in the Old Testament* (London: SCM Press, 1951), 30.

Needless to say, the Hebrews' historical consciousness was not the same as that of modern historians . Undoubtedly tribal memories as a genre were closer to nature myths than to present-day historiography. Yet they represent a significant enough departure from the cosmologically oriented religious setting to constitute a distinct type.

It could be argued, of course, that the God of the Hebrews is just a case of arrested religious development. Creation myths are legion in the world's religions, and usually the creation is achieved by a god or gods who must be in some sense higher than that which they create.[12] In the continuing religious evolution, however, creator gods and high gods are recognized to be an anthropomorphizing of the creative energy that is manifested in all that is. Hence most of the "higher" religions have followed the same path taken by Greek philosophy and identified the divine not with one creator figure but with the power of being and creativity as such. The high god, Yahweh, developed in a cultural backwater, however, where this process of demythologizing did not prove necessary. Yahweh was able to continue as a kind of evolutionary lag, a case of religious and philosophical underdevelopment.

Granting this interpretation for the sake of argument, is it not possible nevertheless to show, using the insights of evolutionary thinking, that the Hebrew understanding of the divine, precisely because it did not go through a process of abstraction that reduced it to identity with a sophisticated version of cosmic monism, was in a position to make a unique contribution to human development? If the Hebrew faith did not complete the evolution of the cosmological religions but remained stranded on an evolutionary plateau, it may nonetheless have proved to be that model of the divine that was "fittest" for a new complex of circumstances, and thus a new evolutionary situation. As Teilhard de Chardin observes, evolution is not a smooth causal process in which that which was given in the beginning simply unfolds in one continuous and uninterrupted line of development. Rather it moves along by fits and starts through a process of testing, trying, shifting, and launching out only to be rebuffed and forced to begin all over again, a process that Teilhard calls *groping*.[13] Through a series of false starts a corridor is finally found through which the process can move onward to greater

---

12. Cf. Eliade, *The Sacred and the Profane*, 165; Parkes, *Gods and Men*, 158.

13. Teilhard de Chardin, *The Phenomenon of Man* (London: Collins; Fontana, 1959), 121.

"complexification." The historical development of evolution is therefore full of blind alleys, paths that were right for a time but were beset by a combination of circumstances that could not be mastered, at which point the "leading edge" of evolution shifted to another seemingly more primitive phylum better able to adapt to the new configuration and survive.

Could not the Hebrew development, especially with the advent of Christianity grafted onto the Hebrew root, be seen as just such a shift in the evolutionary process? More urbane thinking, attempting to reduce whimsical and unpredictable gods to some kind of order, realized that the gods were only less dependable manifestations of an ultimately dependable cosmic order, an order immediately knowable by the mind because human reason participates in the divine logos that underlies the order of nature. As long as the vision of the cosmos as a stable and dependable order remained, demythologized animism provided an admirably suitable model that drew all reality into a rationally comprehensible whole. However, when political events began to dissolve the unity of the Greek world and the chaos around the edges penetrated nearer and nearer the center, the tensions introduced into the monistic model became more and more insufferable. Deeper probing into the nature of being brought not greater assurance of order but, reflecting the Hellenistic mood, the suspicion that a fundamental ambiguity underlies everything. A split within monism became inevitable if thought were to reflect reality as it was experienced. Thus the classic dialectic between mind or spirit and matter became radicalized into a split between good and evil, thereby abandoning the classic Greek assumption concerning the basic perfection, beauty, and goodness of the cosmos. Religion became a means of rising above the ambiguity in a temporary ecstasy that was the foretaste of an ultimate translation that spelled release from this aeon and a return to the less ambiguous center of the cosmos. In a time of breakdown, therefore, the cosmic-monistic model was not able to offer the vision of unity that it initially promised.

THE CHRISTIAN CONTRIBUTION

Into this situation came an unlikely combination the more primitive Hebrew God, who was distinct from the cosmos though ultimately Lord over it, and his Son, who was the means by which the victory over the evil rulers of this present age was to be achieved. In Christ the world was invaded by the life-affirming, transcendent Yahweh, who claimed the world again for God's own, achieving a major preliminary breakthrough in the resurrection, which served as a sign of the redemption to be accomplished in the whole creation. By coming from "outside" this God was able to represent a new possibility over against existence as it was given, an Archimedean point from which the world could be seen from a new perspective. At the same time, through the Son, God was involved in the world, struggling with the powers of disorder to actualize lordship and in the end overcome chaos through the promise of the kingdom of God. Thus, while not denying the evil of the present age, the Hebrew-Christian model was able to place the problematic of human existence on a historical plane and give assurance that the present confusion would be overcome in a historical process, the consummation of which already could be participated in through faith and hope. By introducing a model inconceivable within the monistic framework, the Hebrew-Christian combination opened up a developmental vision of the world, thus enabling thought and belief to move around the impasse, which at that point had blocked the further advance of the animistic, cosmological model. Hence the process continued with the Hebrew-Christian branch now serving as the "evolutionary axis."

MODIFICATIONS

Within a brief span of years the Greek tradition reasserted itself, however, for its monistic vision of the cosmos retained its appeal for those minds seeking the perfection of one all-encompassing whole. Greek thought was grafted onto the Hebrew-Christian stem, producing a new plant that for several centuries bore fruit abundant and varied enough to meet the needs of what became known as "Christendom." The Hebrew-Christian historical vision was to a certain extent modified in the direction of cosmological oneness by sacramentalism and the church's preempting of the eschatological kingdom. At the same time, however, the animistic model was fundamentally abrogated by the transcendent God who never could be entirely equated with the creation, though repeated attempts were made to identify God with being. Hence the two models lived together in a somewhat uneasy truce, the tension between them the source of most of the metaphysical embarrassments and semantic difficulties of the Middle Ages. The reintroduction of Aristotelian thought into the West threatened to intensify this internal tension until Thomas Aquinas, in a superb feat of synthetic reason, superimposed the Hebrew-Christian, Creator-creature model on Aristotle's dialectical monism by identifying the Aristotelian essentially internal causal agent with the transcendent God who operates in the process from without.

Perhaps the most extraordinary triumph of self-contradiction, among many such triumphs in the history of human thought, was the fusion of this conception of a self-absorbed and self-contained Perfection—of that Eternal Introvert who is the God of Aristotle—at once with the Jewish conception of a temporal Creator and busy interposing Power making for righteousness through the hurly-burly of history, and with primitive Christianity's conception of a God whose essence is forthgoing love and who shares in all the griefs of God's creatures.[14]

Aristotelianism proved in time to be fate-laden for the Christian model, for it reintroduced the classic Greek optimism regarding the knowability of the world and its laws (i.e., the demythologized animistic gods), which not only captured the imagination with its aesthetically satisfying monistic perfection but soon demonstrated its efficiency in unlocking the secrets of the natural world. Defections from the Hebrew model were not so much intentional as a result of the obvious success to be gained by employing its alternative. To be sure, there were continuing efforts to combine the two traditions, and John Locke's deistic solution was to serve for more than a century. Yet, as the perfectly balanced cosmic watch loomed ever larger in importance, the watchmaker receded into the background where eventually, the victim of the law of parsimony, he was no longer needed. Laplace's reply to the question concerning where God was to be found in his system illustrates the end of the deist road: "I have no need for that hypothesis."

Absolutizing the universe and its law carried with it its own difficulties however. If order is completely self-contained and mechanistic, what of human freedom? The Romanticists protested as vigorously as they could against the foreclosure of human creativity and freedom implicit in the mechanistic scheme of things. By this time, however, the Creator had been so thoroughly identified with the cosmic watchmaker that the Romanticists' protests had to be directed against the Creator as well as the world. Moreover, they were themselves so fully under the spell of the monistic model that they assumed that the only way out of the locked-in world of the rationalists was by plunging themselves into the nonrational

---

14. Arthur O. Lovejoy, *The Great Chain of Being* (New York: Harper, 1936), 157.

Competing Theological Models for God 13

vitalities of nature, thus seeking to prove that the monistic world has its chaotic and free aspects as well as its rational order. Prometheus was their hero because he had opposed the order of the gods in the name of human self-realization.[15] Dissatisfied with mechanistic monism, the Romanticists were nevertheless unable to appropriate the possibilities for freedom and creativity implicit in duality because the Christian God had become identified with a deterministic scheme of things.

THE RISE OF EVOLUTIONARY THINKING

Rationalistic determinism was to fall, however, with the rise in the nineteenth century of evolutionary thinking, which can be traced in part at least to the recovery of Christian impulses regarding the importance of history in the process of salvation, notably in Hegel. What Hegel really succeeded in doing, however, was to introduce a dynamic element into monism. By injecting historical tension into being he reinterpreted the divine cosmos as a divine history. What may yet prove to be a more radical undermining of determinism came, however, from another side, from the research of one who began as an apologist for an enlightened deism. The impact of Charles Darwin's thinking on the traditional Christian worldview is well known; what is less obvious is the impact of evolutionary thought on deterministic monism, which may in the end prove at least as far-reaching.

Darwin was one of those theological students who, after completing his degree, opted for a specialized ministry. He had intended to settle down somewhere as a country curate. During his studies, however, he was influenced by the English clergyman William Paley, whose *Natural Theology* fascinated him. Paley was by avocation an anatomist of no mean

---

15. A good indication of the very real changes effected by the Hebrew-Christian orientation—in spite of the Romanticists' unawareness of it—can be seen in the change in the response of theatergoers and readers to this classic Greek tragic figure. Prometheus also aroused sympathy from his Greek viewers, who were not always inclined to accept without protest the actions of capricious gods. But they never doubted that Prometheus's punishment was deserved, for his sin was against the order of things. In his hubris he had overstepped his bounds, and punishment was the only way to redress the balance within the cosmos. The Romanticists, however, not only applauded Prometheus's deed but thought his punishment unjust. Without realizing it, they presupposed a transcendent Creator independent enough from the cosmos and its law to be able to redress the balance without having to accomplish it through this-worldly expiation. Cf. Prosser Hall Frye, *Romance and Tragedy* (Lincoln: University of Nebraska Press, 1961), 133.

stature, who used his meticulous research into the intricacies of nature (e.g., his study of the human eye) to reinforce his theological points, seeking to show that an empirical investigation of the natural world would inevitably demonstrate the beneficence of an almighty Creator. Extending his studies to ecology (the adaptation of organisms to their environment), Paley argued that the immense variety of organisms that inhabit a given environment can only be explained by reference to a beneficent Creator who by this differentiation made it possible for more creatures to exist side by side in a limited space. "If all animals coveted the same element, shelter or food, it is evident how much fewer could be supplied and accommodated than what at present live conveniently together. . . . What one rejects another delights in."[16] Paley assumed, of course, that this variety had existed since the original creation and had been maintained by seminal identity. The complexity of organisms and their social interrelatedness thus point to the biblical God of order and love who wills the good of all creatures.

After his theological examinations in 1831 young Darwin, who had also pursued the avocation of naturalist, was persuaded to join an expedition setting out on the good ship "Beagle" to study the western coast of South America. As the ship's naturalist he would have an excellent opportunity to gather further evidence to support Paley's claims. His studies of fossils and living species up and down the coast of South America and in the Galapagos Islands soon convinced Darwin, however, that there were basic fallacies in Paley's notion of special creation, and he returned to England with his deist faith badly shaken. He had gone out assuming a supernaturally established order in the Aristotelian, Thomistic, Lockean pattern, and had found instead an immense variety of seemingly random variations. A different model had to be found to make sense out of the data. The model that finally emerged, under the influence of the geologist Lyell, and Malthus' studies on populations, was what Darwin termed "natural selection," which took into account random variations and the survival of the "fittest" of these variations.

The effect of Darwin's theory of natural selection was to eliminate the whole traditional notion of divine causality and teleology. That happy combination of a supernatural Director of an Aristotelian world that

---

16. William Paley, *Natural Theology: The Works of William Paley* (London, 1824), 485. Quoted in Günter Altner, *Charles Darwin und Ernst Haecke*, Theologische Studien, No. 85 (Zürich: EVZ-Verlag, 1966), 22.

St. Thomas put together had finally come unglued. Not a benevolent, purposeful Providence but a blind, uncaring Chance ruled the world, or so it seemed to many in the latter half of the nineteenth century.

If Darwinism proved traumatic for deist theology, however, it was at least partially because it undermined the monistic-deterministic half of the assumptions of that theology. The notion of a closed, mechanistic universe, so prominent in the classical period of Western scientific development, came under attack with repercussions that continue to the present. The ideas of indeterminacy and chance opened up new possibilities for cognitive models. Indeed, much of the scientific progress made in the last century would have been impossible had not the notion of a rounded-off, complete, and perfected universe, deriving ultimately from cosmic monism, been called into question. As yet, however, there is little recognition that what is involved is basically a theological crisis in science itself, and scientists still continue for the most part to operate with what is essentially an animistic theological assumption, viz., that the universe is self-contained and includes within itself all the reality there is. This theological dogma is the more pervasive because it is so hidden and unrecognized. It is to be found, for instance, in the common assumption that in spite of all the irregularities in the world as it is experienced there is a final order that underlies everything and that all "chance" occurrences will ultimately be explained as consistent with this larger order.

Thus the average scientist finds it as difficult as did his or her animist ancestors to imagine any reality not reducible to cosmic order. When the scientist turns to the theologian for some help in adjusting private beliefs (the realm to which an otherwise irrelevant religion is relegated) he or she is most often searching for a god who will function within the framework of a basic, unquestioned theological assumption. Yet scientific working assumptions are likely to be much less deistic and much more probabilistic and open-ended, and do not actually require—indeed, are in conflict with—the kind of God the scientist assumes is needed. Our attempts to deal with this situation apologetically are not made easier by the fact that practically all the technical language of theology has been mediated to us by the Greek tradition and comes already tainted with monist presuppositions. This language is understandably hard put to describe the reality of a God who is not a dimension of the cosmos. The alternative available to us, biblical language, may be more satisfactory in terms of "the existence it enshrines,"[17] but it is so archaic as to make reception of its meaning more a matter of mystical intuition and the gift of the Holy Spirit than rational formulation and logical discourse. Thus at the crucial point we are left practically speechless.

THE THEOLOGIANS RESPOND

How have theologians sought to move around the impasse posed by the two contradictory models that form the inheritance of the West? We turn briefly to three contemporary figures, each of whom has made a concerted effort to resolve the problem: Paul Tillich, Pierre Teilhard de Chardin, and Jürgen Moltmann.

Perhaps more than any other theologian of our time, Paul Tillich has sought to deal with the issues posed by the two models. "The problem of the two absolutes," he calls it in an essay entitled, "The Two Types of Philosophy of Religion," claiming that Western thought was placed in an intolerable situation when final categories emerged from two directions in the ancient world.

> In two developments Western humanity has overcome its age-old bondage under the "powers." . . . These "powers" were conquered *religiously* by their subjection to one of them, the god of the prophets of Israel; his quality as the god of justice enabled him to become the universal God. The "powers" were conquered *philosophically* by their subjection to a principle more real than all of them [namely, being]; its quality as embracing all qualities enabled it to become the universal principle. . . . The problem created by the subjection of the "powers" to the absolute God and to the absolute principle is "*the problem of the two Absolutes.*" How are they related to each other? . . . *Deus* and *esse* cannot be unconnected![18]

The solution, suggests Tillich, is to be found in the simple statement in which the two absolutes are joined: "God *is*." For the question of the two

---

17. New Testament scholar, Rudolf Bultmann, in his precedent-setting *Keryma and Myth* (London: S.P.C.K., 1953), sought to interpret the New Testament with existentialist analysis to disclose the understanding of life found there.

18. Paul Tillich, *Theology of Culture* (New York: Oxford University Press, 1959), 11–12.

absolutes can be answered only by identifying that fundamental awareness out of which the questions of both being and God arise, that "immediate awareness of the Unconditioned" that is implicit whenever being is sought as the answer to the problem of nonbeing, or whenever the term "God" presupposes that essential power that undergirds everything that is.[19] "God is being-itself" becomes the basic formula of Tillich's philosophical theology by means of which he hopes to overcome the fatal rifts in Western thought and bring values into one coherent whole through a correlation based on a recognition of the essential identity of all cultural manifestations in one ultimate source of meaning and being.

Tillich's remarkable attempt to achieve a mutually enriching and empowering synthesis of the two traditions by identifying their mutual source is one of the great theological contributions of our time. If the analysis of the origins of the notion of being given above is accurate, however, the very concept of being has its home in the rationalization of animism. Being is the animating principle of the cosmos without which nothing that is can exist. When this cosmological divine principle is merged with Yahweh, what is the result? Rather than resolving the problem of the two absolutes, has not Tillich in effect undone the Hebrew contribution and dissolved the Hebrew model of the God who transcends the cosmos? We are left with only one Absolute, to be sure, but it is the absolute cosmos. The cosmic principle is the final reality from which there is no appeal, because in a monism nothing can transcend the ultimate category. Of course it should be noted that Tillich's ontological absolute is no "dead identity." There is movement within being, as being separates itself from itself (in the Son) and reunites with itself (in the Spirit). But this activity all takes place—as in the case of Hegel—within the monistic model. Thus, in spite of the stress that Tillich lays upon the category of "history" in his system, the historically accidental is judged to be meaningful only insofar as it embodies and expresses the awareness of being, the ontological depth, which is the religious dimension of all historical experience. The question may legitimately be raised, therefore, as to whether Tillich's approach is capable of doing justice to history in its sheer happening without first reducing it to ontological categories on the basis of which it can be "interpreted." Is a method that must reduce history to being in order to deal with it able to cope with the "random variations" that constitute history as evolutionists understand

---

19. Ibid., 25.

it? If not, we may be forced to look elsewhere for the answer to the problem of the two absolutes.

One theologian who takes evolution seriously is Pierre Teilhard de Chardin, the French paleontologist-theologian. He has sought to construct a total view of the world that would take into account the absence of causality in the traditional Aristotelian sense in the evolutionary process. Teilhard's "vision" of the cosmos is that of a giant organism that is developing in a process of "complexification" toward the fullest possible realization of its potentialities. Just at the point of complete realization, however, there will be a breakthrough to the *Pleroma*, to the transcendent realm in which God will be all in all and the "divine milieu" will be complete.[20]

Teilhard resists easy classification. Much of his language would seem to place him squarely in the animistic tradition. God would appear to be identical with a combination of "tangential energy," that pushes from behind, and "radial energy" that guides the process of development by magnetically attracting toward the eschaton. The world itself is being transformed into the divine body of Christ in a pattern that gains its inspiration from the doctrine of transubstantiation.[21] Yet Teilhard protests against those who would label him a pantheist and insists that he is merely spelling out what was implicit in St. Paul's description of that eschatological fulfillment in which God would become *ta panta en pasin* ("all in all" [1 Cor 15:28]). "Classical pantheism," says Teilhard, "seduces us by its vistas of perfect universal union," which could result only in fusion and unconsciousness. In that case the end of the evolutionary process would be an absorption of the world by God.

> Our God, on the contrary, pushes to its furthest possible limit the differentiation among the creatures he concentrates within himself. At the peak of their adherence to him, the elect also discover in him the consummation of their individual fulfillment. Christianity alone therefore saves . . . the essential aspiration of all mysticism: to be united (that is, to become the other) *while remaining oneself*. More attractive than any world-gods, whose eternal seduction it embraces, transcends and purifies, . . . our divine milieu is at the antipodes of false pantheism. The Christian

---

20. Teilhard de Chardin, *The Phenomenon of Man*, 322.
21. Teilhard de Chardin, *Le Milieu Divin* (London: Collins; Fontana edition, 1960), 123.

can plunge himself into it wholeheartedly without the risk of finding himself one day a monist.[22]

In spite of these claims, however, Teilhard could still be accused of an internally differentiated monism similar to that of Tillich were it not that his espousal of evolution throws the whole process onto the plane of historical accident. He rejects the *illuminati*, the mystical visionaries who in their eagerness to stress the divine substance do away with the "exacting but salutary reality" of historical accidents, imagining divine action without relation to the "systems of material order in their complex inter-relationships."[23] As a result divine action must be seen by the *illuminati* as supernatural intervention in the natural order that essentially destroys the latter and leaves as residue only the suprahistorical reality clothed in the disguise of what are now essentially disconnected historical events. Teilhard wants to insist that it is precisely in the historical accidents that the world is moving toward God, so that the Christian is not under obligation to abandon the perceptible, accidental, and material but rather to "prolong" them along their "common axis, which links them to God."[24] In this way the possibility of a holistic view is opened up for the Christian, without stopping the normal historical process. The cosmos is unified, but this unity will be fully actualized only at the final consummation.

The link between the historical accidents of the process and the final consummation is what Teilhard calls *radial* energy, which operates in combination with and contrast to the other key force in the evolutionary process, *tangential* energy. The latter is that type of energy familiar to us. It is empirically measurable and is subject to the second law of thermodynamics, entropy. It will continue until finally expended. This is the main drive that is operative in the expansion of the universe. Teilhard presupposes the "big bang" theory of cosmic genesis in the evolutionary process on this planet. The process appears to operate randomly, pushing forward until it meets resistance and then veering in the direction of least resistance. Tangential energy pushes the evolutionary process from behind, as it were. However, the other force, radial energy, operates in a quite different way. It attracts the evolutionary process toward

---

22. Ibid., 116.
23. Ibid., 117.
24. Ibid., 119.

a goal that still lies ahead of the process, toward the Omega Point, the consummation. It is not subject to entropy since its source of power is the magnetic attraction of a goal toward which it is drawing ever nearer. If tangential energy operates in the empirically observable, the without, radial energy operates in the within of things on every level from the inner mystery of the atom to the mind of man, where the evolutionary process achieves consciousness of itself. Radial energy is not discernible by empirical investigation, and its results can be seen only as one looks backward over the history of evolution. Only then does it become apparent that the process has an overall direction, a purposefulness given to it not by an original cause, which in the deist sense predetermined the course of events, but by the goal, the *telos*, which is luring it on. In past developments of the phylum Teilhard can discern a pattern that has given rise to humanity as the leading edge of the evolutionary movement. Following the trajectory of this pattern into the future he is able to predict the developments that still lie ahead, though the path toward the future is not predetermined and the process itself will appear to be completely random. Nevertheless the goal is fixed and will continue to exercise its attracting power on the unfolding history of evolution until, by whatever devious routes are necessary due to the accidents of history, the telos will finally be reached.

While undeniably under the influence of the monistic model, Teilhard nevertheless transcends it, at least preliminarily, in his eschatology. Here a comparison with Tillich is instructive. Eschatology for Tillich is the "prolongation into the absolute" of those realities in history that have most profoundly exhibited ontological power.[25] The "eschatological imagination" projects an ideal age that is the absolute form of those moments of ontological awareness that occur only fragmentarily in history. Thus the eschaton is not part of the historical process as such but rather the rudimentary ontological consciousness cast into the form of a historical myth by the imagination. The eschatological horizon of being is a projection forward from the ontological center, and is therefore, in the first instance, not so much concerned with an actual evolutionary process as it is the expression of an ontological fundament. But that expression will only actualize what is already given. The radically new is not possible. The "end" of history can only be the realization on

---

25. Tillich, "Redemption in Cosmic and Social History," *The Journal of Religious Thought*, vol. III, No. 1 (Autumn-Winter, 1946), 19.

the historical plane of that which already *is* ontologically. Thus Tillich's system is locked in the confines of pre-Darwinian German Idealism and is not able to treat the historically new and accidental with seriousness if it cannot be reduced to ontologically essential elements.

Teilhard, on the other hand, sees each new stage in the evolutionary movement as a realization of the unique on the way to the radically new, the Omega Point. The cosmos is an unfinished organism that will remain incomplete until it is brought to fulfillment through historical development. The real lies not in the depths, therefore, but in the future.

There is one aspect of Teilhard's thought, however, which causes his scientifically oriented readers grave difficulties, and that is the seemingly ideological element that is introduced by his concept of radial energy. For Teilhard it is not too much to say that this concept illuminates the whole; it is the means by which he is able to give the evolutionary movement theological significance. Yet his detractors find it an unnecessary addition backed by no empirical evidence and no demonstrable advantages as a scientific model. A question could be raised from the side of the Hebrew orientation as well, for radial energy would appear to be the point at which, for Teilhard, the divine and the cosmos are identical, a fact that has subjected him continuously to charges of pantheism. The charge is partially false, because radial energy is not simply identical with the world but is rather that force that is at work "within," not satisfied with the world in its present form but transforming it in the light of its telos.[26] But the charge is also partially true in that the eschatological expectation is for the universalization of the within in a Christic diaphany in which God becomes "all in all." Teilhard can defend himself by insisting that at that point the world will have been taken up into God and completely spiritualized so that God will be all there is. Such a vision may save him from the technical charge of pantheism, but it only serves to reinforce the suspicion that his ultimate eschatological model is monistic. Hence, like Tillich, Teilhard is unable to offer us an orientation that finally does justice to the biblical distinction between God and the world, a distinction that the eschaton serves not to dissolve but to reestablish and fulfill.

Jürgen Moltmann is a third contemporary thinker who has focused attention on the competition between the traditions that have informed the life and thought of the West. He draws a contrast between

---

26. Cf. Teilard de Chardin, *Le Milieu Divin*, 152.

"epiphany religions," on the one hand and "faith rooted in promise" (*Verheissungsglaube*), on the other. The former is similar to what I have termed the animistic-monistic tradition, while the latter designates the Hebraic type of faith. Epiphany religions are preoccupied with repeating the sacred past through cultic celebrations of the appearances of the gods in order that the gods might again draw near and effect the renewal of the cosmos. Epiphanic humanity lives as closely as possible to the gods in order to avoid the threats of historical meaninglessness by dwelling in that which is eternal.[27] The appearance of Yahweh to the Hebrews, however, is "linked up with the uttering of a word of divine promise," a promise that points to a future fulfillment in time and space. Israelite faith is thus not so much an escape from history but a turning toward future history as the place where the problems of history will be resolved by means of history.

Moltmann seeks to do theology from an eschatological perspective, so that eschatology is not just an appendix to an otherwise complete system but a perspective that qualifies the whole enterprise. In his analysis of various theological alternatives Moltmann casts his net wide and manages to catch most of the big theological fish playing in epiphany territory, though many of them (Karl Barth, for instance) would heartily resent his classification. Relying on Ernst Bloch's analysis of the phenomenon of hope and his "ontology of the not yet," Moltmann attempts to show how both Barthian theological positivism and Bultmannian existentialism have abandoned the dimension of future fulfillment in favor of a type of immediacy that he claims parallels that of the epiphany religions. In opting for Bloch, Moltmann has chosen a philosophical orientation that opens up the possibility of appropriating evolutionary thinking, but without the necessity of an ideological concept, such as radial energy, to achieve some ontological continuity between traditional theological notions of causation and the random variations in evolution. The connection between the present and the future is in terms not of a cryptic principle at work in the cosmos but simply the drive toward realization in the cosmos itself, that is, Teilhard's tangential energy. The evolutionary process is essentially goal-less; it cannot anticipate the future but can only react to the possibilities available in the present situation, moving in the direction of least resistance. Nevertheless, evolution is a constant transcending of what has been, a constant adjusting to new

---

27. Cf. Jürgen Moltmann, *Theology of Hope* (London: SCM Press, 1967), 98.

environmental conditions, in terms of which various aspects of single or societal organisms can come into their own, aspects that were previously only tendencies. Moltmann describes the process in this way:

> The stringency of the causality of natural science is renounced and the transition in historic movements is described not as a transition from *causa* to *effectus*, but from possibility to reality. What stands between possibilities and realized realities is not a causal necessity, but tendency, impulse, inclination, trend, specific leanings toward something, which can become real in certain historic constellations.[28]

This means that the evolutionary process is itself open to being influenced. Indeed, what we experience today is no longer pure natural evolution but "cultural evolution," the selection and encouragement by human beings of those tendencies and trends that we deem advantageous to our own enhancement. The meaning and purpose in the evolutionary process is therefore introduced by humanity, which is not to say that meaning and purpose are completely subjective, for both humanity and our decisions are part of the "objective" process, responding to tendencies and making possible new trends. We are the place where the process transcends itself and becomes aware of itself.[29] Humanity is therefore that creature who can hope and plan, who can transcend the present movement in the awareness of new possibilities that are never fully realized. We remain dissatisfied with every present achieved by the process and push on toward the new.

Accepting Bloch's analysis and description of humanity as that creature who hopes, Moltmann is nevertheless concerned that hope, if it is to provide the genuinely teleological element in the historical process, be not just the transcending of every given—which evolution would accomplish in any case—but directional. This is the point at which he must modify Bloch's general phenomenology of hope with the specific content of the Christian promise. Christianity gives humanity not just self-transcendence—which after all would be meaningless were it infinite but undirected—but a promise, not just hope in hope but a goal in terms of which the process can be evaluated and judged at any stage

---

28. Ibid., 243.

29. Cf. Julian Huxley's definition of humanity as "evolution become conscious of itself," Teilhard de Chardin, *The Phenomenon of Man*, 243.

along the way. Eschatological hope overcomes historical relativism by means of a destination to be reached through the historical process.

Is this promised kingdom not just as mythological and ideological as Teilhard's radial energy? Is it not an "illusion"? To be sure, it is not subject to empirical verification because presently it does not exist; yet it cannot be classified as illusory because it functions as a self-fulfilling prophecy, having its effect upon the shape that the future takes. If humanity indeed operates as the director of *cultural* evolution, then hopes, aspirations, plans are the agencies that select out for cultivation those tendencies that are congruent with our desires for the future. Far from being illusory, hope is the greater "realism," for it alone "takes seriously the possibilities with which all reality is fraught. It does not take things as they happen to stand or to lie, but as progressing, moving things with possibilities of change."[30] Hope makes possible that which shall be!

In his theology of hope Moltmann has provided a concept of God that at least partially satisfies the demands of evolutionary thinking without merging God in some way with creation. The reality of the world and of history are not abrogated by being reduced to an ontological essence, like Tillich, or by being deified, like Teilhard. Instead, Moltmann grants the world the independence it has as creation, without the necessity to transform it finally into something other than world. At the same time, the reality of God is not neglected but conceptualized in analogy to the future. Like the future, God is real and is constantly influencing the form that our present takes, but is nonetheless always beyond our grasp, never fully realizable in any present actuality. What is less clear in Moltmann's treatment is the nature of the promises. He insists that the promises are the only form in which we "have" God in the present, yet he refuses to speculate about supernatural intervention in the course of history to effect events such as exodus and resurrection that give rise to these promises, leaving one to conclude that the promissory events are in some sense *historical accidents* and in that regard the same as all other events in history. Is it possible, however, to be fully conscious of the historical relativity of revelatory events and at the same time receive them as acts of God? If the promises are explicable on the level of historical accidents is not their divine authority undermined? Or, to put it in the form of a challenge to Christian faith, are we willing to allow the accidents of history (an underdeveloped Hebrew deity, a strong wind across a marsh,

---

30. Moltmann, *Theology of Hope*, 25.

the execution of a nonconformist, an empty tomb, and a few visions) to mediate to us our understanding of what is to be trusted in the present and hoped for in the future? Is an evolutionary variation, an ancient semitic high god whose memory happened to survive because he was fittest to speak to the configuration of that particular historical moment, to be the norm by which the whole of history is measured and judged? To these nagging questions of historical relativism Moltmann provides no clear answer, and we are forced to press on alone.

Historical accidents, in themselves quite explicable in immanental terms, become nevertheless the means by which we are taught to trust history and even to hope in anticipation of the realization of the possibilities inherent in the accidental. How does this come to pass?

The first point to be made is a general one: every new event has the effect of undermining the absoluteness of past events, which no longer can be understood simply in terms of themselves or their previous context but are now made relative to the new moment that transcends them and throws them into a new light. Thus it is possible to say of such a moment that in it the power of "transcendence" is felt, that is, the past is thrown into question, relativized, placed in a new context. While this may explain how events can transcend the past, it does not clarify how they can transcend the future. Would not every new moment in history as such be a transcending of the past, as is assumed for instance by process philosophy? If every moment is in turn subject to being transcended, how can any final claim be made for those historical occasions that have been decisive for Christian faith? The very experience of transcendence in the form of historical relativity would seem to be a denial of Christian claims.

Transcendence as described thus far is an experience within the historical process that in many respects parallels transcendence as experienced by primitive man. Indeed, in a variety of ways contemporary man is caught up in a historical monism that resembles cosmic monism. He understands himself as part of a historical process in which every moment transcends the last, and yet the process as such has no discernible goal. This is the form the monistic model takes as it emerges from evolutionary thinking. It differs from previous monisms in that it views the cosmos not as a closed, completed, perfected reality but as an ongoing process in which new possibilities are constantly opening up. Yet it parallels the cultic situation of primitive religion in that life is renewed only as it joins the vitalistic forces of the cosmos now located on the ever-advancing frontier of progress. Thus contemporary devotees are obligated to rush from one new doctrine to the next, drawing from each whatever dynamism is available to sustain life until the next moment and the next new wind of doctrine come along. One lives close to the gods by living breathlessly on the evolutionary edge. But such a life is inevitably directionless, for evolution as such can have no goal because natural selection operates only in terms of the circumstances given in the present and has no way of anticipating what circumstances may obtain in the next moment. An evolutionary model is clearly not enough unless it is basically modified by the Hebrew-Christian insight.

Just as the Hebraic understanding of the distinction between Creator and creation made a strategic contribution to the release of humanity from bondage to cosmic monism, so the same distinction as it recurs in Christianity—expressed on the historical plane as eschatology—may well offer an alternative to the progressive, yet in basic respects still locked-in, world of historical monism. The Hebrew-Christian model explains how the promises that have come to expression in historic events transcend not only the past but the future, and why these decisive events are therefore themselves in principle unsurpassable. The historical accidents of exodus and crucifixion-resurrection are not just moments of transcendence in the sense already described. They do not just throw the past into a new light, they are also understood as establishing a continuing relationship between humanity and one who is the Lord of history, that is, one who already stands at the end or goal of the process. By the very nature of their content, moreover, the historical accidents preserved by the Christian memory make it possible to grasp ultimate reality as both transcendent and personal, both discrete and related. This personal factor makes it possible, in turn, to conceive of the relationship as extended in time while preserving the independence of the partners. Thus transcendence is experienced not just as momentary inspiration destined to be dissipated and made obsolete by the next historical moment, but as *covenant*, as a relationship created in the present but signifying a commitment into the future to one who from God's side maintains the bond with humanity in history while at the same time standing at the goal of history. This kind of experience of transcendence, which might be termed *covenantal-eschatological*, becomes a "*promontory*" jutting out into the flux of history to provide a vantage point from which the goal of history can be glimpsed. Such promontories are themselves historical, made of the same stuff, so to speak, as the rest of history; yet, as signs of a covenant with the one who stands over against the historical process as well as standing in it, they provide that essential Archimedian point necessary to gain leverage on history, both critically and teleologically. The covenantal promise, since it comes from the goal of history, proves inexhaustible in history. No earthly kingdom is able fully to actualize it, so that those living under the promise are never satisfied with the status quo and press forward toward the eschaton. At the same time, the promise serves as the principle of cultural selection whereby evolution is guided, new history shaped, and the creativity of God comes to bear on history through the people of the promise.

Now it should be apparent that the Hebrew-Christian orientation is not necessarily in conflict with evolutionary modes of thought and may indeed serve to modify the latter in such a way as to overcome the historical monism implicit in a point of view that strictly speaking operates willy-nilly and cannot anticipate the future. In proposing such a new alignment, however, one is only too conscious of the continuing problems that plague biblical and theological language, problems that are in part endemic to any attempt to conceptualize a reality that transcends history and that bursts historical categories as well as spatial, and that will therefore always partially elude us—as does the future. Thus the temptation to absolutize any model, including the Hebrew-Christian, should be obviated in the awareness (negatively) of the limitations of all models and (positively) of the advantages to be gained from the continuing dialectic between those models that have in the past proved so resourceful in the development of thought. The theologian's task in any case is to keep the options clear lest, in the effort to overcome the tension between the "two Absolutes," the continuing contribution of the one or the other be lost. A pluralistic age will not only demand alternatives but will profit from the dialectic between them.

If the "historical accidents" of the Christian memory do provide, however, the *promontory* that enables contemporary humanity to trust and to hope, as have our precursors in the faith, the Christian faith will have demonstrated its "fitness" and "truth" in the form most readily acknowledged by the pragmatic mood of our time. And it will also supply the required grounding for entering into the dialogue with other religions called for today.

2

Introduction to Paul Tillich[1]

PAUL TILLICH WAS FIRST and last a theologian, a theologian with a passion for discussing issues and arguing theological points late into the night. But he was a theologian with a difference. His preoccupation was not theology for its own sake but theology for the sake of a richer, more humane existence in a society and culture unaware of its own religious dimensions and theological roots. He saw himself as an interpreter of culture to itself, an interpreter equipped with insights and a method that enabled him to penetrate the surface of things and open them up from new angles of vision in such a way that observers cannot remain simply observers but suddenly discover not only an accurate description of the world but of themselves as well.

Tillich has for this reason been called an existentialist theologian, but the label is accurate only if one's definition of *existentialism* is broad enough to include the roots of modern existentialism in nineteenth-century German idealism and notably in Friedrich Schelling, who was Tillich's special mentor. From Schelling—on whose thought Tillich wrote not one but two doctoral dissertations—Tillich derived his basic notion of the ground of being, being-itself, the power of being, the fundamental source of everything that is, which functions as the absolute in his system to which everything else is relative. This absolute is not available to the ordinary reasoning process, dependent as it is upon experience of the empirical world, which is anything but absolute. Instead,

---

1. Previously unpublished lecture in the series, "Shapers of Contemporary Thought," for students of all faculties of Emory University.

it must be approached phenomenologically as a dimension intuited in our experience of the finite world but which transcends it. Tillich calls it "the dimension of depth," or "the ground of our being."[2]

Paradoxically, our consciousness of being ordinarily emerges from our encounters with its opposite, the threat of non-being.[3] It is at those moments when we feel our existence threatened, when the taken-for-granted routine and securities of life suddenly dissolve or become problematic, that we become most keenly aware of a power within us that opposes those threats and negates the negative. Thus a close brush with death may make us more conscious of our own aliveness; we want to grasp life, sense it, savor it, cherish it, rejoice in it, in a way scarcely experienced by us before we met its opposite. Likewise, if someone close to us is threatened with death, we suddenly become aware of how much that person's life is intertwined with our own and what a gap there would be if he or she no longer existed. Indeed, we are seldom aware of how important ideas, values, and beliefs are for sustaining our lives until they too are endangered by counter-arguments, doubt, or ridicule. When that which undergirds threatens to become a void we suddenly become conscious of its significance. Tillich calls this the "shock of non-being."[4] Through the shock of non-being we are enabled to focus on the experience of being. (Put most simply, the chair that most impresses itself on your consciousness is the chair that, when you go to sit down, isn't there!) According to this Tillichian version of the *via negativa,* our knowledge of God is more likely to come by the route of indirection rather than directly. This is because the being of God is being-as-such and is not an object ranged alongside of other objects "out there" in the world of objects. God is prior to all subjects and objects as the presupposition of their being and our knowing. Following Augustine, Tillich suggests that God is present to our experience in a way analogous to *light* and *truth.* We do not normally focus on light in itself, yet we see everything else in the light. We cannot isolate truth as such, yet we presuppose truth in every process of reasoning. Even if we deny the reality of truth we affirm it, claims Tillich, for our argument against truth would have cogency only if it is true. Again, to put this Augustinian line of thinking most

---

2. Paul Tillich, *Systematic Theology* (Chicago: University of Chicago Press, 1951), vol. 1: 112, 116.

3. Ibid., 64.

4. Ibid., 110.

simply, "you cannot see the ground on which you are standing." The nature of God is such that God cannot ever be reached as the object of a question and not its basis. "God is the presupposition of the question of God."[5] Along with thinkers as different from him as Charles Hartshorne and Karl Barth, Tillich prefers the ontological argument for God to the other traditional arguments employed in the history of philosophy and theology because, in spite of its difficulties, it does more justice to the nature of God's being. Note that I said the ontological *argument* for God and not proof for the *existence* of God. For Tillich, this is an important distinction. The ontological argument is a demonstration using rational language, not a proof in the incontrovertible sense. And it is a demonstration of God's necessary being, not of an object in space. When we ask the question of God, says Tillich, we are asking "about that which is by its very nature above existence."[6] To reduce God to an object in existence about which we endlessly could debate whether the object is there or not would be as atheistic as to deny God's existence. (To be sure, this statement has to be held in tension with his discussion of the way God is present to us in existence, a subject to which we will turn later when we consider his doctrine of symbols.)

What does Tillich gain by this kind of ontological approach that identifies God with the power of being? It enables him to bring the ultimate categories in the religious and philosophical traditions to which he is heir into a unified picture: *deus est esse,* God is being. This equation allows him to inform the abstract category from the philosophical tradition with the concrete imagery and content of the Judeo-Christian tradition, and at the same time to protect the ultimacy of the reality to which the Scriptures testify by the critical principles inherent in the process of philosophical abstraction. "God is being-itself" is for Tillich an abstract translation of the first commandment, "I am the Lord your God . . . you shall have no other gods before me"(Exod 20:2,3).

Moreover, this identification of God with the power of being universally present in all human experience gives him a way of speaking of fundamentally religious motivations, imperatives, and values operative in persons and movements that do not think of themselves as being religious. By definition, concern with issues that determine the being or not being of persons and societies is *religious* concern. For most of us

---

5. Ibid., 205.
6. Ibid., vol. 2:23.

most of the time as we routinely go about our day-to-day business, ultimate questions remain very much in the background. Creative persons bring these questions to the fore, however, and struggle with them in the face of the debilitating and destructive elements they see at work in the world. They have a passionate concern to discover and give expression to a power or powers that can oppose and overcome the threats to human life and meaning. One of Tillich's favorite examples of this kind of passionate concern on the part of a creative artist is the modern classic that Tillich visited frequently in the Museum of Modern Art in New York City, Picasso's "Guernica." This painting, which comes out of the Spanish Civil War, portrays in stark black, white, and grays, the agony of a defenseless Spanish village, arbitrarily chosen to demonstrate the effectiveness of saturation bombing by the Spanish fascists' new allies, the German and Italian air forces. In this painting, claims Tillich, Picasso, out of the depths of his own soul, gives expression to a powerful divine and human protest against demonic and cynical injustice and destruction. There is nothing in the human situation that would guarantee that Picasso's intuition of what is just and true will in the end win out over the very real forces of evil and oppression. And that fact is what makes the ultimate concern expressed here a risk, an act of faith. This act of faith is twofold. It is, on the one hand, a willingness to portray the human situation in all its stark, senseless horror, without in any way seeking to smooth it over or cover it up. That suggests an underlying confidence that facing the human situation, as grim and meaning-destructive as it may be, will not finally destroy us. This confidence is grounded in an immediate awareness of the power of being and is what Tillich calls "absolute faith," the immediate certainty that is not subject to doubt, which he explains in his book, *The Courage to Be*.[7] And the faith manifested here is the courage to affirm the meaningfulness of human existence in spite of everything that testifies to the contrary. That is "existential faith," faith that in a concrete situation throws its lot in with what it believes manifests the ultimate before there is any certain evidence that the cause will indeed prevail.

In developing these distinctions Tillich was not just spinning theories. In 1933, he was in mid-career, having worked his way up to a prestigious professorship in philosophy of religion at the University

---

7. Paul Tillich, *Dynamics of Faith* (New York: Harper, 1957), 102–5; and *The Courage to Be* (New Haven: Yale University Press, 1952).

of Frankfort. Then came the Nazi takeover, and he found himself dismissed along with eleven colleagues who were Jewish, among them Karl Mannheim, Erich Fromm, Max Horkheimer, Theodore Adorno, and Herbert Marcuse. Later Tillich was proud of the fact that he was the first gentile fired by the Nazis. For six months he was without a job. During that time he was summoned by the government minister of education and assured that there was a good possibility that he could be reinstated if he withdrew his criticisms of the Nazis and his defense of the Jews. This he refused to do. It was then clear that, in spite of his deep-rooted attachment to his homeland, he had no future in Germany. Fortunately Reinhold Niebuhr was aware of Tillich's plight and invited him to come to the United States to assume a teaching post at Union Seminary in New York. (Hannah Tillich recalls something of the trauma of those days in her book, *From Time to Time*.[8])

Tillich was unpopular with the Nazis not just because of his Jewish associations but because of his identification with Religious Socialism. Religious Socialism was a movement primarily within Protestant circles in Germany that saw in Marx's criticism of capitalism an authentic prophetic witness, a fundamentally religious protest against the dehumanization brought about by the capitalist economic system in the West. Tillich's criticism of capitalism was grounded in an historical analysis that began with an examination of the breakdown on the intellectual front of the unity of medieval culture. One by one the various fields of human knowledge at the end of the Middle Ages declared their independence of the church and its doctrinal and moral tutelage. Developing according to their own autonomous rationality, the natural sciences were able to demonstrate the advantages of their new freedom through rapid advances in the knowledge of the physical universe, which resulted in increased ability to manipulate the environment and make it serve human technological aims. Economics, which previously had been controlled by moral considerations deemed necessary to maintain the balance of justice in society, claimed for itself a similar autonomy from religious and moral control. It assumed that there were economic laws as predictable and invariable as physical laws waiting to be discovered that, if isolated and comprehended, would provide the basis for a fully rationalized economic system. The economic order has proved to be considerably more intractable than the physical order, as we all

---

8. Hannah Tillich, *From Time to Time* (New York: Stein and Day, 1972).

well know and continue to discover to our frustration and dismay. But the fundamental break was made. Economics was wrenched out of the social organism as a whole, and questions of societal justice and moral principle were no longer allowed to exercise determinative control over a free market. Liberty for the marketplace was the dominant theme of the liberal parties of Europe, freedom from controls by the church and controls by government. Only with complete freedom can production and profits—presumed to be the chief goals of the economic system—be maximized. The market was to be allowed to function according to its own laws based on the costs of labor and materials and the balance of supply and demand.

That the capitalist system has had remarkable success in the production of goods no one would deny. But at what cost? The system inevitably sets group against group, claims Tillich, as each struggles to get a larger share of the goods and the profits. *Class warfare* and *imperialism* are the inevitable result. A struggle ensues between the owners of the instruments of production and labor, a struggle not to be decided on grounds of moral right but purely and simply on the basis of who can mobilize the most power. This inevitably includes, of course, the power of the state, so that there is a continuous jockeying for control over the state and its legislative and judicial processes. Where the economy exercises this kind of autonomous authority no other institution in the society can avoid being bent to serve the interests of the competing parties. Hence the cogency of Marx's insight that the institutions of any society become a reflection of the dominant ideology of the economic base. In order to guarantee free access to raw materials at advantageous prices, imperialism—economic, political, and finally military—is called for. Should it be necessary to justify this imperialism to those whose overly tender consciences are made uncomfortable by the vestigial remains of Christian values, it can always be pointed out that imperialism is bringing the benefits of western capitalistic civilization to the whole world. And if the market sags at home because people do not really need what the system is producing, advertising campaigns are cranked up to create needs and lure customers into showrooms with generous rebates.

The result of all this is pervasive alienation and cynicism. Not only are laborers alienated from their work and from what they produce, and therefore constantly pressuring for more money to make up for the meaninglessness of work (thereby shifting life's meaning to the impersonal goods money can make it possible to accumulate), producers are forced cynically to find ways to "con" consumers into buying what they do not need, and the public is understandably cynical about not only management and labor but also the politicians and public servants that both attempt to subvert.

That this remarkable bumble bee of an economic system flies at all is nothing less than amazing, but with our combination of checks and balances and long experience with pluralism and social chaos, we seem to be able to make a go of it. Abroad, however, where the checks and balances do not exist to the same extent or can be more easily subverted, American capital appears to follow the more classic pattern described by Marx of collusion with the forces of oppression. For years, with our inveterate tendency to think of ourselves and our motives more highly than we ought to think, we were able to obscure this truth from ourselves and pretend innocence. Now we know better.

Tillich had a catholic kind of yearning for a unified society—but not at the expense of sacrificing the legitimate rights of the individual. This tension between autonomy and heteronomy, between individual self-actualization and participation in the larger whole, was the dialectic that was fundamentally at stake in his analysis of the economic situation. He saw western civilization at the end of an era that began with the legitimate revolt of the intellect against institutions such as the church that did not allow sufficient space and sufficient grace for the various fields of knowledge to pursue their development in freedom. The church resisted, not because resistance to these autonomous developments was inherent in the Christian gospel, but because the church did not have a large enough umbrella under which to provide a meaningful orientation to the mind and spirit of a maturing humankind. The church confused the size of its dogmatically pre-defined umbrella with the size of the universe. Western Christendom collapsed in principle when theology no longer infused society with principles comprehensive enough not only to accommodate new ideas but to enrich them and increase their creativity by putting them into an overarching context in which they could relate with other areas of knowledge as well. When religion no longer has a *big* idea it tends to opt for a *rigid* idea, substituting absoluteness for comprehensiveness. The result is growing alienation between religion and culture to the eventual detriment of both. The various disciplines in their splendid isolation refine their in-group language more and more and understand each other less and less, until finally some irreverent soul has the temerity to ask whether the truth-claims of language that can be understood only intramurally are sufficient to sustain human life. That's a question that rightfully ought to be asked of us in our respective disciplines as well as in the church.

Autonomy gone to seed is demonic, claims Tillich. He sensed that the forces of autonomy were reaching the outer limits to which they had been carried by the centrifugal forces released in the Renaissance, Reformation, and Enlightenment. He and his cohorts in the Religious Socialist movement were anticipating a new *kairos*—the New Testament notion of "the fullness of time" to be distinguished from *chronos,* the prosaic time that clocks can measure. It would be a creative moment that would be determinative for the future because it would be the watershed from which a new cultural synthesis would emerge. Tillich and his friends were hopeful that an enlightened socialism would provide the necessary emphasis upon the social dimensions of human existence neglected in the capitalist era. They were appalled, however, by the heteronomous tendencies they saw at work in communism that they felt had betrayed Marx's original humanism. Thus Tillich found himself fighting on two fronts, attempting to make the case within the church for socialism to people who had been turned off and frightened by the atheism of Marxist rhetoric, and attempting through his critiques of heteronomous tendencies in the Socialist and Communist Parties to recall those movements to what he felt to be their legitimate contribution.

Someone who operates on the boundary between two camps is likely to find himself one day in no-man's-land, which is where Tillich did find himself when the whole enterprise of Religious Socialism and its hopes for a new *kairos* of the human spirit were aborted after the German masses opted, not for the continuation of the liberal democracy of the Weimar Republic, and not for some authentic form of socialism, but for a fascism that promised law and order and an ideology based on national chauvinism. Tired of the endless chaos of autonomy, the masses chose the security of heteronomy. But they were soon to discover that in a technological society the latter can be even more demonic than the former. In any case, in Germany the door was closed for Tillich. And he made his way to the United States with his wife and young child to begin over again at the age of forty-seven.

The English language was not the only thing in the new country that gave Tillich problems in communicating. Few of his colleagues and none of his students had been steeped in the Teutonic idealism that was his intellectual home. And *socialism* was a word so subject to misunderstanding that one was well advised not to mention it outside a limited number of *avant garde* drawing rooms in New York City much less unfurl it as the motto on one's theological banner. This meant that Tillich was forced to refocus the direction of his research and writing and to concentrate on the theological task *per se*, which eventually resulted in the publication of his three-volume *Systematic Theology* that established him as one of the foremost theologians of the twentiety century. His work on systematics did not prevent him from continuing his preoccupation with theological interpretation and criticism of culture, however, and from his pen flowed a steady stream of articles and creative insights that may yet prove to be his most important contribution.

Among the interpretations that have proved most fruitful in interdisciplinary discussion is Tillich's analysis of human *anxiety*. In his ontological scheme of things, to exist is to move out of undifferentiated unity with original being into a definite shape and form, to move out of innocence into experience. And experience is inevitably ambiguous. This is the profound meaning contained in the biblical story of the Fall, he suggests.[9] The Fall is in one sense a fall *up*, a realization on the part of human beings of their potential for independent action and shaping their own destiny. At the same time their act of independence is a fall *down*, for it entails a loss of innocence and original unity with all things and entrance into a world of estrangement, a world in which they will henceforth be subject to the threats of non-being. To exist is to be vulnerable. And the richer, the broader, the more extended one's existence is in the realization of possibilities, the more one is exposed to destructive forces. The pathological reaction to this situation of inevitable anxiety is regression and withdrawal to a more manageable, self-defined and presumably defensible territory. Schizophrenia is the extreme form of the self-definition of the limits within which one is willing to cope. Obversely, the willingness to risk vulnerability, the willingness to stick one's neck out for unpopular causes, requires what Tillich labels, "the courage to be," that fundamental confidence in the power of being and truth that enables us to take on anxiety and transcend it while not de-

---

9. *Systematic Theology*, vol. 2:23, 29–44.

nying its reality. Tillich identifies Jesus of Nazareth as the prototypical example of this kind of courage. According to the Pauline interpretation, Jesus did not grasp at equality with God but freely identified himself with humankind in all its vulnerability up to and through death itself, maintaining all the time his complete openness and obedience to the power of being in which he trusted. "Therefore God also highly exalted him," writes St. Paul in an ecstatic hymn of praise, "and gave him the name / that is above every name, / so that at the name of Jesus / every knee should bend, / in heaven and on earth and under the earth, / and every tongue should confess / that Jesus Christ is Lord, / to the glory of God the Father" (Phil 2:9–11). Tillich calls Jesus the "New Being," because he unites in himself both complete humanity and complete openness to the divine power that sustained him.[10] He did not succumb to humanity's temptation to avoid anxiety by withdrawing to a self-created world cut off from threatening relations to fellow humans or to God. But in utter trust in God that sustained him even through his questioning of God, he conquered in principle the sinful tendency of humanity, that is, the tendency for us when confronted by anxiety to cut ourselves off from the very power that can enable us to face and overcome anxiety.

Though a Christian is one who testifies to having been grasped by the power of being through the Christian story and the Christian symbols, Tillich is able to see phenomenological parallels operative in other religions as well, just as he sees religious concerns at work in persons and movements that claim no religious allegiance or are even antireligious. The power of the New Being is present wherever forces of reconciliation are at work overcoming the alienation that characterizes human existence. While he can speak of the unique significance of Jesus as the decisive historical kairos that ushered in the Christian era, his utilization of Johannine Christology, which sees Christ as the manifestation of an eternal principle, the *Logos,* makes it possible for Tillich to recognize this same principle active in other religions without denying the significance of the Christian revelation. This combination of conviction about the salvation available through Christ coupled with openness to the claims of legitimacy put forward by other religions has made Tillich attractive to persons seeking some way to overcome the dogmatic intolerance so often associated with religions without lapsing into complete relativity and indifference with regard to religious claims to truth. Tillich and the

10. Ibid., 2:90.

historian of religion, Mircea Eliade, were avid *Gesprächspartner* during Tillich's years at the University of Chicago, and the results are evident in Eliade's tribute in Tillich's posthumous volume, *The Future of Religions*.[11]

Another area in which Tillich's influence assumed major proportions was in the emergence of the cross-disciplinary field the theological interpretation of literature, an enterprise that has been institutionalized as a discipline in its own right in the Theology and Literature programs that have sprung up across the country. Tillich's conviction that religious passion had in many cases migrated outside the churches and was to be found instead in the artists and writers who sensitively describe and reflect the malaise of the culture, its loss of depth, and its yearning for new sources of authentic meaning, made literature fair game for a theological hermeneutic. At about the same time, the rise of the "new criticism" attempted to go beyond previous literary criticism's preoccupation with social and historical analysis, style, and questions external to the text, and focused instead on the text itself to let it speak. This provided fertile soil for the flourishing of an expressionist reading of literature that saw in the work of art the creative reflection of the depths that ordinary analysis simply fails to reach. The text read from an expressionist standpoint puts a claim on the reader in much the same way that Picasso's picture puts a claim on the viewer. It demands participation if one is to "understand." The remarkable success in applying this method to the field of literary criticism would seem to ensure the continuing importance of this kind of cross-disciplinary effort.

Of interest to a wide range of disciplines is Tillich's analysis of *symbol*.[12] In our ordinary use of the term we tend to assume that a symbol is only a mental construction or convention that stands for something else that is the real thing. In Tillich's language, such a construction or convention would be a *sign*, not a symbol. A *symbol* is a meaning-complex that participates in and is able to mediate that for which it stands. For example, the deliverance of the Hebrews from slavery in Egypt has always been a potent symbol for African American Christians, and when the story is retold, those who hear it are grasped by their own participation in the event. The event mediates to them conviction concerning the providence of God and God's identification with the oppressed of the world against their oppressors. They sense that they are in touch with

---

11. See Paul Tillich, *The Future of Religions* (Harper, 1966/1987).
12. *Systematic Theology*, vol. 1:239–52, vol. 3:356–61.

what is ultimately real, which empowers them to "keep on keeping on" in a hostile world. Middle-class blacks who have made it in the system may find that the story has become less meaningful, less empowering, to them. Why? Because the story does not speak with the same immediacy to their situation. They are making it on their own. They are not so sure they want to be delivered from their present situation. Whites, on the other hand, are likely to take the story as an occasion to argue over miracles—did the sea really part when the children of Israel passed through?—or as a charming but meaningless ancient tale, or as dangerously subversive if one ventures to ask, who are the modern-day pharaohs of this world? The same symbol can have a variety of meanings, depending upon the situation. Does that mean that symbols are completely relative? Not at all. In our illustration, only one group, African Americans, are able genuinely to participate in the symbol and receive the benefits of sustenance, freedom, and meaning that the symbol is potentially able to mediate to all who take it seriously. Our avenue to the power of being and meaning is inevitably through symbols. That is why, when the symbols that sustain a culture and give it overall shape and direction no longer are powerful, the culture languishes as well.

Tillich is sensitive to the fact that this is precisely what has happened in our own time to many of the symbols of the Judeo-Christian heritage. Their power to inform life and provide a coherent picture has eroded for so many that secular ideologies and superficial concerns have moved in to take their place. What makes the situation even more insidious is that the substitutes, such as nationalism or "our way of life," often usurp what is left of the Christian symbols and appropriate them, making it difficult to tell the genuine article from the cultural substitute. This is a situation ripe for doubt. Yet doubt in such a time is not a disaster but rather a sign of life and hope, according to Tillich. It arises from our immediate awareness of what the genuine article would have to be if it were to provide the kind of depth of power needed to live meaningfully. This kind of doubt makes us unwilling to accept the claims of those who would press the symbols upon us as something we have to affirm just because we are Christians, or Jews, or Americans, or African Americans. Such claims actually reverse the flow of power and require us to sustain the symbols rather than the symbols sustaining us. In effect we breathe life into the symbols rather than the symbols breathing life into us as we are grasped by their power. Doubt under such circumstances is the surest sign of faith, that is, the best indication that we are still in touch with a source that we know is not adequately mediated by traditional symbols in the form they are now presented to us, and therefore we refuse to accept the heteronomous claims advanced for existing symbols.

On the other hand, Tillich reminds the doubter that there is no way toward affirmative participation in the power of being that does not lead through symbols, and for most persons in our society the best place to begin is through a thoughtful re-appropriation of the basic symbols of the religious tradition by participating in a community for whom these symbols are meaningful. Normally one does not appropriate the symbols of faith in one fell swoop. You feel your way back into them, beginning with those symbols that still have some residual power for you and exploring the depths of their meaning more fully.

His excitement over the various ways in which people are doing just that—struggling with the heritage, accepting it, rejecting it, transforming it—was something that Tillich retained to the end of his life. On the evening before a disabling heart attack, he was in a symposium at the University of Chicago on the Death-of-God theology. The animated debate continued afterward in a faculty home, where Thomas J. J. Altizer's oft-quoted claim that Tillich was the spiritual father of the Death-of-God theology was up for discussion. Tillich was nonplussed. He could see how these young theologians could claim that traditional symbols of God may be heteronomous and unable to mediate divine power, and thus how such symbols can even function demonically, keeping people in subjugation who have no alternate access to the divine. But such a protest is itself a manifestation of the power of being and the living reality of a God who transcends all symbolic representations. From Tillich's standpoint the Death-of-God theology was involved in fundamental contradictions that would result in its own demise if it did not move beyond semantic obfuscation. Though Hannah Tillich urged her husband to leave the party earlier, the debate went on past midnight.

And so, at the age of eighty-nine, Paul Tillich died as he lived, fighting a battle on two fronts, against the heteronomous conservatives and the autonomous radicals, appreciative of the concerns that motivated them both, but convinced to the end that there is a way that transcends them both and offers unity and truth.

3

Paul Tillich, the Conservative Revolutionary[1]

ALTHOUGH THE ISSUES OF revolution are no longer on the theological agenda in the same form they took in the 1970s and 1980s, they cannot be avoided by today's theologian who wishes to take seriously developments in theology throughout Latin America and other parts of the world. The need for basic social, political, and economic changes is as acute as ever. Yet in places where revolutions have been successful, the results have seldom fulfilled expectations. Is there a theology of revolution that takes seriously the post-revolutionary situation? Latin Americans have resisted this question, suspecting that behind it lies the demand for a guarantee of stability and "normalcy" that no revolutionary movement can give, even if it wished. Nevertheless, the development of a conservative theory of revolution that is comprehensive enough to anticipate the post-revolutionary situation does not seem to be an unreasonable expectation. This essay will suggest that in the ontological analyses of Paul Tillich is found one line of thinking that could contribute to such a theory.

In many ways Tillich would seem a congenial figure for those who find in Marxism the chief instrument of analysis for social change. Tillich's dismissal from his professorship at the University of Frankfurt soon after the Nazi rise to power in 1933 came not, as one might suppose, because he was a Christian philosopher-theologian, but because he

---

1. Originally published as "Tillich's Understanding of Revolution," in *Theonomy and Autonomy: Studies in Paul Tillich's Engagement with Modern Culture,* edited by John Carey (Macon, Ga.: Mercer University Press, 1984), 267–80. Used by permission of Mercer University Press.

was a *socialist*.² Though not a socialist political figure, he was considered a leading theoretician of the movement called *Religious Socialism,* which was enough to brand him as an undesirable in the new, anti-Bolshevist, Nazi state.

The roots of the Religious Socialist movement in Germany go back to the nineteenth-century British Christian socialists, Carlyle and Kingsley, whose influence spread to Switzerland and resulted in the work of Hermann Kutter and Leonhard Ragaz. This Swiss movement had profound impact on the generation of theologians emerging during and just after the First World War: Barth, Thurneysen, and Gogarten. (Gerhard Sauter has shown that it was equally influential for Bonhoeffer.³) The nascent dialectical theology proved uncongenial to the positive interpretation of culture that many of the German Religious Socialists wished to achieve, however, and they turned more and more to the theological tutelage of George Wunsch and Paul Tillich. The German movement actually arose in three different circles, one centered in southern Germany, which sought to reform the church and bring about a rapprochement with the working class; a second in Berlin, which was sharply critical of the traditional indifference of the Prussian state church to social and political issues; and a third in Cologne, which disavowed allegiance to any church and attracted Catholics and freethinkers as well as Protestants to its ranks. In 1924, the three groups came together to form the Federation of German Religious Socialists. It was natural that Tillich, coming out of the middle-of-the-road Berlin group, should have an important role in the federated movement from the beginning. He was not an activist, not an organizer, a marcher, or a picketer. Rather, he saw his function as that

---

2. Paul Tillich, *Political Expectation,* ed. James Luther Adams (New York: Harper and Row. 1971), includes translations of several of Tillich's early political writings and socialist thought. More extensive sources are to be found in *The Socialist Decision* (New York: Harper and Row. 1977), the original of which was published in 1933 and occasioned Tillich's dismissal from the University of Frankfurt, and in the following volumes of Tillich: *Gesammelte Werke*—vol. 2: *Christentum und soziale Gestaltung*; vol. 3: *Das religiöse Fundament des moralischen Handelns*; vol. 6: *Der Wiederstreit von Raum und Zeit*; vol. 9: *Die religiöse Substanz der Kultur*; and vol. 10: *Die religiöse Deutung der Gegenwart. Gesammelte Werke* (Stuttgart: Evangelisches Verlagswerk, 1959) (hereafter GW).

3. Gerhard Sauter, "Zur Herkunft und Absicht der Formel 'Nicht religiöse Interpretation biblischer Begriffe' bei Dietrich Bonhoeffer." *Evangelische Theologie* 25 (June 1965): 283–97.

of a theoretician, whose job it was to provide the theological base and rationale for the practical efforts of other members.

What was the movement attempting to accomplish? Tillich described it well in his introduction to *The Protestant Era*. Religious Socialism understands itself not as a party, but as

> a spiritual power trying to be effective in as many parties as possible, . . . standing unambiguously against every form of reaction. . . . Religious Socialism is . . . neither political Marxism in the sense of Communism, nor "scientific" Marxism in the sense of economic doctrines. We have, however, learned more from Marx's dialectical analysis of bourgeois society than from any other analysis of our period.[4]

Marx provided an interpretation of history that Tillich found closer to the classical Christian doctrine of humanity, "with its empirical pessimism and its eschatological hope,"[5] than any alternative point of view.

It would be a mistake to assume that Marx provided Tillich's fundamental orientation, however, for it was only within a more ontological framework that Tillich was able to appropriate and interpret Marx and affirm the Marxist contribution. What was that framework?

TILLICH'S ROOTS IN SCHELLING

Tillich's ontology is derived primarily from his chief mentor, the nineteenth-century German philosopher, Friedrich Schelling (1775–1854), on whose thought Tillich wrote both his philosophical and theological doctoral dissertations.[6] According to Schelling's so-called *Identitätsphilosophie*, all seemingly opposite, contradictory, disparate, and dialectical elements of experience are rooted in an *absolute* ground of *being—the Source of all being*—that is the underlying foundation

---

4. Paul Tillich, *The Protestant Era* (Chicago: University of Chicago Press, 1948), xviii.

5. Ibid., xiv.

6. Tillich's philosophical dissertation at the University of Breslau, 1910: Paul Tillich, *The Construction of the History of Religion in Schelling's Positive Philosophy*, trans. Victor Nuovo (Lewisburg PA: Bucknell University Press and London: Associated University Press, 1974). Tillich's theological dissertation at the University of Halle, 1912: *Mysticism and Guilt-Consciousness in Schelling's Philosophical Development*, trans. Victor Nuovo (Lewisburg, Pa.: Bucknell University Press and London: Associated University Press, 1974). The original German version of the latter is reprinted in GW, vol. 1: *Frühe Hauptwerke*.

of subject and object, ideal and real, nature (i.e., matter) and spirit. *Identitätsphilosophie* thus finds the source of all reality in this Absolute, in light of which all appearances must be judged as relative, and from which they issue forth.

From Kant, Schelling learned that this Absolute is not available to the ordinary reasoning processes, dependent as they are upon the experience of an empirical world that is anything but absolute. It must instead be approached through intuition, which allows the mind to penetrate behind the world of appearances and differentiation to that one, primeval power of being that sustains all that is.

If the source of all reality is to be intuited as one, however, that one cannot be unambiguous; it must be the source of the darker sides of life as well as the brighter, the destructive elements in existence as well as the creative. Thus Schelling, like his predecessors in the monistic tradition, Meister Eckhart and Jacob Boehme, found it necessary to posit a final ambiguity in the Absolute. If the opposites are to coincide in the Absolute, the *Source* must give rise to disparate manifestations. The notion that the Absolute realizes itself through a variety of manifestations may be the impulse that Schelling contributed to Hegel's philosophy of history. R.G. Collingwood speculates that Hegel, who borrowed more freely from his contemporaries to compound his magnificent system than is today generally realized, was influenced at this point by Schelling, his younger colleague at Berlin, who published his dynamic understanding of the Absolute long before Hegel's system unfolded.[7] Hegel was in fact known earlier as a disciple of Schelling, and one of his earliest writings was a comparison of the thought of Schelling and Fichte.[8]

The later Hegel was not able to retain ultimate ambiguity in his Absolute, however, and it was the recovery by Kierkegaard of that ambiguity that Tillich credits (in a lecture on "*Schelling und die Anfänge des existentialistischen Protestes*"[9]) with being the origin of Kierkegaard's protest against the Hegelian brand of idealism. In the state library in Copenhagen are the notes that Kierkegaard took while attending Schelling's Berlin lectures on the "Philosophy of Revelation," in which Schelling brought to clearest expression the dialectic between "negative"

---

7. Cf. R. G. Collingwood, *The Idea of History* (Oxford: Clarendon Press. 1949), 111.

8. G. W. F. Hegel, "*Differenz des Fichte'schen und Schelling'schen Systems der Philosophie*," in *Gesammelte Werke*, vol. 4 (Hamburg: Felix Meiner Verlag. 1968).

9. Reprinted in Tillich's GW, vol. 4: *Philosophie und Schicksal*, 133–44.

and "positive" philosophies.[10] This provided the basis, Tillich claimed, for Kierkegaard's attack on Hegel. (According to Kierkegaard's own testimony, however, he was relatively unimpressed by Schelling's lectures.)

Although no similar claim can be made for the historical relation of Schelling to Marx, Schelling's protest against the Hegelian uncritical identification of being with thought was a factor in making Tillich open to the Marxist critique of Hegelianism and the bourgeois culture that it reinforced.

SCHELLING'S ONTOLOGY

Before proceeding further, let us take a closer look at the fundamental structures of Schelling's ontology that reappear in Tillich. Frustrating as this ontology may be to the non-Germanic mentality, Tillich's insights into the nature of revolution are inseparable from it. As we have already observed, Schelling's basic category, especially in his late period, is the *Ungrund (which above I have termed, the Source), is* the Absolute that is *ungrounded* in anything else and is therefore the final ground upon which all else rests. Actually the term originated with the early seventeenth-century German philosopher and mystic, Jakob Boehme, who also contributed to Schelling the notion that this final source in which all things are united contains two contraposed principles that are in eternal tension. These Boehme identified as the wrath of God and the love of God. For Schelling they became "nature" and "spirit." Neither principle can be actualized, except as absolute being separates from itself and moves into the world, into the realm of conditioned being. The world is the *explicatio dei*, the sphere in which originally undifferentiated being takes on form and definitive character.

How does this transition from the unconditioned Source to the world of conditioned, existing entities come about? Schelling developed his doctrine of *potencies* to explain the process. With its internal, polar tensions, the *Source* seethes with primeval forces and powers that are constantly pushing toward realization in concrete existence. Nature and Spirit emerge from potentiality into the actuality of finite matter and finite mind by virtue of this drive. The process of self-realization, with its concomitant actualization of freedom, always falls short of completion, however. Hence the Absolute now appears in a new role, that of absolute

10. Ibid., 136.

perfection, the idealized goal or *telos* that is never reached. And what is this *telos* but the memory of the Source from whence the process sprang? Herein lies the irony of existence: in order to actualize itself in the world, being must separate from itself in a movement that includes distancing itself from its origin in the Absolute and the acceptance of finitude. Any finite form achieved will necessarily fail to satisfy being's memory of its unconditioned Source. Life is the actualization of freedom; yet freedom, accompanied as it inevitably is by alienation, can never provide complete satisfaction, which the ontological consciousness intuits as reunification with the Source in perfection (Schelling's philosophical equivalent of the kingdom of God). Therefore, all existing things are subject to the melancholy fate of seeking self-realization in the ever-greater actualization of freedom, yet forever falling short of fulfillment in perfection.

TILLICH'S APPLICATION

Now we are ready to turn to Tillich to see how he reworked and applied this ontology. In Tillich's own system, Schelling's Source becomes "the Unconditioned" or "the Unconditional" *(das Unbedingte)*, the original "Ground of Being," or simply "Being-itself." Tillich then distinguished between essential and existential dimensions of being: *essence* corresponds to Schelling's potencies in their primeval, unrealized stage; *existence* corresponds to the actualization of the potential as being separates itself from its origins in essence and takes on concretion in the world. This movement frees essence for self-expression, but only at the price of the ontological gap that separates all existing things from their original essence. Tillich's *polarities* (dynamics and form, individualization and participation, freedom and destiny) speak of the tensions present in both essential and existential dimensions of being. The lack of balance between these elements can result in the breakdown of existing structures accompanied by the threat of nonbeing.

One more set of Tillichian terms must be explained before turning to Tillich's appropriation of the Marxist analysis: the combination *heteronomy, autonomy,* and *theonomy*. These are the categories he found most useful for interpreting the historical process. The impulse that creates history is to be found in the ontological drive for self-expression. A human being is "not bound to the situation in which he finds himself," but can transcend any given state of things, leaving behind the security of what is for the sake of what can be. "It is just this self-transcendence that is the first and basic quality of freedom"[11] and the possibility of coming to expression in existence. At the same time there is within society a conservative element, a resistance to change, which arises out of the awareness that change brings the destruction of presently given structures without any guarantee that new forms will emerge that will be more adequate. *Heteronomy* is the resistance to change and has its origin in the anxiety that existence could be overwhelmed by chaos. This anxiety is not without justification; it is an accurate intuition of the dangers implicit when new, creative powers threaten the present forms of existence. "To lose structure is to lose the possibility of being," says Tillich in an early essay on "The Demonic," so that it is not surprising that throughout history the conservative forces in all societies have been motivated by "the terror of the breakdown of structures."[12] Their answer has been to resist change by shoring up the traditional order by whatever means are at hand to maintain the status quo, even after it has become an alien law, a *heteros nomos*, which must be imposed from without. Any methods required to preserve the appearance of stability seem justified because, for this mentality, the alternative is chaos—*après nous le déluge*.

The dialectical opposite of heteronomy in the historical process is *autonomy*. If heteronomy is the defense of existing structures and institutions to counter the threat of nonbeing, autonomy is the attack on those same structures in the conviction that they no longer represent the essential depths of being. This attack is fueled by the universally present, but not universally realized, potential within human beings to be aware of essential ontological forms and powers. To be sure, this awareness is usually sparked into consciousness by an encounter with the force of nonbeing, which lacks the power to inform life with meaning and yet heteronomously demands loyalty. In this encounter, the law within—*autos nomos*—rises to the surface and enters consciousness as the awareness of alternative, more authentic possibilities of being. Once aware of the alternatives, the autonomous reason and imagination feel with especial keenness the burden of heteronomous pressures to conform to traditional but empty authorities and values. Finally the autonomous spirit, convinced of the ultimate triumph of the alternatives that it intuits as grounded in the essential dimension of being, and which cannot

---

11. Paul Tillich. *Systematic Theology*, vol. 3 (Chicago: University of Chicago Press, 1963), 303.

12. Paul Tillich, *The Interpretation of History* (New York: Scribner, 1936), 77–122.

forever be denied, casts its lot with the forces of revolution regardless of the consequences. As the cracks and fissures in the status quo become more and more obvious, and the threat of nonbeing becomes evident to wider circles, autonomy's claims gain increasing credibility, until at last the previous order crumbles and autonomy can celebrate its triumph. The history of the race would seem to indicate, however, that as soon as a new autonomy successfully establishes itself it quickly succumbs to the temptation to impose conformity upon the recalcitrant elements in its own environment, thus taking on the marks of a new heteronomy.

The exceptions to this pattern are those rare moments in history when the new order that emerges does not seek to guarantee itself by extending its power and control over existence heteronomously but remains in constant contact with, and open to continuous revision from, the all-empowering depth dimension. Such a moment is theonomous, for *theonomy* is Tillich's term for a culture in which essence and existence are united under the conditions of existence, but without the alienation and estrangement that usually flaw existence. (Note the parallel between his interpretation of the characteristics of a theonomous culture and his Christology of the "New Being.") The institutions of such a culture are not alien to humanity's inner being but are regarded as the concrete expression of our own essence as well as the essence of all reality. Where this combination occurs, the valid claims of both heteronomy and autonomy are met: the concern for structures (heteronomy) and the concern that structures express essential being and meaning (autonomy). Such a moment in history is a *kairos*, a fullness of time that becomes a watershed for the future.

THE SOCIALIST KAIROS

Tillich and his friends in the Religious Socialist movement were convinced that a kairos was appearing on the horizon. They saw in the combination of the socialist critique and the authentic Christian substance of culture congruent elements that together could lead to a new order, a new configuration of social, political, and economic structures and values. With this the cause of justice could be served, human integrity enhanced, and the power of being brought to new and genuine expression. In order to effect such a combination, lines of communication would have to be opened up between Christians and Marxists. The common assumption that the church and the socialist movement stand in absolute contradiction to each other would have to be overcome. Toward this end Tillich called attention to elements in Marxism that by his definition constituted authentic religious protest against the heteronomous character of bourgeois culture and the capitalist economic spirit, and therefore sought to interpret for the church the genuine religious motifs in Marxism. At the same time he sought to show Marxists that socialism was not in opposition to religion as such, but only to the bourgeois form that religion had taken in the church. Within socialism are genuine religious elements, he argued, which need to be recognized for the sake of the socialist cause.

The first contribution of Religious Socialism was to expose the heteronomous nature of capitalist society and the offshoots of it found in the church. Capitalism emerged at a certain point in history as a structure by which society, utilizing the tensions within itself, was able to maximize the production of goods. Yet by absolutizing the conflict between classes and freezing the development of being in its present forms, capitalism has become heteronomous and feels obliged to maintain itself ever more rigidly in view of the increasing proletarian protest. Tillich agreed with the Marxist analysis that class warfare is part and parcel of the capitalist orientation. The owners of the instruments of production will inevitably be in opposition to those who are dependent upon those means of production for their own existence.[13] The heteronomous situation becomes even more demonic when the owners also control the structures that are meant to ensure justice; for justice will be interpreted in terms of what is good for the owners and for the kind of stability in society they desire. The depth dimension of justice is cut off, and the new, the creative, is not allowed to call into question the waning power of the old structures. Thus the institutions of justice can themselves become tools of oppression to keep down more authentic expressions of being.

Moreover, capitalism extends its control to society's other representative of the depth dimension, the church, so that the church is allowed to function at the superficial level only. It is used as a means of perpetuating the religious symbols, experiences, and values of the past, which have in the meantime lost their depth of significance and their ability to inform life with meaning and power. The old forms are continued heteronomously, imposed on each generation in the name of the Absolute. What has in fact become absolute is the bourgeois culture, which has

13. Tillich, *Political Expectation*, 48.

usurped the place of divinity and cut humanity off from the true depth dimension of being by persuading us that the only possibilities for socially approved existence lie with the establishment and with the surface of things. Do not probe the depths, says heteronomy, for forces are there that will destroy everything we hold sacred.

With the voices of the official representatives of the Unconditioned—namely, the agencies of justice and the church—stilled, it is inevitable that essential being, if it is to find new expression, will have to seek out a new instrument, a new agent and bearer of the power of authentic being. The Religious Socialists agree with Marxism that history is driven forward by certain groups who are "the real bearers of historical destiny," and who through their actions carry the meaning of history into practice.[14] Historical leadership has passed therefore into the hands of the proletariat, that group within society that, at least in its self-conscious leaders, has become more intensely aware of the inauthenticity of present existence and is seeking to inaugurate a new era. Tillich identified this awareness of the proletariat, which is grounded in a deep sense of justice aroused by experiencing blatant injustice, as inherently religious, for religion is present wherever sensitivity to the depth dimension is aroused.

While critical of the heteronomous culture that capitalism has produced, Tillich is not uncritical of the dangers inherent in the autonomous nature of socialism.[15] This is consistent with the role he sees Religious Socialists playing in both church and politics. He refused to join a socialist party, claiming that Religious Socialists are called not to commit themselves to any one party position, or to specific economic programs that the parties may develop, but are free agents who interpret socialism so that a deeper understanding of the socialist cause and goals can emerge. Suspicious of the church because of its alignment with the status quo, the socialists have thrown out the religious factor as a significant element in the interpretation of human existence. The result is that socialism has cut itself off from a conscious interpretation of its own religious roots and its continuing source of power. Where the roots are not cultivated they tend to shrivel, and socialism will become just

---

14. Tillich, *The Protestant Era*, 254.

15. Cf. Tillich's article on Religious Socialism ("*Socialismus: 2. Religiöser Sozialismus*"), written for the second edition (1930) of the encyclopedia, *Religion in Geschichte und Gegenwart*, and translated in *Political Expectation*, 40–57.

another in the long line of autonomies that have turned into heteronomies. Religious Socialism attempts to intervene in this process by keeping alive within Marxism an awareness of the depth dimension.

Needless to say, Tillich was not successful in his efforts. Religious Socialism was squelched soon after the Nazi victory, and Tillich found himself job hunting. Fortunately, H. Richard Niebuhr had visited him in the summer of 1932, and had already begun to make plans to woo him to America, communicating to his brother, Reinhold, Tillich's availability. And Reinhold Niebuhr made a place for him at Union Seminary in New York. In this respect, Tillich's situation was better than that of many of his less well-connected colleagues. When he arrived in this country, however, he found little enthusiasm for his version of socialism. American socialists were put off by the heavy layer of philosophical rhetoric in which his theories were ensconced, while his reputation as a socialist made churchmen wary of him. Admittedly, he always remained too much the thinker to have played an active role in revolution; and perhaps he would have fallen under Marx's stricture against Feuerbach, who also wanted to understand the world in its deeper sense. The revolutionary does not want to interpret history; he wants to make it! Of course, Tillich and the Religious Socialists wanted to make history too, but they were too circumspect, too reflective, and finally too bourgeois to succeed. As Bonhoeffer wrote from his prison cell:

> Tillich set out to interpret the evolution of the world itself—against its will—in a religious sense, to give it its whole shape through religion. That was very courageous of him, but the world unseated him and went on by itself: he too sought to understand the world better than it understood itself, but it felt entirely misunderstood, and rejected the imputation. (Of course the world does need to be understood better than it understands itself but not religiously as the Religious Socialists desired.)[16]

TILLICH'S CONTRIBUTIONS

In spite of his seeming failure in his attempts to win socialism to an ontological-religious interpretation of itself and to win the church to a religious interpretation of socialism, there may be important lessons to

---

16. Dietrich Bonhoeffer, *Letters and Papers from Prison* (New York: Macmillan, 1965), 108.

be learned from Tillich's analysis of the revolutionary situation, lessons that could prove quite useful in our attempts to come to terms with revolutions both in the church and in the world:

1. If being is in its very nature dynamic, characterized by inner tensions that keep it constantly seeking new forms of expression, there is no such thing as permanent stability in any political, social, and economic structures. In the final analysis, only those structures will endure that allow for a high degree of continuous evolution and internal change, those that can accommodate a "permanent revolution."

2. Anxiety is the normal human reaction to change. This anxiety is realistic in that it is grounded in the awareness that existence is possible only through structures, and where structures are threatened nonbeing may take over completely. Anxiety's reaction is to attempt to stop change, to clamp the lid down and buttress the status quo. If Tillich's analysis is correct, however, such a reaction only intensifies the pressure for change. Although heteronomous, repressive measures may for a time give the appearance of maintaining "law and order" better than a more permissive approach, the explosive force of the revolution, when it comes, will be in direct proportion to the amount of energy that has been required to suppress change.

3. Other factors being equal, the more explosive a revolution is, the less chance there is for new forms to capture and give positive expression to the essential power that bursts forth. Yet if authentic new forms are not soon forthcoming that are capable of conserving the genius of the revolution, its positive contributions will be dissipated. Energies will be drained off, and the revolution will end in a confusion of conflicting autonomous authorities and insufferable anarchy, which will give way to the call for a new heteronomy. And so the vicious cycle continues. For heteronomy to survive it must either stamp out the hopes of the people so completely that there is no energy left for dissatisfaction, or it must by propaganda and actual efforts convince most of the people that positive changes are being made at the fastest rate possible under the circumstances. The run-of-the-mill fascist dictatorship is able to do neither of these successfully.

4. Successful revolutions are always partially disappointing. This is because in their origins revolutions are a search for an ultimate

form, for a total solution, for perfection; but any actualization is less than perfect. It participates in the ambiguity of existence and soon finds itself subject to most of the same corrupting influences in other guises that have dogged the existence of its predecessors. Moreover, the gap between the actual world and what we intuit in ontological consciousness as potential is the fundamental tension that makes us dissatisfied with any given forms and drives us on in a constant search for the new. The quest for utopia is grounded in essential being, according to Tillich, and will continue beyond every revolution as an irradicable part of the human makeup.[17] Utopian consciousness remains the disquieting burr under the saddle of every system, and as such its continuing contribution ought to be recognized and channels provided for its positive expression.

5. Responsible revolutionaries will operate out of an awareness of all of these factors. They will understand, for instance, the anxiety of conservative opponents because they have had to face and overcome the same anxieties in themselves as they have demolished the old sources of security, launched out into the unknown, and risked chaos. Understanding the motivations of heteronomy, they will seek ways to meet its valid concerns without, of course, sacrificing the essential goals of the revolution. Their objective will be the shaping of theonomous structures, not the exploitation of new power to gain revenge for past injustices by perpetrating new injustices and imposing new heteronomies.

In the final analysis, Tillich was a *conservative* revolutionary. From his ontological perspective he saw the inevitability of revolution and wanted to give it a positive value. At the same time, if revolutions are to be of maximum benefit, they should take the form of controlled reactions rather than atomic explosions. Indeed, he insisted that revolutions be productive, that they promote their creative elements, and that they find means by which to build in constant change.

It is not surprising, therefore, to discover that the foremost conservative revolutionary in America, Martin Luther King Jr., wrote his doctoral dissertation on Tillich.[18] Though his autobiographical reflections

---

17. Cf. Tillich, "The Political Meaning of Utopia," in *Political Expectation*, 125–80.

18. Martin Luther King Jr., "A Comparison of the Conception of God in the Thinking of Paul Tillich and Henry Nelson Wieman" (doctoral dissertation, Boston University, 1955).

in *Strength to Love* make meager reference to Tillich, it is apparent that Tillich's revolutionary conservatism may have been an important factor in shaping King's own efforts and philosophy, and in his realism about goals and methods. He pointed to the finite character of freedom as one of the things he learned from Tillich. And he thought it important to take into account the anxiety of those who felt the status quo crumbling around them, an anxiety shared both by the demonstrators and the defenders of the structures against which they were demonstrating.[19] This insight informed, and at times tempered, Dr. King's whole approach. It enabled him to sympathize with the anxieties of his opponents as well as those of his followers, and lent his movement a humaneness that few revolutionary movements possess. Thus the contribution that Tillich, the conservative revolutionary, consciously sought and failed to make in the Germany of the 1920s and early 1930s, may have succeeded in an unexpected and indirect way on another continent in another time.

---

19. See Martin Luther King Jr., *Strength to Love* (New York: Harper and Row. 1963), 137.

4

Friedrich Gogarten

Consistent Twentieth-century Pioneer[1]

History is one of those all-important—if somewhat mystifying—words in current theological discussion. And no modern theologian has devoted himself more persistently to clarifying what we mean when we say "Christian faith is historical" than has Friedrich Gogarten. Gogarten's concern has been twofold: to rethink the traditional doctrines of the church in historical rather than metaphysical categories and to show the relevance of Christian faith—understood as a kind of interactive history—to a humankind that has become conscious of the overwhelming responsibility it carries for present history.

Born in 1887 in the Ruhr industrial city of Dortmund, Gogarten received his university training in Berlin, Jena, and Heidelberg. After serving as an assistant pastor in Bremen, he took a small country parish in Thuringia, bought himself a complete edition of Luther's works, and began to steep himself in the thought of the Reformer. Up to this point Gogarten had been a rather conventional "liberal" in the tradition of German idealism. His first book was on the religious thought of Fichte. But his absorption in Luther resulted in an abrupt break with the past, a break that first found expression in his sermons. The peasants

---

1. Originally published as "Friedrich Gogarten" in *A Handbook of Christian Theologians* (Cleveland and New York: The World Publishing Co., 1965), 427–44. The original publisher has gone out of business, with no successor. Every effort has been made to trace the owner and/or administrator of this copyright. The publisher regrets any omission and will, upon written notice, make the necessary corrections in subsequent printings.

who dutifully listened to those sermons might not have been aware of an emerging theological position, but students from the university at nearby Jena soon began making pilgrimages to the village church to hear the young pastor and spend the day discussing theology.

"The Crisis of Culture,"[2] an address delivered in 1920, first brought Gogarten to public attention. Spengler's *Decline of the West* was a best seller and no one in post–World War I Germany needed to be reminded that civilization was in crisis. Gogarten's task was rather to clarify the relation of religion to the crisis. And here he differed sharply with many of his fellow theologians. The question they faced was this: Can Christianity as a Western religion survive the downfall of Western civilization? Many concluded that while Christianity as a historically conditioned form of religion may not survive, that matters little if the essential religious truths expressed in Christianity are preserved. And this is assured, they reasoned, for Christianity like all religions is an expression of the deep, inner religious consciousness of humanity. And this consciousness will persist even if Christianity passes away with Western civilization.

Gogarten's response is not so much a defense of Christianity's present forms as an attack on a liberalism that sees the crisis as limited to these forms. Liberalism is not radical enough. It continues to think of the religious consciousness of humanity as a kind of storm cellar from which humans can emerge after the crisis has blown over. But this is hardly the biblical understanding, which never conceives of crises as simply external, nor as excluding any part of humanity—least of all our religious consciousness. The real crisis, asserts Gogarten, is not defined by the instability of Western civilization but by that which shakes all foundations: the judgment of God. And the religious consciousness is no place to hide from this judgment, for it begins precisely with humanity and its religion—with a humanity that has named the depths of its own spirit "God," and thus completed the circle of reality within itself. For this humanity—its culture, *and* its religion—there is no road to renewal that bypasses death. There are no "good" elements that might be salvaged. For this culture's highest good—the human spirit—is just that which has usurped the place of God. Therefore the death sentence must be pronounced; the *no* must be said. And at the present moment it may have to be said so loudly there seems little room left for a *yes*. But the *no*

---

2. Friedrich Gogarten, translated as "The Crisis of Our Culture" in *The Beginnings of Dialectic Theology*, ed. James M. Robinson (Richmond: John Knox, 1968), 283–300.

of God's judgment is not the *no* of cynicism; it is not ultimately negative. "The death sentence is the entrance into life."[3] It is said in order that the *yes* might be said, the *yes* of God's new creation.

This new creation does not signal the end of crisis, however. If the life of faith means continually receiving oneself from the hand of the Creator, it is a life lived always at the end of human possibilities, never self-sufficient, always dependent for continued existence on help from beyond. Thus the fundamental crisis is permanent, written into the very nature of Christian faith itself.

This awareness of the radical character of the crisis, along with the dialectic of judgment and grace under a sovereign God, made it natural for the young German pastor to join forces with a young Swiss pastor, Karl Barth, who was also disengaging himself from earlier theological idealism and striking out on a new course. In 1922, together with Eduard Thurneysen and Georg Merz (later joined by Rudolf Bultmann and Emil Brunner), they founded a journal that was to provide a forum for this new direction in theology known in Europe as "crisis theology" or "dialectical theology" and in America as "neo-orthodoxy." The journal took its name from the title of one of Gogarten's articles, "*Zwischen den Zeiten*" ("Between the Times").

FAITH AND HISTORICAL RELATIVITY

The book that was to secure Gogarten a permanent place in the theological world, *I Believe in the Triune God*, was published in 1926. Subtitled "An Examination of the Relation between Faith and History," it is a vigorous attack on the historicism tempered with idealism of Troeltsch, Harnack, and Seeberg. Their historical research had forced them to face the *relativity* of Christian ethical and doctrinal positions traditionally considered absolute. They finally had to ask, is there anything in Christianity that is absolute? Troeltsch's answer is characteristic of the general view: Christianity is "the historical concretion of a universal truth."[4] The historical form, marked as it is by the peculiarities of a particular time and place, is not absolute. It is only the shell within which

---

3. Ibid., 291.
4. Ernst Troeltsch in Gogarten, *Ich glaube an den dreieinigen Gott* (Jena: Diederichs, 1916), 96.

dwells an essential idea that is timeless. The absoluteness of Christianity is to be found in the universal value of its history-transcending essence.

But this solution does not satisfy Gogarten. Can an approach that grants validity to historical events only as they can be reduced to a universal essence unconditioned by time and place do justice to Christian faith? If Christian faith is the product of God's creative activity, and if this activity not only takes place in history but *makes* history, then the "essence"of faith most certainly cannot be non-historical. Quite the opposite, *faith is history*.[5]

This claim is basic to Gogarten's whole approach. But it needs explanation, for certainly he does not mean by *faith* much of what passes under that name. Indeed, he protests those views that have gradually diluted the distinctively Hebrew-Christian understanding of the relation between humanity and God, substituting for it aesthetic experience, participation in a world spirit, or religious intuition. Nor is Gogarten any more friendly toward a sterile dogmatism that mistakes assent to theological propositions, however important, for faith. All these views are deficient because they fail to see that faith cannot be defined exclusively in terms of human feelings, intuition, convictions, or ability to assent. Faith is faith only as God is actively involved, only as it is happening *between* God and humanity. "The final, most profound, yet simplest fact is that you cannot have God without God."[6] Faith in God must be called forth by God, the God who communicates trustworthiness and elicits faith and obedience. Faith is therefore an event, a relationship in which the Creator is active with the creature.

It follows that "faith is history" does not mean that faith is simply *past* history. For just as *faith* must be carefully defined, so *history* cannot be understood in the ordinary schoolroom sense. It designates instead the process of interaction in which being and meaning are created ever anew. Therefore faith is present history, history now taking place. And if it is not present history it is nothing.

Gogarten recognized in the I-Thou approach being developed by Grisebach, Buber, Ebner, and Heim an interpretation of history akin to his own. And Bultmann's *Jesus and the Word*, the first edition of which appeared in 1926, applies a similar methodology to New Testament studies. The reality of history is neither the reality of ideas in the mind of

---

5. Ibid., 17–18.
6. Gogarten in Robinson, *The Beginnings of Dialectic Theology*, 298.

the interpreter, who by virtue of these ideas makes the facts fit together in a meaningful pattern (subjectivism and idealism), nor the reality of the "facts" in themselves in their detached isolated state (objectivism and positivism). The truth cannot be known by coming down on one side or the other of a fence between subject and object. It is found instead in the interaction between subject and object—or better, in the case of God and humanity, between Subject and subject. Reality is an event that happens in the "between" in history.

Thus the problem of relativity as it concerns Christian faith is solved not by escaping from history into a realm of absolute ideals and universals but by living in history the *responsible* life of faith. And faith is itself a kind of relativity, man's relativity to God in every new moment.

In his next major work, *Politische Ethik* (*Political Ethics*), Gogarten examines the implications of this view of history for the relationships between human beings. Here again relativity is the problem. Historical research had mercilessly exposed the relativity of supposedly absolute ethical norms and standards. Seeking to rebuild on the wreckage, Christian ethical theorists were tempted to search for universal principles within Christianity that would be valid beyond the relativities of Christianity as a historical religion, on the assumption that if such universals could be found a system of Christian ethics could be formulated that would have all-embracing validity and lasting authority. From Gogarten's standpoint, however, historical contingency—while undermining an absolutist ethic—is not inimical to ethics as such. Indeed, the fact that history is composed of contingent relationships is what makes it unavoidably ethical. One has one's ethical being in creative encounters—being is always being-from-the-other *(Von-dem-Andern-sein)*—and continuing existence in being-with-another *(Mit-dem-Andern-sein)*. These are not secondary modes of existence preceded by a primary mode of being-in-and-for-oneself *(An-und-für-sich-sein)*; rather, individuality is secondary and the interpersonal is primary.[7]

Accordingly, ethical decisions and actions are the result not of adhering to abstract, non-historical standards of what one does or does not do, but of responding to each situation out of the being that one is in the relation to God and neighbor. The Christian life is a life of openness and obedience. The two go together. Obedience is understood not as strict

---

7. Gogarten, *Politische Ethik* (Jena: Diederichs, 1932), 26, 173. Thus "thou-I" would be a more appropriate characterization of Gogarten's approach.

compliance with laws and ideals but as that kind of openness that marks the genuine listener (*obedience* means literally "to hear toward") whose action is a creative response to what is heard. In ethics as elsewhere, therefore, the problem of relativity is overcome not by substituting nonhistorical absolutes for the relativities of history but by facing each situation as a call to responsible action in history out of the existence one has in faith. Thus Gogarten provides us with one of the earliest formulations of a "contextual ethic," which has become a hallmark of much contemporary, theologically based ethical thought.

Not content to rest on the level of individual relations, Gogarten pursues the implications of his position for an ethic of the state. Contemporary Western theories of society and the state have their roots in the individualism of rationalism. They are I-oriented. The fundamental mode of existence is understood as "being-in-and-for-oneself." Society and the state are thus secondary, artificial realities created by humanity for the furtherance of welfare, goals, and ideals. Over against this Gogarten sets an understanding of the state as a fabric of inter-responsibility in which each has his or her being in being-for-another.[8] The state is given power over the individual member to ensure that the needs of the body politic will be met by forced obedience, if necessary, where the individual is irresponsible regarding duties. Such obedience is not true obedience in the intended sense, of course, but is necessary to maintain order in at least an external sense even if fallen humanity does not will it.

Discernible here is the influence of Luther's doctrine of civil authority, which grounds the magistrate's authority and power in the Fall. His Lutheran unwillingness to risk anarchy was to make Gogarten less prone to criticize the state in the first years of the Nazi regime than were many of his friends in the circle of dialectical theology. During the same period there was a gradual parting of the ways theologically between Gogarten and Barth, the latter accusing Gogarten, Bultmann, and Brunner of leaving the common ground of the earlier dialectical theology and making theology too dependent upon philosophical presuppositions.[9] This led

---

8. Hence Gogarten's preference for the title "political ethics" rather than the usual "social ethics." The *polis* is an organic whole in which each member has a function and duty for the maintenance of the body politic, rather than merely an association of individuals. See *Politische Ethik*, 115-16, 147-49.

9. See *Zwischen den Zeiten* XI (1933): 311.

to the discontinuation of the journal *Zwischen den Zeiten*, as well as the partnership that had created it.

Though continuing to teach (at the University of Breslau, from 1931 to 1935, and at the University of Göttingen, from 1935 until his retirement in 1955), Gogarten published no further major work until after World War II.

FAITH AND SECULARITY

In most of his major postwar works, Gogarten continues his interest in history, but whereas his concern earlier had been to overcome idealism and answer the problem of historical relativism, he now turns to what he considers *the* problem confronting a technological age: the relation of Christian faith to secularism. And he does this by developing the implications of a theology of history for the traditional theological questions of Christology and soteriology (in *The Proclamation of Jesus Christ*), law and gospel (in his magnum opus, *Man between God and the World*), faith and works (in *The Fate and Hope of the Modern Era*), and subjectivism versus objectivism (in *The Reality of Faith*).

While the popular attitude toward secularism regards it as the archenemy of the faith, Gogarten asks whether a certain kind of secularization is not implicit in the Christian gospel itself. For example, the secular view sees the world as depopulated of those spirits once thought to have the world's well-being under their control. The task of maintaining the order of the world passes out of the hands of the demons, angels, "principalities and powers," and into the hands of humanity, which takes over the responsibility of ordering and caring for the world in accordance with human needs and desires. Such a secularization is, however, by no means foreign to the Christian faith, in which humanity is understood as receiving its being from the creative Word of God that calls us, not just into existence, but into an existence-in-responsibility. The world is directly involved in this responsibility, for the being into which we are called is, in Pauline terminology, the being of a *son* (or daughter) (Gal 4). A son is distinguished from a child in that, whereas the child is completely dependent upon the parent for continued existence, sons or daughters—who have come of age and received an inheritance to manage—have the ability to stand on their own, to be independent (*selbständig*), no longer bound to the parent by the necessities of physical survival. The inheritance bestowed upon humanity is the *world;* we are given dominion over it and charged with the responsibility to "till it and keep it" (Gen 2:15). Our position with regard to the world thus frees us for a mature and non-compulsive relationship with the Creator, while the filial relation to the Creator frees us for a mature and non-compulsive attitude toward the world.[10]

Now we are in a position to understand the context of Gogarten's recurrent insistence that the examination and ordering of the world be delivered to the human reason with no strings attached.[11] His regular conversations with his physicist colleague at Göttingen, Carl Friedrich von Weizsäcker, convinced him of the very real necessity of clarifying the relation of formal and technological reason to faith, especially as it bears on the responsibility of the scientist. Again he finds the answer in Luther's understanding of faith and works and the doctrine of the two realms. Faith has no business anxiously hovering over reason lest reason discover something about the world that would undermine faith. A faith that could be so undermined would actually be pre-Christian, that is, it would in effect assume that the world has a power over one's salvation that the early Christian message specifically denied that the world possesses. In genuine faith humanity receives the world and its existence as steward of the world—but not information about the world. The latter is *our* responsibility and is to be gained through our efforts. Nor need we justify ourselves before God by piously limiting our reason in the pursuit of this task. We are justified by faith alone, that is, by the sustaining relationship with the Creator, which frees us to explore the world with true "objectivity," unhampered by the subjective necessity of justifying our existence by our works.

However, contends Gogarten, if faith is not present, if humanity does not continue to receive existence from the God, then the crucial balance—reason operating within faith—cannot be maintained. Freedom and openness are destroyed, anxiety sets in, and a now heteronomous "faith" seeks to extend its authority and control over an autonomous "reason," and vice versa, in the anxious effort to reestablish the wholeness and unity of life lost with the death of genuine faith. It matters little which side in this struggle is victorious, for neither is what it was and is

---

10. Note the similarity between Gogarten's development regarding the place of the world in Christian faith and Dietrich Bonhoeffer's later seminal idea of "the world come of age."

11. E.g., *The Reality of Faith* (Philadelphia: Westminster, 1959), 90.

meant to be. Both have been fundamentally perverted. Humanity without faith remains a son or daughter, to be sure, but a son or daughter who has betrayed the Father. Humanity without faith retains mastery over the world, but as a master who is in the ironic position of having to squeeze meaning and being out of that over which we are lord. Thus the change is not so much the loss of what we previously were as turning what we were into its negating opposite.[12] Just as honor betrayed becomes dishonor—that is worse than the mere absence of honor—so sonship betrayed becomes worse than the mere absence of relationship; it becomes a corrupted relationship, one of alienation and estrangement.

When this shift comes about and humanity looks to the world for being and meaning, the world begins to take on a religious nature. That which was secular now becomes the source of life in a religious sense remarkably parallel to the ancient world, though without benefit of the ancient mythology. The reality is the same, however. We are subject to the powers of the world; they control our meaning or lack of it. Nor are "materialists" the only ones who fall under this subjugation. Indeed, the two classic examples of bondage to the world are religious: the Greeks' bondage to the cosmos and the Jews' bondage to the law. In both instances one's being was assured only if one adhered rigidly to what was understood as a religious order of things. Absolute conformity brought salvation. Is the picture so different today? Meaning, place, and position are guaranteed with conformity to a group, class, or national self-image that grants participants being—but only as long as they continue to conform. Nonconformity results in rejection and threatened loss of being. Worldviews are propounded that promise to reduce the world to a meaningful and manageable whole—but only if one adheres to the assumptions and laws by which their originators seek to introduce order. Stray from the path and chaos reigns again. In this misuse of reason, meaning can be had only at the price of conformity to the law of the world of the human mind. Gogarten's early rejection of idealism was based on the conviction that it was really a form of worldliness; it imposed a subjective scheme of things upon reality and insisted that reality conform to that scheme. A fullscale example of the same phenomenon was National Socialism. Operating on the basis of a quasi-mythological world view, Nazism methodically destroyed all opposition to its ordering of the world in conformity with its own

12. Cf. Romans 1:22–25.

self-image. All such religio-secularistic attempts are inherently totalitarian. Any opposition calls forth a neurotic response simply because as long as opposition persists the system is in principle undermined, for it has failed to accomplish what it promises: to reduce all of reality to conformity with itself.

Thus the problem of secularism is not its irreligion but its continual tendency to become religious. *It is not secular enough.* Secularism in its various modern forms does not preserve the truly the secular nature of the world but tends to give to the world—whether this be the material world, the world of religion, or the world of its own mind—the honor due God alone. Christian faith proposes to keep the world truly secular and thus safeguard human freedom toward the world through a certain kind of existence, existence as a mature and responsible human being under the Creator. Where this existence-in-faith is not present, however, the freedom for which we were created cannot be present. We still remain human, to be sure, and as human we are that being who has our being *in relation,* that creature who must be fulfilled from beyond ourselves. But this is precisely our difficulty. If not fulfilled through a free relation to our Creator, we will—we *must*—turn to another source of fulfillment; we enter into a compulsive relation to the world.

In the fateful situation of corrupted relations, God acts to restore to us the possibility of authentic relations. And God does so in and through the true Son.

CHRISTOLOGY AND SOTERIOLOGY

In developing his doctrine of Christ, Gogarten insists that Jesus' divinity must be understood in and through his humanity. Jesus' revelation of God is to be found in his history rather than in a metaphysical nature in which he is "consubstantial" with the Father. Or, expressed another way, his history *is* his metaphysical nature through which he reveals God to us and brings about reconciliation. In his history the incarnational event—God assuming our flesh—takes place. What is the nature of this event?

Jesus of Nazareth is fully a human being, but since he is a human who is completely responsive and obedient to the one he calls Father, his being is being-from-the-Father. Lived out of this relation, his life is the concrete expression of the divine will. In the history of Jesus of Nazareth the eternal will of God is enacted. He is that Son who *is* the second person of the Trinity, for in his life the eternal relation between the Father and the Son in the being of God becomes historical.[13] The basic difference, therefore, between ourselves and Jesus is not the difference between natural man and a supernatural being but the difference between sinful history and faithful history, between sonship betrayed and sonship lived out.

But to this must be added that Jesus' relationship is with the One who wills to restore estranged sons and daughters to fellowship. Consequently, the Son who received his being from the Father reflects in his sonship the concern of the Father for the brothers and sisters. He enters into relationship with them and thus also receives his being from their sinful being. Having his being *entirely* from God, Jesus turns toward humanity and, in fulfillment of the second half of the Great Commandment, receives his being *entirely* from humanity. (This illustrates how "being" as used by Gogarten cannot be understood substantially or quantitatively but as the quality of historical existence.) Thus his full divinity and full humanity are the result of the same divine will and are a description of the same history. He is "made to be sin" (2 Cor 5:21), while at the same time remaining "without sin" (Heb 4:15) in perfect obedience to God. Scriptural passages such as these, which for a substantialist approach must remain inexplicable, take on new meaning and relevance when seen as history. The doctrine of the two natures of Christ is meant to be not an unintelligible mystery but an account of Jesus' life with God and humanity. At the same time, it is an account of the way in which humanity is restored to that filial life with God for which we were created. Since true sonship is not available apart from faith, the question becomes: How does the action of God in Jesus Christ make faith—and true relationship—possible?

Acting in accordance with the will of God, Jesus turns toward the brothers and sisters, participating in their being-in-sin through his relationship to them. In so doing, he experiences more radically than can any of us the intensity of the alienation between humanity and God, for he experiences it within his own history. On him the full weight of the curse of this alienation falls, coming to expression in the cry of dereliction. Is it surprising that the cross was interpreted by the early church as judgment, as the place where Christ as the representative of humanity takes upon himself the judgment that should rightly fall on all? This is

---

13. See "Gottheit und Menschheit Jesu Christi," *Zwischen den Zeiten* X (1932): 3ff.

how it looks from our side. On the cross the man who has received his being from a humankind-against-God is reduced to nothingness. But the cross is not only "the disclosure of the guilt-laden fate of perverted being that lies upon man and his world"; it is also the turning of this fate. It is not only the sign of divine judgment but also "the sign of the salvation brought to man by the crucified One." It is not only the condemnation of our sin and our reduction to *Nichtigkeit;* but "on the cross the forfeited sonship is bestowed anew."[14] The humanity-against-God is reduced to nothingness—but in order that we might be raised and restored by the God who quickens the dead (Rom 4: 17).

We participate in this history that takes place in Jesus Christ as we encounter the Word directed toward us from the Father and communicated to us through the Son. For the one who hangs on the cross as the representative of humanity is also the Son who is the representative of God. In the encounter with the Son, we meet that which both reduces us to nothing and raises us to new life and new relatedness. For in the relation with Christ we receive our being from the One who receives his being from God and whose being is therefore "historically identical" with that of God the Father. In this way we participate in the salvation made available to us in Jesus Christ. But this participation is not metaphysical, nor mystical, nor is it a matter of the moral influence or spiritual interpretation of a story, nor any approach that views atonement as taking place exclusively, or even primarily, either in the supernatural world apart from us or within our minds. It is fundamentally the reconciliation of persons. It is the event that takes place as we are confronted by the One who in his life, death, and resurrection is God's judgment upon our life apart from God and is at the same time God's turning toward us in forgiveness and restoration to true relatedness in the faith relation.[15]

In this historical event of atonement we are released from our bondage to the world and restored to our intended place over it through the reestablishment of the faith-relation to God. Once again we receive our fundamental meaning and being from the Creator and are thus enabled to live in creative freedom toward a world that has been "secularized," stripped of its idolatrous pretensions. (This transformation can be expressed mythologically as the vanquishing of the demonic cosmic powers through the cross of Christ, a victory in which we benefit by

---

14. *The Reality of Faith,* 123, 125.
15. See Gogarten, *Demythologizing and History* (London: SCM Press, 1955), 68–79.

virtue of our relation to the Victor (cf. Rom 8:38f.; Eph 1 and 2; Col 1 and 2). Thus salvation is at the same time the secularization of the world, that kind of secularization that, according to Gogarten, is at the heart of Christian faith.

Modern secular*ism* on the other hand, developing out of the reorientation that took place in the Renaissance and Enlightenment, has purged the world of gods and devils by splitting all reality into "subject" and "object," the subject taking charge over the world as its object in a way it previously had never dared to do. The world is to be examined in and for itself, disregarding all supernatural associations, in order to define and isolate the intramundane law. The result of this methodology has been a technological advance without parallel. Unfortunately, however, technological control, though it does guarantee the burden of responsibility, does not guarantee meaning. The result is a situation in which we *alone* are responsible for the world—there are no more gods with whom to share the burden—while at the same time the ultimate meaning of this responsibility eludes us. We feel increasingly victimized by a world about which we are accumulating ever greater amounts of objective information. Yet every attempt to derive meaning from within the world proves finally unsatisfactory. At the end of the subject-object era the *object* has become the real, the vis-à-vis *(Gegenüber)* from which the subject has to receive its being because it is the only reality apart from the subject. As a result, the subject is relativized by that over which it is supposed to exercise dominion. And the values of the subject are now "only relative," "only subjective."

The bankruptcy of the subject-object orientation as an exclusive approach to reality is clear. It has ended in a situation in which we are the victim and captive of that toward which we should—and indeed *must*—be free if we are to carry out our responsibility for "tilling and keeping," for ordering and maintaining the world under the Creator.

FAITH AND DEMYTHOLOGIZING

It should now be apparent why Gogarten felt called upon to enter the "demythologizing controversy" on the side of Bultmann. The real issue at stake, says Gogarten in *Demythologizing and History*, is the nature of faith and its relation to history.

A charge commonly lodged against Bultmann and his followers is that they have, by the application of rigorously critical methods to the

New Testament, reduced the amount of objective, factual material in the gospel records to the point where the bridge between the historical Jesus and the preaching about him has collapsed. If the first Christians were not concerned with reporting the facts objectively in their preaching, but instead made generous use of the language of the then-current world views *(Weltanschauungen)* and of the ancient conception of the physical universe *(Weltbild)* in interpreting and proclaiming what they experienced, we are left with little or no solid ground in reliable fact to which we can point as reinforcing the claim of faith that God has acted decisively in objective history through the life, death, and resurrection of Jesus Christ. And if this be the case, how can we continue to speak of Christianity as a "historical" religion in any more than a strained and indeed mythological sense?

But Gogarten must question both assumptions: the objectivism of history and the subjectivism of faith. The demythologizers no less than their opponents affirm that "the great acts of God are set before all human existence indestructibly, indissolubly, and irremovably."[16] But the reality and permanence of these events, as they are understood in the Bible itself, lie not in their independent objectivity but in their being used by God in communicating the divine intention toward humanity. This is made especially clear, as we have seen, in the revelation in Jesus Christ. The genuine history of Jesus *includes* his relation with God. His very being is being-from-the-Father. Moreover, the being he receives as the Son is God's being-for-humanity. So that *the history of Jesus is God's turning toward humanity to save!* But obviously neither the relation of Jesus to God nor the intention of God toward humanity enacted through the Son is available through an "objective" approach, not because they are irrecoverable but because both are recoverable only in and through a method appropriate to transmitting the kind of history with which we are here concerned. For this history has a verbal *(worthaft)* character; it intends to communicate. And its reality cannot be grasped apart from a reception of this communication. This is why preaching, far from breaking the connection with the historical Jesus, is actually the conserver and effectuator of the genuine history of Jesus. For whoever would understand this history must be involved in it as it becomes the living Word of God to us. This history can be grasped and understood only as its reality becomes present, as it happens here and now. To attempt to reduce this

---

16. Ibid., 67.

to "objective" history is to engage in a "miserable rationalization of the New Testament history ... [by which] the New Testament message loses its own historical character."[17]

Likewise, faith for Gogarten cannot be labeled "subjective," for faith is not a subject's affirmation of an object but rather its being confronted by the Word from beyond itself and incorporated into a relationship—into a new history fundamentally conditioned by the history of Jesus Christ (as that history has just been described). Faith therefore transcends subjectivism by virtue of the fact that it is a historical mode of being, a being-from-the-other and with-the-other. Apart from this "other" and the interaction there is no genuine faith.

What happens in revelation and faith thus bursts the bonds of the subject-object approach and simply cannot be comprehended by it. To attempt to do so can lead only to a distortion of the genuine reality involved. The demythologizers recognize this and explicitly operate in a different context in their theological formulations. However, they do continue to use the objective approach where it is appropriate, namely, in historical critical research. The resultant alternation between methods is the source of much confusion to many of their opponents who themselves operate for the most part unconsciously in a subject-object context that is neither so strictly employed in criticism nor so clearly superseded in theological formulation. Thus much of what is said and written in the controversy is unfortunately beside the point. Rather than the destruction of historical truth, the demythologizers see their task as making possible a proper confrontation with a history understood not as a supernatural object but as the divine Word. Their negative contribution is in making it impossible to confuse faith with assent to certain thought forms of the first century. Consequently they have to be critical of the *form* of expression of the first century, but only in order to open up the genuinely historical *content* that was and is being communicated: God's Word to humanity.

Because of his defense of the existentialist stance in theology, Gogarten's name is today often linked with that of Bultmann as it once was with Barth. In some respects the present classification is more justified than the earlier one, for Gogarten's Lutheran bias and philosophical interests made him something of an anomaly in dialectical theology. It would be a mistake, however, simply to equate Gogarten with Bultmann.

17. Ibid., 76.

Several of the so-called "post-Bultmannians" are dependent upon Gogarten for their theological orientation, especially Gerhard Ebeling, Brunner's successor at Zurich,[18] and Ernst Fuchs, upon whom the mantle of Bultmann has fallen at Marburg. And Gogarten is credited with anticipating systematically in *The Proclamation of Jesus Christ*[19] many of the conclusions to which these younger critics of Bultmann have since come on the basis of textual evidence. Perhaps it is his foremost American admirer, Carl Michalson, who in *The Rationality of Faith*,[20] a programmatic study of faith's relation to history, has given most explicit expression to Gogarten's central concern. For underneath Gogarten's earlier attacks on idealism, as well as his more recent conversations with secularization, lies but one aim: to examine systematically the implications for theology of the truth that reality in general, and the reality of the Christian faith in particular, must once again be viewed as it was in the biblical period—as inter-active history.

---

18. See Gerhard Ebeling, *The Nature of Faith* (Philadelphia: Muhlenberg, 1961).

19. Gogarten, *Die Verkündigung Jesu Christi* (Heidelberg: L. Schneider, 1948). For an account of the "post-Bultmannian" development see James M. Robinson, *A New Quest of the Historical Jesus* (London: SCM Press, 1961).

20. Carl Michalson, *The Rationality of Faith* (NewYork: Scribner's, 1963).

5

Parallels Between Jürgen Moltmann and John Wesley[1]

I WOULD LIKE TO share with you an unlikely personal journey that took me from a twenty-first century theologian to the rediscovery of the eighteenth-century founder of Methodism. My first meeting with Jürgen Moltmann was in 1963 at the Faith and Order assembly of the World Council of Churches in Montreal. We discovered that we both had studied at the University of Göttingen with the same Doktorvater (doctoral advisor), Professor Otto Weber. This made me eager to explore Moltmann's book, *Theologie der Hoffnung*, when it appeared the next year. Convinced of the importance of the book and not wanting to wait for an English translation, I announced a graduate seminar on the German text in the spring quarter of 1966. Four students who had just passed their German foreign language examination signed up. They struggled mightily with the text and were not impressed when I assured them that Moltmann's German was considerably clearer and easier to understand than was Karl Barth's. But they faithfully worked through and discussed the chapters of that text.

My fascination with Wesley did not begin until ten years later when Dow Kirkpatrick enlisted me to take over his position as American co-director of the Oxford Institute of Methodist Theological Studies, a meeting at that time held every four years at Oxford University for

---

1. "Moltmann and Wesley," originally published in *Hoffnung auf Gott—Zukunft des Lebens: 40 Jahre "Theologie der Hoffnung,"* (Gütersloh, Germany: Gütersloher Verlaghaus, 2005), 129–143. Permission granted, Gütersloher Verlaghaus.

European and American faculties in Methodist theological colleges and seminaries. We expanded the 1977 meeting to include Latin American delegates, focusing on the theme "Sanctification and Liberation," the dialogue between Euro-American theologians and the emerging Latin American theology of liberation. The contributions of Moltmann to the thinking of the Latin Americans were immediately recognizable, although the Latin Americans were sometimes loath to admit it, concerned as they were to claim their independence from Euro-American influences. But one Latin American, José Míguez Bonino, a president of the World Council of Churches and a Methodist systematic theologian from the Protestant Institute of Advanced Theological Studies in Buenos Aires, was not hesitant to celebrate the connection with Moltmann, quoting in one of his books this classic passage from *Theology of Hope*:

> Faith, wherever it develops into hope, causes not rest but unrest, not patience but impatience. It does not calm the unquiet heart, but is itself this unquiet heart in human beings. Those who hope in Christ can no longer put up with reality as it is, but begin to suffer under it, to contradict it. Peace with God means conflict with the world, for the goad of the promised future stabs inexorably into the flesh of every unfulfilled present.[2]

That session of the Oxford Institute drew themes from Wesley on issues of justice: poverty and economic justice, social change, women's liberation, and liberation in the African-American religious tradition, published as *Sanctification and Liberation: Liberation Theologies in the Light of the Wesleyan Tradition*.[3] Editing that volume, I was struck by the fact that these were all themes that Moltmann addressed as well. Recalling this, when I was invited to be one of the contributors in the celebration of the fortieth anniversary of the publication of *Theology of Hope*, I thought it might be of interest to examine more closely some of the issues and theological concerns shared by Wesley and Moltmann. Looking at these themes in Moltmann may give Methodists a new perspective on the resources available in their Wesleyan heritage.

Of the many possible parallels between Moltmann and Wesley, from human rights to women's rights, I have chosen three: *goal orientation*, *ecology*, and *religious pluralism*.

---

2. Jürgen Moltmann, *Theology of Hope* (London: SCM Press, 1967), 21.

3. Theodore Runyon, ed., *Sanctification and Liberation* (Nashville: Abingdon Press, 1981).

GOAL ORIENTATION

The first parallel found in both Moltmann and Wesley is a teleological structure of salvation. For both the kingdom of God is not simply a heaven beyond this world but is breaking into this world as present participation in a future fulfillment. The form this takes in Moltmann is eschatological. History is not circular, a meaningless round without direction and purpose. History has a goal, and that goal is God's reign over all of life. The coming kingdom of God rights the wrongs that human sin has introduced into God's creation. It is an intervention implicit in God's covenant with the people of Israel, anticipated by the hopes of the prophets, initiated by God's Son, and spread abroad by the Spirit. The children of Israel carried with them their nomad God of the covenant who journeyed with them through the wilderness into the promised land. But there they were tempted by the local agricultural gods, the Canaanite gods of the eternal round of the seasons, of seedtime and harvest, the gods who in their new context could guarantee fertility and the success of their crops. Nevertheless the Israelites, inspired by their prophets, clung to the God who had been faithful to them during their wanderings in the desert and resisted the allure of the epiphany gods of the Canaanites. They clung to the promises of fulfillment in the future.[4] It was in this soil that early Christianity was planted and that prepared the way for an amazing turn of events that established the future-orientation of Jesus' disciples. For it was the resurrection that now gave history a direction in a new covenant and, after the utter defeat of the crucifixion, a new hope. The resurrection is the first fruits of the victory that is yet to come in its fullness but that sustains life and hope in the power of the Spirit. The outpouring of the Spirit at Pentecost guarantees that the God who accompanied Israel to the promised land will continue to accompany the people of the new covenant into the future and toward the kingdom. The Christian community broadens the reach of covenant faith. It is no longer limited just to the Jewish nation but extends the good news of Jesus' resurrection to all humanity everywhere. For Jesus is the beginning of the renewal of the image of God in all humankind. He is the opening to a new destiny for all who would be his disciples and be led by his Spirit on their way into the new future.

---

4. Moltmann, *Theology of Hope*, 96–106.

By emphasizing the decisive role of the Spirit in this way into the future, Moltmann corrects the tendency in Karl Barth, and indeed in most of western Christianity, to proclaim a "binitarian" gospel, a gospel of the Father and the Son, downplaying the role of the Spirit. In the case of Barth this was understandable, given the social context in which Barth's theology developed. A totalitarian Nazi state needed to be countered by a resolutely absolute and sovereign God, and an exclusive revelation in Christ, excluding Nazi claims to revelation in the state and Aryan race. But Western theology in general, both Protestant and Catholic, has neglected the role of the *Spirit* ever since the division in 1054 between Eastern and Western Christendom over the filioque clause[5] introduced by the Western church into the Nicene Creed. The Eastern church argued that this in effect made the Spirit subservient, not ascribing to the Spirit full equality in the Godhead. Moltmann has played an important role in the efforts of the World Council of Churches to resolve the unnecessary conflicts arising from this age-old division.

Turning now to Wesley, how does Wesley do justice to the eschatological thrust, the theme of hope, and the goal orientation of the Christian gospel? We have to begin by recognizing that eschatology was not a major theme for the founder of Methodism, probably because the trumpeters of the currently popular "Left Behind" theme were in Wesley's time the so-called "French prophets," Huguenot refugees from France who, under the strain of decades of Catholic persecution, had turned to an apocalyptic gospel that predicted an early judgment and cataclysmic end to this evil world. Wesley also avoided the apocalyptic predictions of the leading New Testament scholar of his time, Johann Albrecht Bengel, on whom Wesley otherwise relied extensively in his own commentary, *Notes on the New Testament*. Bengel predicted the inbreaking of the millenium on June 18, 1836. From Wesley's standpoint, that was too long to wait. Such a prediction puts the kingdom too far into the future and misses the possibility of a goal closer at hand. Justification and sanctification for Wesley describe the way the kingdom is breaking in even now. The justifying grace of God makes reconciliation possible. And grace in the heart of the believer—"we love because he first loved us"—inaugurates a new history that begins with justification and includes the quickening of the spiritual senses and the renewal of the image of God. This image now reflects and

---

5. Nicene Creed: "We believe in the Holy Spirit, . . . who proceeds from the Father *and the Son*" *(filioque,* italics added*).*

mirrors back to God and out to neighbors the love we are receiving. But the fulness of salvation still lies ahead. The goal is *entire* sanctification. Love to God and neighbor is that with which sanctification begins, and the comprehensive and transforming increase of this love is the goal toward which sanctification is constantly aimed. The perfection of this love lived out is "Christian perfection."

Moltmann is accurate when he says that pietism in general, and Wesley as a representative pietist, tends to reduce eschatology to the interior life of the individual, thus missing the biblical understanding of eschatology. Biblical eschatology sees Jesus' resurrection as God inaugurating a new era, not just in the interior life of the individual, but in world history. The kingdom that Jesus ushers in is one in which God's will shall be done "on earth as it is in heaven." To be sure, there are times when Wesley describes the kingdom in a pietistic way.

> It is called "the kingdom of God" because it is the immediate fruit of God's reigning in the soul. . . . It is called "the kingdom of heaven" because it is (in a degree) heaven opened in the soul. For whosoever they are that experience this, they can aver before angels and men [quoting a hymn of Charles Wesley:] "Everlasting life is won: Glory is on earth begun."[6]

But he can also say that in the Lord's prayer,

> "Thy kingdom come" is offered up for the whole intelligent creation, who are all interested in this grand event, the final renovation of all things by God's putting an end to misery and sin, to infirmity and death, taking all the things into his own hands, and setting up the kingdom that endureth throughout all ages.[7]

While the eschatological hope is for the destruction of the forces of evil, it is not for the destruction of this world but its transformation, not the annihilation of the present creation but its renewal. The apocalyptic message of the French prophets in Wesley's London was that as soon as the proper number of individuals had been rescued, God would destroy the planet, much as apocalypticists today proclaim. Wesley could not deny that there were passages in the New Testament that could be used

---

6. John Wesley, *The Works of John Wesley*, Bicentennial edition; hereafter *Works* or *Works* (Bicentennial), Albert C. Outler et. al., eds. (Nashville: Abingdon Press, 1984), vol. 1:224. Direct quotations used by permission.

7. Ibid., vol. 1:582.

to reinforce this view. But this was not, he insisted, "the whole tenor of Scripture." Those passages that speak of future destruction should be balanced with those that speak of God's efforts to redeem the earth, not by annihilating it but by renewing it. God will not "despise the work of [his own] hands." God takes neither delight in the death of a sinner nor in the destruction of anything he has made. But Wesley had to oppose not just the apocalypticists but also the quietists, who claimed, "religion does not lie in outward things but in the heart, the inmost soul; it is the union of the soul with God." God is not concerned with "outward services, but [only with] a pure and holy heart." To these claims Wesley answers, "The root of religion lies in the heart. But if this root be really in the heart it cannot but put forth branches," and these branches "partake of the same nature, and consequently are not only marks or signs, but substantial parts of religion."[8] Thus persons who participate in the life of God in the soul become the agents of God in the world.

> "Ye are the salt of the earth." It is your very nature to season whatever is round about you. . . . This is the reason why the providence of God has so mingled you together with other men, that whatever grace you have received of God may through you be communicated to others. . . . By this means a check will in some measure be given to the corruption that is in the world.[9]

Indeed, the branches of true religion bring forth the "outward practice of justice, mercy and truth." And Wesley goes on to say, "true Christianity cannot exist without both the inward experience and the outward practice of justice, mercy and truth."[10] Yes, justice is experienceable; or perhaps it is more to the point to say that injustice is experienceable as we feel the protest mounting within us at the sight of injustice and the lack of mercy, as Wesley witnessed it at the slave market in Charleston where he sensed that trust was betrayed and truth trampled underfoot. The outward practice of justice, mercy, and truth is dependent upon inward experience, for as Moltmann says in *Experiences of God*, "Only the person who has discovered a stable identity in himself

---

8. Ibid., 541–44.
9. Ibid., 537.
10. Ibid., vol. 4:174.

will protest against social injustice and resist political oppression and be prepared to make the necessary sacrifices."[11]

Therefore, the goal of the Christian life is for Wesley entire sanctification, a goal that lies not in the distant future or in another world, but a goal meant to direct our faith and actions in this life and in this world. This is a goal realizable through the perfecting work of the Spirit. Here Wesley departs from the main emphasis of Luther who was so important for Wesley's understanding of justification. For Luther, discovering and appropriating the grace and forgiveness of God in Christ is the supreme goal, and justification is the greatest gift. It was Wesley's realization of this that he describes in his account of Aldersgate. "I felt I did trust in Christ, Christ alone for salvation; and an assurance was given me that he had taken away *my* sins, even *mine*, and saved *me* from the law of sin and death."[12] But with time and distance from Aldersgate, Wesley realized that God's purpose in redeeming and reconciling us in Christ was not just to forgive our sins, important as that is, but to restore us to what we were created to be, namely, to serve as the image of God in the world through the empowering Spirit. This understanding of the sanctifying work of the Spirit was something to which Wesley had been introduced by the ancient Eastern Fathers during his Oxford years, but for which at that time he had not had the proper undergirding. That foundation was supplied by Luther and the experience of radical grace. Then the two aspects of salvation, justification and sanctification, finally fit together.

> The righteousness of Christ is the whole and sole *foundation* of all our hope. It is by faith that the Holy Ghost enables us to build upon this foundation. God gives this faith. In that moment we are accepted of God, and yet not for the sake of that faith, but of what Christ has done and suffered for us.[13]

But God has more in store for us. God not only justifies, not only reconciles, but opens up hitherto unimagined possibilities for *growth* in grace. And so Wesley urges, quoting Heb 6:1,

> Go on to perfection. Yea, and when ye have attained a measure of perfect love, when God has . . . enabled you to love him with all your heart and all your soul, think not of resting there. That

---

11. Jürgen Moltmann, *Experiences of God* (Philadelphia: Fortress Press, 1980), 60.
12. *Works*, vol. 18:250.
13. Ibid., vol. 1:459.

is impossible. You cannot stand still; you must either rise or fall—rise higher or fall lower. Therefore the voice of God to the children of Israel, to the children of God is "Go forward" [Exod 14:15]. "Forgetting those things that are behind, and reaching forward unto those that are before, press on to the mark for the prize of your high calling of God in Christ Jesus!" [see Phil 3:13–14].[14]

This is the goal orientation in Wesley, the teleology that parallels the structure in Moltmann's eschatological orientation. Of course the hope in Moltmann's case is for world history and is more cosmic in scope, whereas in Wesley the hope is more for growth in grace in the life of the individual. Moreover, Wesley argued, if there is no expectation of a sanctification that in the future is entire and complete, present life cannot be nurtured and shaped by this hope.

> Constant experience shows, the more earnestly they expect this, the more swiftly and steadily does the gradual work of God go on in their soul. . . . Whereas, just the contrary effects are observed whenever this expectation ceases. They are "saved by hope," by this hope of a total change, with a gradually increasing salvation. Destroy this hope, and that salvation stands still, or, rather, decreases daily.[15]

Now this could be understood as fitting into the pietistic framework of the salvation of the individual. But Wesley sees it as being empowered by the Spirit, which he claims immediately turns us outward. The renewed image of God is not something that inheres within the individual but, like a mirror (a simile he borrows from the Eastern Fathers), always reflects the light it receives from beyond itself back to God and outward to others. "Love cannot be hid any more than light, and least of all when it shines forth in action."[16] This is what Wesley means when he insists that "Christianity is essentially a social religion, and that to turn it into a solitary religion is indeed to destroy it."[17] He was reacting of course to the quietism of his former mentor, William Law, who advised withdrawing from all social contacts in order to perfect the soul. "Directly

---

14. Ibid., vol. 3:501.

15. John Wesley, *The Works of the Rev. John Wesley*, Jackson edition; hereafter *Works* (Jackson), Thomas Jackson, ed. (Grand Rapids: Zondervan Publishing House, 1872), vol. VIII:329.

16. *Works* (Bicentennial), 1:539.

17. Ibid., 1:533.

opposite to this," claims Wesley, "is the gospel of Christ. Solitary religion is not to be found there." To be sure, Christ withdraws to pray, and the Christian makes daily communion with God a part of his or her schedule. But "'holy solitaries' is a phrase no more consistent with the gospel than holy adulterers. The gospel of Christ knows of no religion but social; no holiness but social holiness. "'Faith working by love' [Gal 5:6] is the length and breadth and depth and height of Christian perfection."[18] This is why good works are, for Wesley, not a substitute for faith but an extension of faith into the world. "In truth, whosoever loveth his brethren, not in word only, but as Christ loved him, cannot but be 'zealous of good works' [Titus 2:14]. He feels in his soul a burning, restless desire of spending and being spent for others."[19] This is the energizing activity of Spirit at work in and through the Christian.

And so, we see both in Moltmann and in Wesley an emphasis upon hope and a teleological direction, an emphasis that joins in questioning traditional Protestant theology and its lack of this expectation toward the future. And we see in both an emphasis upon the Spirit as God's empowering of the journey toward the fullness of faith and hope.

ECOLOGY

We turn now to two modern-day issues to which Moltmann has devoted much attention. *First, the ecological crisis.* With his concern for the recovery of the message of hope in present-day Christianity, it is not surprising that Moltmann is concerned about those things that undermine hope for the future. He was one of the first theologians to develop a comprehensive ecological theology, which became the basis for the Gifford Lectures in 1984 and 1985, at Edinburgh University, and were published in 1985 as *God in Creation.* He dedicated this book both to Emory University and to the University of St. Andrews from which he had received honorary degrees. Emory students were the first to hear the trial run of these lectures when Moltmann was guest professor in 1983.

He traces the ecological crisis back to the use we have made of the command in Genesis to "subdue the earth" and have "dominion" over it. The modern era, with its advances in science and technology, has understood this as a license to exploit nature. He takes as his challenge

---

18. *Works* (Jackson), XIV:321.
19. Ibid.

to replace such thinking. "Today," Moltmann says, "the essential point is to understand this knowable, controllable and usable nature *as God's creation*, and to learn to respect it as such."[20] What are the implications of a theology of hope for the ecological crisis? Is there hope for the earth? Traditional eschatological thinking has considered the future of the earth unimportant. Moltmann's eschatology is more akin to Luther's. When asked what he would do if he knew the end of the world were coming tomorrow Luther replied, "I would go out and plant an apple tree today." Moltmann sees the gospel message not in the end of the world but in the new beginning in the resurrection of Jesus, "the firstborn from the dead" (Col 1:10). This opens up a new future for human beings who know themselves through Christ to be created anew in the image of God.

The connection between the image of God and ecological responsibility takes us to where Wesley enters the discussion. To be sure, the environment was not an issue in Wesley's day. Londoners may have complained about the smoke from the many coal fires in winter that made their eyes smart, but we find nary a comment from Wesley on that issue. Are there nevertheless theological insights in Wesley that speak to today's concern? Indeed there are. It was Moltmann who first called my attention to a quote from Wesley's third discourse on the Sermon on the Mount in which he calls upon us to "survey heaven and earth and all that is therein as contained by God in the hollow of his hand, who by his intimate presence holds them all in being, who pervades and actuates the whole created frame, and is in a true sense the soul of the universe."[21] When we deal with the natural world we are dealing with God. For the eyes of faith, "God is in all things. . . . We are to see the Creator [reflected] in every creature. And we should use and look upon nothing [in the natural world] as separate from God, which indeed [would be] a kind of practical atheism."[22] But is Wesley treading dangerously close to pantheism here? Is he failing to maintain the basic biblical distinction between Creator and creation? No, says Moltmann in what could be used as a defense of Wesley, because the trinitarian God is not divorced from creation but is present as *Spirit* in creation and in every creature. All things are in God, and God is in all things.

20. Moltmann, *God in Creation* (San Francisco: HarperCollins ed., 1985), 21.
21. *Works* (Bicentenial), 1:517.
22. Ibid., 1:516-17.

> The trinitarian doctrine of creation therefore does not start from an antithesis between God and the world. . . . It proceeds differently, starting from an immanent *tension* in God himself: God creates the world, and at the same time enters into it. He calls it into existence, and at the same time manifests himself through its being. It lives from his creative power, and yet he lives in it. . . . The God who is transcendent in relation to the world, and the God who is immanent in that world, are one and the same God.[23]

Wesley's doctrine of the Spirit therefore allows him to maintain God's sovereignty over creation while at the same time being fully in it without any danger of pantheism. We can see the Creator reflected in every creature.

One aspect of the trifold image of God in humanity is what Wesley calls the *political image*, the vocation of humanity to be the guarantor of justice and order in the world. Just as God is Lord over the whole creation, so humanity serves as "prince and governor" of this world and the "channel of conveyance" of the blessings of the Creator to the earth and its creatures.[24] Our attitude toward the natural world cannot be arbitrary and capricious, therefore, but must be exercised as a conscious imaging of the care of the Creator. Here again Wesley is trinitarian, for he identifies Christ, the Word through whom all things were created—"without him was not anything made that was made" (John 1:3)—not only as the origin of all things but as the one through whom they continue to be upheld.

> [Christ] is now the life of everything that lives in any kind or degree. He is the source of the lowest species of life, that of *vegetables;* as being the source of all the motion on which vegetation depends. He is the fountain of the life of *animals*, the power by which the heart beats, and the circulating juices flow. He is the fountain of all the life that man possesses in common with other animals. And if we distinguish the *rational* from the animal life, he is the source of this also.[25]

Humanity is therefore part of the "family of nature," that member of the family who, as the political image of God, carries responsibility

---

23. Moltmann, *God in Creation*, 15.
24. *Works*, 1:440.
25. Ibid., 3:95.

for the care of the rest of the family. Wesley's favorite way of describing humanity as the political image is as a "steward."

> We are now God's stewards. We are indebted to him for all we have. . . . A steward is not at liberty to use what is lodged in his hands as he pleases but as his master pleases. . . . He is not the owner of any of these things but barely entrusted with them by another. . . . Now this is exactly the case of everyone with relation to God. We are not at liberty to use what God has lodged in our hands as we please, but as God pleases, who alone is the possessor of heaven and earth and the Lord of every creature. . . . [God] entrusts us with [this world's goods] on this express condition, that we use them only as our Master's goods, and according to the particular directions which he has given us in his Word.[26]

The implications are clear. We don't *own* the world. It is not our private property. God alone is "possessor of heaven and earth." We are stewards, whose integrity in our essential being and calling as the political image is to manage faithfully God's own property. And as Wesley says, "Let not those designed to save the earth destroy it."[27] God has equipped the political image with the capacities of *reason* and *will* and *freedom*, so we have the equipment to manage the earth responsibly. We have the rational ability to analyze all the statistics on deforestation, the loss of wetlands, the acid rain, the depletion of natural resources, the loss of fertility of the soil, the pollution of lakes and rivers. We can project statistically what these depletions and losses will mean to future generations. The figures are all there. We know we are robbing our grandchildren. We know the earth needs, as Moltmann says, a sabbath rest to recoup before the trends become irreversible. We *know*, but we don't *do* because our reigning ideology, capitalism, says we must have ever greater production to have ever greater profits to beat the competition. In other words, the market system robs us of the freedom God gives us to set priorities different from what the system dictates. And we use our reason and will to thwart the stewardship for which reason and will were given us. This is *sin*. Reason is used to rationalize our own selfishness, will is used to pursue our own objectives regardless of what it does to our neighbors here and abroad and future generations, and freedom is used to ignore our calling and responsibility. Sin is the corruption of good

26. Ibid., 2:283–84.
27. *Works* (Jackson), XI:124.

gifts to serve evil ends, and then to claim those ends are good because they appear to be good for us and our economy at the present moment. One of the important contributions of Moltmann's theology is to remind us that we have a covenant with generations yet unborn. Moltmann and Wesley are one, therefore, in saying that if we intend to preserve hope and exercise the political image, we must do long-range planning and make the sacrifices that are necessary to be the stewards God created us to be.

RELIGIOUS PLURALISM

Another current issue that both Moltmann and Wesley address is *religious pluralism*. This is an issue we cannot avoid. There are now more Muslims than Presbyterians in the United States. And religious pluralism is a fact with which Christians will have to live not just in the wider world but at home.

Moltmann admits he feels torn when he asks himself whether he should devote himself as a Christian theologian to the dialogue among the world religions, to seek some meeting of minds that can provide a religious foundation for world peace. Or should he devote himself as his first priority to the Christian mission to proclaim Christ and his kingdom. After all, Matthew's gospel says, "Go and make disciples of all nations," not "Engage in conversation with all religious groups."[28] Or is there a way to have both genuine dialogue and genuine mission? It should not surprise you to know that Moltmann thinks it possible to have both. He is not too optimistic, however, about the possibilities for genuine dialogue. After engaging in a number of these dialogue sessions, he reports that such talks are discouraging if the focus is on theological topics. "A Christian theologian puts questions—a rabbi, a mullah or a swami readily replies. But they ask nothing [in return] . . . because they aren't interested in Christianity. Many . . . reject interfaith dialogue because self-criticism is foreign to them,"[29] and they are unwilling therefore to allow any criticism of their position. He concludes that dialogue is really a Western idea that presupposes an environment where "it is impermissible to make anything absolute—except pluralism."[30] This

---

28. Moltmann, *God for a Secular Society* (Minneapolis: Fortress Press, 1999), 226.
29. Ibid., 234.
30. Ibid., 233.

does not mean that meaningful dialogue is impossible, however. There can be what Moltmann terms "indirect dialogue" about ethical, social, and ecological topics of common concern.[31] Here dialogue is based on "shared perceptions of the perils in which the world stands today, and the common search for ways out of those perils. . . . What changes are necessary if the religions are to become forces which affirm humanity's life and preserve the world?"[32]

You won't be surprised to hear that Wesley approaches this issue from a direction similar to that of Moltmann, with pneumatology, the doctrine of the Spirit, in the forefront. His doctrine of *prevenient grace* is grounded in his understanding of the Spirit and the activity of the Spirit. This shapes both his understanding of mission and his approach to non-Christian religions. He was convinced that wherever we go and whomever we reach with the Christian message, the Spirit has preceded us. We can be assured that there is no one in whom the Spirit of God has not already been at work. The openness of persons to our message is often in fact because this prevenient grace has already been active in their lives, causing them to raise questions and making them receptive to new sources of meaning. According to Wesley, "every degree of grace is a degree of life,"[33] and prevenient grace brings with it "some degree of salvation."[34] Salvation is a healing process in which, from the moment one begins to cooperate with divine healing powers, one enters upon the way. Thus everyone who is open to the Spirit, to God's inward voice, can come to a rudimentary saving relationship with God. Wherever there is an awareness of God, he says, that

> enables everyone who possesses it to "fear God and work righteousness," whosoever in every nation believes thus far, the Apostle Peter declares is "accepted of [God]" [Acts 10:35]. He actually is at that very moment in a state of acceptance, . . ."the wrath of God" no longer "abideth on him."[35]

God's own work of prevenient grace is thus the basis for detecting the work of the Spirit in other cultures and religions. Wesley would seem

31. Ibid., 235.
32. Ibid., 237.
33. Wesley, *The Letters of the Rev. John Wesley, A.M.*, Telford edition (London: Epworth Press, 1931), 6:239.
34. *Works*, (Bicentennial) 3:204.
35. Ibid., 3:497.

to be saying, using Peter as his authority, that something akin to the beginning of justification, insofar as it is acceptance by God, is possible through the Spirit apart from explicit knowledge of Jesus Christ. Yes, that is the case. And in the version of the Articles of Religion he sent to the Methodist movement in America, he struck out Article 18, "Of obtaining eternal salvation only by the Name of Christ." Interestingly enough, however, he is *not* saying that acceptance by God is *apart* from Jesus Christ. Why? Operating from a Trinitarian perspective, the second person of the Trinity is the one who gives incarnate expression to the grace that is eternally active in the Godhead and is the basis for this acceptance. Nor is he saying that with prevenient grace revelation is complete and that the relationship is all that it can be.

If grace is always and everywhere operative, however, what then is the point of proclaiming Christ? Has not Wesley undermined the very thing he declares to be basic to Christian mission, to "share Christ"?

The Christ who is to be shared is the Christ who is the Incarnation of God's mercy and the declaration of God's love extended to all humankind. He is the "friend of sinners" of every race and in every land. It is Christ who gives divine grace its human shape and human form. This is what makes it possible for Wesley to hold together both openness and conviction in his attitude toward those outside Christian faith. And he does this by distinguishing between the "faith of a *servant*" and the "faith of a *son* [or *daughter*]."[36] The source and shape of these relationships is what makes the difference. From Wesley's standpoint, the relationship of the sincere non-Christian through the promptings of the Spirit in prevenient grace is that of a *servant*. If taught by the inward voice of God the essentials of loyalty to God and obedience to what he or she understands to be the will of God, the non-Christian fears God and practices righteousness, and thus is not condemned but accepted of God. Yet the character and quality of that relationship has not been shaped by Christ, and God wants something *more* than the servant relation. That *more* is supplied by encountering God through Jesus Christ. Hence the reason and motivation for mission is not lost but instead intensified. The mission to non-Christians does not begin, however, with the negative threat of condemnation. It begins instead with a positive promise: God has more in store for you. "You shall see greater things than these," greater things than in your sincerity you have seen thus far. For through the

36. Ibid., 3:497.

revelation of the heart of God by the Son and the Spirit is made possible the faith relationship the Father desires, with a *son* or *daughter*, that is, with a *child* of God. Through the revelation in Jesus of Nazareth, God has opened the divine heart and shared the divine life in the Spirit intended for all humankind. Experiencing this overwhelming love enables one to testify with the words of St. Paul, "The life which I now live in the flesh I live by faith in the Son of God, who loved me, and gave himself for me"(Gal 2:20). And Wesley adds, "Whosoever hath this, 'the Spirit of God witnesseth with his spirit that he is a child of God.'"[37] "Because you are sons," continues Paul in Gal 4:6, "God has sent forth the Spirit of his Son into your hearts, crying, Abba, Father. So you are no longer a servant but a child, and if a child then also an heir." It is out of this experience of the love of God that we are motivated to share this love with the world. Conviction and openness can be held together because the *source of both is love*!

> If you love God, you will love your brother also; you will be ready to lay down your life for his sake; so far from any desire to take away his life, or hurt a hair of his head.... Be zealous for God; but remember that ... true zeal is only the flame of love.... While you abhor every kind and degree of persecution, let your heart burn with love to all mankind, to friends and enemies, neighbors and strangers, to Christians, heathens, Jews, Turks, Papists, heretics; to every soul which God hath made.[38]

This burning heart of love turns Christians toward the whole world in mission, not to impose ideas or Western culture but to share in very concrete ways the love we have received. The Spirit will accompany this witness and do the convincing.

On the basis of this combination of factors Wesley was able to hold together both a deep commitment to tolerance and openness, on the one hand, and on the other, an equally thoroughgoing conviction concerning God's re-creative power directed toward the world through the Son and the Spirit. And so, from both Moltmann and Wesley we see how the doctrine of the Spirit opens up new ways of being confident about the importance of the Christian message to the future of a religiously pluralistic world.

37. Ibid., 3:498.
38. *Works* (Jackson), XI:191.

Although I don't want to say Moltmann is a Wesleyan, or that Wesley is an early Moltmannian, it seems to me they are closer to each other than the 60,000,000 sons and daughters of Wesley have been to a major European theologian in many a decade.

Part II

Biblical Foundations for Theology

6

The Human Being as a Theological Animal
A Biblical Argument against Creationism[1]

IN THIS CHAPTER I will attempt first to show how human beings are inevitably theological creatures and then to analyze how the theological impulse, operative in the faith of the Hebrews in exile in Babylon, expressed itself in this story of creation we find in the first chapter of Genesis. In this creation account I will observe how biblical faith drew on the scientific knowledge of its time in order to express its own distinctive perspective. If this can be demonstrated, it should be applicable to the debate between creationists and evolutionists in our time.

The interests of theologians and cultural anthropologists converge when we take as our focus the human being: that creature who has to have meaning to flourish. Humans labor under the impulse to organize and order their lives, and this ordering process appears to be, if not impossible, at least much more difficult without some notion of the larger purpose, direction, and context of life. As humans we need to know how we fit into the big picture, not only to make sense out of daily life but to meet and overcome crises.

This need for meaning appears to be biologically grounded. How can such a claim be supported? The German anthropologist, Arnold Gehlen, observes that the human animal, when compared with other

---

1. Originally published as "The Human Being as a Theological Animal: A Biblical Argument against Creationism," in *Images of Man*, edited by J. William Angell and E. Pendleton Banks (Macon, Ga.: Mercer University Press, 1984), 81–91. Used by permission.

species, is "instinct poor," or relatively underdeveloped with regard to the multitude of instincts that guide the lives of most creatures.[2] This is not to say that we do not have instincts, or that the instincts we do have are not a powerful factor in our actions and reactions, as Nobel Prize-winner Konrad Lorenz has amply demonstrated. Nor does it deny that we learn a great deal about human behavior by examining animal behavior, as anyone who has taken a course in experimental psychology knows. Yet there is a very real difference between humans and other animals, which at first glance would seem to place humans at a distinct disadvantage. As Ernst Cassirer says, "A child has to learn many skills which the animal was born with."[3] Because of our relative lack of instincts, our lack of preprogrammed behavior patterns, we lag behind the rest of the animal world. As Cassirer observes, we fall far short of the geometric accuracy of the honey bee. In the construction of their cells, honey bees "act like a perfect geometer, achieving the highest precision and accuracy. Such activity requires a very complex system of coordination and collaboration."[4] Yet the honey bee cannot take much credit for its superior achievement; it inherited it all. It was preprogrammed in its brain, and therefore involves no special skill it has mastered. It just does what comes naturally, while you and I struggle to draw a simple circle—and never quite succeed.

If we humans are underendowed when it comes to instincts, we have been given as compensation an unusually large cranial capacity to house what has been called "that cancerous growth at the upper end of the spine," our brain. Each of us has billions of open circuits ready to receive whatever information we feed them. What this remarkable brain enables us to do, which most animals better equipped with instincts cannot do, is to extemporize; to imagine alternative possibilities; to organize the information continuously being fed to us and make sense out of it by incorporating it into the patterns already there; and to project new options on the basis of what we already know.

What does this have to do with the initial claim that human beings are theological animals? Each of us is constantly expanding the amount of information absorbed. As we are constantly bombarded with information, we are forced to make sense of it, to organize it into a whole that has

---

2. Arnold Gehlen. *Anthropologische Forschung* (Hamburg: Rowohlt, 1961) 18–19.
3. Ernst Cassirer, *An Essay on Man* (New Haven: Yale University Press, 1944), 43.
4. Ibid., 223.

coherence and consistency. The way we do this is by "contextualizing," by putting the new information we receive into a context with which we are basically already familiar. Yet in this process the contexts themselves constantly are being expanded and forced to take in new information that requires adjustments in perspective. Our horizons constantly are being pushed outward as we absorb more and more data; therefore we all, consciously or unconsciously, yearn for an ultimate context within which everything has its place and everything can be understood.

Our very biological nature, which leads us to assemble ever larger worlds of meaning, makes us seekers after the logic of God— "theologians" if you will—who must find ever more comprehensive frameworks that can do justice to our experience and knowledge. The concept of "God" is for all of us, whatever our level of sophistication, a "limit concept," that which lies at the outer boundary of our knowledge, and also beyond it, and enables our world to have coherence.[5] Put most simply, biologically we are that animal who is destined to be a theological creature, a *homo theologicus*.

Note carefully what I am claiming and, just as carefully, what I am not claiming. I am not yet talking about the concrete revelation of God in Jesus Christ but about the God-concept, which is as operative for Christians as for all other human beings. Therefore I am not saying that anyone with half a brain is a Christian, or that everyone believes in the Christian God, or that everyone, by virtue of being human, is a little bit saved. No. I'm simply saying that any human being "with any brains at all" must deal with the God-question. And implied in this is also the assertion that it is better to deal with the God-question consciously and openly and honestly than to be unaware that this is in fact what one is doing.

I am not saying that to believe consciously in God, or in a god, is to know everything there is to know about the ultimate context within which our lives are lived. Theologians and saints down through the ages, as well as the Bible itself, have always testified to what they call the continuing mystery of God. Because God both constitutes the outer horizon of our knowledge and at the same time lies beyond our knowledge and

---

5. Cf. Anselm's ontological argument for God as "that than which a greater cannot be conceived." *The Ontological Argument*, ed. Alvin Plantiga (Garden City, NY: Doubleday Anchor Books, 1965), 3.

beckons us out into the beyond, the mystery of God continues at two levels: the level of what we know, and the level of what we do not know.

Speaking first from a Christian perspective about what we know: we claim that in Jesus Christ we are given a clue to the *character* of the ultimate context within which we "live, and move, and have our being." Jesus names that ultimate context "Father," and he enables us to trust God as our Creator, Father, and Lord, the one who reconciles us to himself through the love that the Son directs towards us. But to know this God is not to remove the mystery any more than to know another person is to remove the mystery of that person. Just the opposite is the case: the more we learn about another person, the more we discover there is to learn. And even though through their commitment to us we may know persons in the core of their being, in the will and integrity that is at the very center of who they are, nevertheless there is always more to learn layer after layer—for the mystery of a single human being is inexhaustible. How much more is this the case with God. The holy mystery of God grows more profound as our experience of God increases and our knowledge of God in Christ deepens.

The further out we push, the further toward the infinite we are led; the more our knowledge of the outer horizon expands, the more we become aware of the unknown that lies beyond and the more the mystery of the beyond remains inexhaustible. To be able to name God, therefore, is not to be able to limit God. Although our knowledge grows with our constantly expanding horizon of understanding, the ultimate context is always greater. God always remains transcendent Lord. As the psalmist cries out, "O Lord, our Sovereign, how majestic is your name in all the earth!" (Ps 8:1).

What about the certainty that faith is supposed to bring? Does all this talk about ultimacy and mystery undermine the confidence, the certitude, the assurance that faith promises? Not at all. What remains constant in the midst of continually expanding horizons and growing understanding is the character of the *relationship* that God maintains with God's creation and creatures. The Bible names the quality of that relationship "covenant." Furthermore, this reality of covenant is so central to the Bible that the Scriptures themselves are divided into the original covenant and the renewed covenant or, in the Latin, the Old Testament and the New Testament.

What is a covenant? It is a relationship of loyalty and steadfastness entered into by two parties who vow to be solid and dependable and at the same time flexible and capable of being enriched. This is the model the Old Testament uses to characterize first the relationship between Yahweh and Israel, and then, by extension, God and all humankind. God pledged himself to Noah, to Abraham, to Moses, and elicited from the people in response a pledge of faithfulness and loyalty. According to the biblical writers, this mutual pledging is the paradigm for what human marriage ought to be. Indeed, marriage offers perhaps the best analogy for understanding both the trustworthiness and the room for growth in covenant. In marriage two persons pledge themselves one to the other under God. Each commits self to the other in a sacred trust, and thereby they give their relationship a firmness and dependability. At the same time that bond with each other is meant to be not only ongoing but enriching. As the two persons mature in experience and understanding, their relationship will grow and deepen as well. Assurance and security are not foreign to an expanding faith in God, but provide the psychic base, strength, and continuity that are necessary to make such growth possible. God is "the faithful God who maintains covenant" (Deut 7:9) amidst all the changing circumstances of life.

HOW THE BIBLE ARGUES AGAINST "CREATIONISM"

Having laid the groundwork for the fundamental need of human beings to identify an all-encompassing horizon within which all the experiences of life can become meaningful, and having seen how, in the Judeo-Christian tradition, continuity is provided by the covenant relationship, we may now move to practical application and to the current debate over evolution versus creationism, and a biblical argument against creationism.

If the horizon that we confess as ultimate is not able to encompass the new information we have about reality, one of two things tends to happen: (a) we either declare that whatever cannot fit within our present concept of God does not have to be taken seriously or does not exist; or (b) we discover that our concept of God is not as big as our concept of reality—in effect, God suddenly seems less relevant because God no longer encompasses, transcends, and makes sense of reality as we know it. God is no longer God. God is no longer "that than which a greater cannot be conceived" (St. Anselm). Is there a clue within the Bible itself to an approach that can avoid these twin pitfalls and provide a more satisfactory alternative? I am convinced there is, and the remainder of the chapter will spell out this third alternative.

One of the main sources for understanding the biblical view of human nature and human existence is found in the first two chapters of Genesis. Before turning to those accounts, however, it is important to remind ourselves that even though the creation stories speak of primeval history, they are not the most ancient materials in the Old Testament. The covenant traditions concerning Abraham, the fathers, and Moses, are older still. The earliest story of creation in the second chapter of Genesis is already shaped by the covenant motif in the stories of Abraham and Moses; and God is portrayed as entering into a covenantal relationship with Adam. What is seen here is an example of the human theological drive at work. A central hallmark of Hebrew faith, the covenant relationship with God, has been expanded outward to encompass the very creation itself, so that no part of human existence will lie outside the province of the meaning-giving covenant. In this sense Exodus really comes before Genesis, and provides the theological context within which the stories of origins and of the fathers and mothers are told, equating the God of the covenant with the ultimate source of all that is.

Turning to the creation stories themselves, Hebrew scholars have known for generations that there is not just one but two stories here, the more ancient one—the story of Adam—probably dating in its written form from the tenth century BC, while the more recent one dates from the time of the exile in Babylon in the sixth century BC and begins with the familiar words of Genesis 1:1(KJV), "In the beginning. God...." It is not necessary to know Hebrew in order to spot these differences. Open your King James Bible and you will notice the contrasts in style between the two chapters as well as differences in the order of creation. Genesis 1 begins with a watery chaos; the dry land does not appear until the third day, followed by plant life, animal life, and then the creation of man and woman. In Genesis 2 creation begins with dry land, followed by the introduction of water, the creation of a man, plant life, animal life, and then the creation of a woman.

Scholars have also known for a long time that Genesis 1 bears striking resemblances to the ancient Babylonian story of creation, the *Enuma elish,* with which the Jews would have been familiar during their exile in

Babylon. In the Babylonian story you will find the watery deep encountered in Genesis 1, the division into the waters above and the waters below, and the same order of creation as in Genesis 1. What is more interesting than these similarities, however, are the differences between the Babylonian and Hebrew accounts. And it is these differences that provide a possible clue to the reason for the writing of Genesis 1.

When the Jews were carried into exile in Babylon, they brought with them a perfectly good story of creation that had probably been a part of their oral tradition since the twelfth century BC, and written down since about 950 BC. It begins at Genesis 2:4b with the words, "In the day that the Lord God made the earth and the heavens. . . ." That ancient story identified the primordial link between God and the first human creatures as a covenant relation. Adam was given responsibility to order the world, to "till it and keep it" (v. 15), to name and care for the animals, and to maintain the law of the Creator. The story said what needed to be said about covenant responsibilities, but admittedly it lacked the poetic power, the grandeur and sweep, of the Babylonian story. The Babylonians, after all, had written of the cosmic order and were the proponents of the most advanced "science" of the time,[6] and this science was what the Jewish children were learning, so to speak, in the Babylonian public schools. What should the Jews do? They could, of course, set up an intellectual ghetto and try to keep their children from being contaminated by the new science. Instead they took a more courageous and biblically consistent approach. In response, the Hebrew priests composed a creation story that appropriated the magnificent cosmic sweep of the Babylonian story—they incorporated the science of the day—but they reinterpreted the Babylonian picture of creation in such a way as to put it within the context of the Hebrew covenant God. The facts of the new science were different, to be sure, from the traditional Hebrew story, but that evidently bothered neither the exiles nor the editors who put these two stories together in the form we have them today. It would have been simple enough to alter one story to fit the facts of the other. For them, however, it was not the facts but the relationships that mattered.

The original Babylonian story placed a decidedly different evaluation on human existence. Humans came into existence, according to the Babylonian account, because the gods became tired of taking care of the

6. Cassirer, *Essay on Man*, 46.

world. The lesser gods therefore invoked the high god, Marduke, to create some slaves who would assume the burdens of toil. Marduke heard their plea. He punished a lesser god, Kingu, who had been guilty of causing a revolt among the gods, by cutting his arteries and with the blood created human beings as slaves. Marduke then imposed the services of the gods upon humankind, and set the gods free to be the leisure class.[7]

This story was absolutely inconsistent with the Hebrew revelation of humankind's place within the ultimate context. The birth of Hebrew faith and of the Israelite nation occurred in the exodus as the Hebrews were led out of slavery, not into it. There was no way they could agree with a doctrine that viewed humans essentially as slaves! So while the Jewish writers accepted much of the Babylonian cosmology, they rewrote the relationships between Creator and humanity. In the Genesis 1 account, human beings are placed in the world not as slaves but as governors over the earth. Indeed, they are called the very "image of God," and are to exercise dominion and care over the earth as God does over the whole of creation. They are given responsibility for the other creatures and for the management of the fruits of the earth. Thus Genesis 1 defines our humanity in terms of our stewardship of the world, our faithfulness to the Creator for the things that have been entrusted to our care.

Now notice how the new version parallels, as far as these vital relations are concerned, the older story almost exactly. In Genesis 2 the man is part and parcel of the earth; he is shaped from the dust of the ground. But he receives his life through the breath of God, and he is summoned to stewardship for the garden and care of the other animals. The one possible improvement Genesis 1 makes over Genesis 2 is that responsibility is given to male and female together, not just to the male. Otherwise the relationships are basically the same in the two chapters. Although the picture of the world in Genesis 1 was borrowed in large part from the Babylonian cosmology, that cosmology was utilized to advance the basic Hebrew understanding of the ultimate nature of things.

Now perhaps you can begin to see my line of reasoning. If we want to take the Bible seriously, I suggest we make the Bible our model and do what the Bible does! The Bible does not dig in its heels and simply reject the new picture of the cosmos developed by the Babylonians, even though that picture differed in its presentation of the facts from the

---

7. Norman Gottwald, *A Light to the Nations* (New York: Harper and Row, 1959), 573.

traditional Hebrew story. But it took the details of the Babylonian cosmology, the science of the day, and put them into the ultimate context of the Hebrew covenant between God and humanity.

An objection could be raised at this point, however. One could ask, Isn't it just the other way around? Is not the covenant being set in the context of the Babylonian picture of the cosmos, and thus the Babylonians define the ultimate horizon. But such an objection both discloses our modern mind-set and exposes it as inadequate. We tend to assume immensity of space, and the furniture that occupies that space is more important than relationships. We automatically identify ultimacy with bigger, with a larger space. But is that not contrary to reality as we actually experience it? If you think of your own home, it is not the furniture in your house, the space, that defines you so much as the relationships, the covenants. The Jews knew this, and although for centuries they were without a space they could call their own, they still maintained their identity because that identity was given in the covenant relation. It is relations, not facts and furniture, that are truly ultimate and all-determinative.

I am suggesting that we would be wise to follow the example of the writers of Genesis 1, and that is to be open to whatever modern science can tell us about the facts of the cosmos, keeping fully aware that these facts are constantly subject to revision; a description of the universe one hundred years hence will have quite another shape than the one scientific knowledge dictates at the present time. Our faith does not tie us to any one description of the world. Rather, like the Hebrews in ancient Babylon, we are free to take the descriptions most in accord with the scientific data of our time and put those descriptions into the ultimate framework of our covenant with God. To state it more simply, there is a division of labor involved. Scientific theories are attempts to discover and describe the *how* of creation, but they cannot tell us the *why* or the *what for*—that is the theological task. As T. S. Eliot describes it, a thousand policemen directing the traffic cannot tell you why you come or where you go.[8] The scientist's job is to sit at the intersection and count cars. There is no way the scientific approach can supply the ultimate context as long as it remains purely descriptive.

---

8. Inspired by T. S. Eliot, "Choruses from 'The Rock,'" in *Collected Poems, 1909–1935* (New York: Harcourt Brace and Co., 1936), 191.

From the standpoint of the creationists, however, this is just the issue. Some evolutionists have turned evolution into a religious—albeit atheistic—dogma, into a complete worldview that they promote as they teach evolutionary theory. Where this happens it can be justifiably challenged—not by attempting to discredit the science of the scientist, but by questioning the *theology* involved in the interpretation of the ultimate context. The appropriate place for this challenge to occur is in the university, where conflicting religious philosophies are debated and examined for their cogency and ability to illumine human existence. It is unfair and inappropriate to ask teachers on the secondary-school level to enter into this debate. They are neither prepared nor are their pupils mature enough to understand the issues involved. Yet this debate is what creationists are, in effect, requesting. For if the Christian view of the ultimate context is presented, then in all fairness the claims of other religious groups and of atheism must be presented as well; and that is not what the creationists have in mind. Therefore, Judge William Overton was probably right when in his Arkansas decision he saw the creationist position as an attempt to use science courses in the public schools to buttress a certain Christian religious perspective.[9]

If the creationists insist on fighting the battle on the level of factual accuracy, they would put the Bible itself in an untenable position. One would then have to set Genesis 1 against Genesis 2. Was it seven days or was it one; was the order of creation dry land, water, man, plants, animals, and finally woman; or was it watery chaos, land, plants, animals, and finally man and woman together as the image of God? If priority were given to facts, the facts in these accounts conflict, and in the end would discredit the Bible. No sincere Christian wants to do this, for we desperately need the biblical understanding of the relationships between human beings, God, and the world. Indeed, the understanding of ourselves as stewards of the creation is absolutely essential if the planet is to survive. And this is one value derived from the biblical account that no scientist would wish to deny.

I will conclude with a plea to the creationists. Do not put the argument on such a level that the Bible will inevitably be questioned and even discredited by thinking young people. Take a cue from the Bible itself. Let the horizons expand to include the best information that the modern-day Babylonians can supply. Do not insist that children espouse

---

9. *New York Times.* 6 January 1982, 1.

a tenth or a sixth-century BC cosmology in order to be true to their religious heritage. Whoever wishes to be loyal to God must allow God to be the ultimate context to which our minds aspire. Religion can be effective only as it is inclusive enough to integrate all of the available information without the necessity of denying or excluding any theories concerning the *how* of this universe. But this openness to scientific knowledge must be accompanied by a commitment to the rigorous intellectual task of putting the *how* within a consciously religious framework of the *why* and *what for*—as the writers of the first chapter of Genesis did—in order to enable the Scriptures once again to exercise their powerful understanding of human existence.

In conclusion, I cannot do better than to quote the French paleontologist and priest, Pierre Teilhard de Chardin, whose scientific research in the 1930s and 1940s into the facts of paleontology has been largely superseded today but whose theological insight remains as profound as ever.

> Look from the standpoint of two thousand years of Christian experience and you will see [that] the two stars, [science and religion] whose divergent attractions were disorganizing your faith, are brought into conjunction. Without mixture, without confusion, the . . . Christian God will, under your gaze, invade the universe, our universe of today, the universe which so frightened you by its alarming size or its pagan beauty. . . . If you are able to focus your soul's eyes so as to perceive this magnificence, you will soon forget, I assure you, your unfounded fears in face of the mounting significance of [scientific knowledge]. Your one thought will be to exclaim "Greater still, Lord, let your universe be greater still, so that I may hold you and be held by you [in a covenant] made ever more intense and ever wider in its extent!"[10]

---

10. Pierre Teilhard de Chardin, *The Divine Milieu* (London: Collins, 1964), 47.

7

Creation, Covenant, and Kingdom

The Human Condition in Biblical and Theological Perspective[1]

To attempt to identify the Christian theological understanding of human nature today is to focus on a moving target. Most traditional theological analyses drew their major inspiration from the biblical stories of origins, the stories of Creation and Fall. These motifs have for centuries provided rich thematic materials to describe doctrinally and artistically both the divine origins of the race and the ambiguity of the human creature, whose capacities for freedom and creativity on the one hand and evil and corruption on the other are evident.

Another motif closely linked with Creation and Fall is *covenant*. For the biblical writers, both the original calling of humankind in Creation and the original sin of humanity in the Fall are to be viewed within the larger framework of the covenant relation to God. The motif of covenant sets forth the basic relationality in terms of what it means to be human. Without it none of the other categories can properly be understood.

However, two of the most influential recent theological movements, the theology of hope and the Latin American theologies of liberation, propose a different starting point for analyzing the human condition. Taking their cue from the priority Jesus gives to the theme of the coming

---

1. Originally published as "Kingdom, Creation, and Covenant: The Human Condition in Biblical and Theological Perspective" in *Changing Views of the Human Condition*, Paul Pruyser, editor (Mercer University Press, 1987), 12–27. Used by permission.

kingdom of God, they see this kingdom as the context within which everything else, including human nature and society, must be viewed.[2] Moreover, they understand that the kingdom Jesus anticipated was not interpreted by him as otherworldly but as a renewal of the earth. Divine justice and love will penetrate and transform this world until "The kingdom of the world has become the kingdom of our Lord and of his Messiah, and he will reign forever and ever" (Rev 11:15). How would our understanding of human nature be changed, ask the liberation theologians, if the fundamental angle from which we view humankind were not the past but the future, not what has been but what, by God's grace and the power of the Spirit, can be?[3]

It seems obvious that any attempt to do justice to current theological understandings of human nature must take seriously the perspectives introduced by the theologies of hope and liberation. To fail to do so would be to continue to define humanity in provincial Western European and North American terms. At the same time no theological interpretation can neglect the traditional themes of creation, fall, and covenant, for this combination lends depth to and makes for a more comprehensive and convincing picture of the human condition.

Nevertheless, the methodological point of the liberationists is well taken. It does make a difference where one starts. If we begin where theology traditionally has begun, by tracing the dismal history of the race from its origins down through the ages (as does St. Paul in Rom 1:18–3:18), we will doubtless be impressed by not only the persistence of human sinfulness but also the impossibility of doing anything about it

---

2. See Jürgen Moltmann's now-classic *Theology of Hope* (New York: Harper, 1967) and Jon Sobrino's *Christology at the Crossroads* (Maryknoll N. Y.: Orbis, 1978). In one sense eschatology is by no means a recent theological discovery. The kingdom of God played an important role as an ideal in post-World War I liberal theology, and H. Richard Niebuhr analyzed the historic significance of the doctrine in his *The Kingdom of God in America* and in *Christ and Culture*. Yet for most Americans eschatology remained associated with otherworldliness and premillennialism. And the theme of the 1954 Evanston Assembly of the World Council of Churches, "Christ, the Hope of the World" (see the preparatory materials in *The Christian Hope and the Task of the Church* [New York: Harper, 1954]), seemed abstract and passive for Americans who were accustomed to the activist approach to all problems. The relevance of eschatology and hope therefore did not become apparent until the recalcitrance of both national and international problems had dissipated all natural and easy optimism.

3. Cf. Jose Miguez Bonino, *Doing Theology in a Revolutionary Situation* (Philadelphia: Fortress Press, 1975), 132–53.

and the unlikelihood of any improvement in the future.[4] Such an analysis unfortunately lends itself to use by conservative forces as a theological argument against any change. The motivation for change is undermined by the solemn reminder that every reform, every alternative form of human organization, will be subject to the same original sin that infests the present order. "Better be content with the evils we know," counsels the voice of realism, "rather than risk the new evils that would be introduced by change." Such a reading, however, turns a theological analysis all too readily into an ideology to reinforce and support the status quo, and in so doing robs the future of its promise.

THE TURN TOWARD THE FUTURE

If we begin instead with "the kingdom of God and his righteousness" (Matt 6:33) and make this the starting point for our interpretation of human nature, the results may be quite different. If, rather than focusing on origin and first cause, we turn our attention to the final cause and the power of the "absolute future" to change the present—as do Catholic theologian Karl Rahner and Protestant theologian Jürgen Moltmann—the results may be quite different. This is not to deny the continued conditioning and even determinism exercised by the past. The effects of genetic makeup, social environment, and past experience never can be denied. Yet a doctrine that takes seriously the power of the kingdom will see persons and society not simply as the result of past conditioning but as in process, subject to the freeing effect of future possibilities. The future can also "condition," and does so in such a way as to break open otherwise rigidly determined situations. The philosopher Ernst Bloch calls this "the ontology of the not yet," the power of that which does not yet exist to transform present things. From a Christian standpoint this is an analogy to the creativity of the God who "gives life to the dead and calls into existence the things that do not exist" (Rom 4:17). Therefore, "hope alone is to be called 'realistic,'" writes Moltmann, "because it alone takes seriously the possibilities with which all reality is fraught. It does not take things as they happen to stand or to lie, but as progressing, moving things with possibilities of change."[5]

---

4. Cf. Karl Barth's commentary on this section of the epistle in *The Epistle to the Romans* (New York: Oxford University Press, 1933), 42–91.

5. Moltmann, *Theology of Hope*, 25.

In similar fashion the Latin American theologians of liberation turn to the future, to the kingdom of God, as their starting point. Where did the Christian faith itself begin, they ask. Did it begin with a discussion of creation and original sin or with the announcement that a new creation was at hand, that a transformed existence had become available to those whose lives were directed toward God's new order, which was marked by the intercession of Jesus Christ? Early Christians asserted that the forces of evil and death had been decisively defeated through the cross and resurrection and that a new age was dawning. Evident as it was to them that the kingdom had not yet arrived in its fullness, it was nevertheless possible to participate in the first fruits of the age to come through faith, hope, and the power of the Spirit. We confront this same theme in Jesus' own ministry and message. Is there any phrase more central to his preaching than the repeated call to "seek first the kingdom of God and his righteousness"? To turn to the kingdom of God as the locus from which to derive an understanding of human existence is for these Latin Americans not an escape. If the kingdom of justice and peace is God's intention for human flesh, it is the ultimate reality and truth toward which this world must tend if it is finally to be sustained. Moreover, awareness of this truth heightens consciousness of the discrepancies between God's intended order and this present order. It robs the rulers of this world of the kind of legitimacy that religion as the preserver of order has traditionally lent them, and it makes the masses aware of God's stake in change.

The radicalizing of the Latin American churches under the impact of this theological shift is familiar. In many countries the church has moved to the forefront of those demanding change in the age-old patterns of political, economic, and military power that were once blessed by the church and declared to be the will of God. The fact that this vision of an alternative future was first introduced by the Marxists should not invalidate its truth, insist these theologians. In the Marxist analysis the church recognizes its own heritage in disguise. The church lays claim, therefore, to that which is rightfully its own on the basis of the critical power of the biblical message of the kingdom of God. Moreover, the church, insofar as it is true to its own vision, must champion humane means toward humane ends—something that often has been lacking in Marxist approaches.

The implications for educational theory of this reorientation of the church's leadership role have been made clear by Brazilian educator Paulo Freire in *Pedagogy of the Oppressed*.[6] Whereas traditional education fits persons into a preexisting order by giving them information and skills that enable them to adjust and function productively within the needs of the present system, now education asks critical questions about the nature of the system itself. Previously, the education of the illiterate gave access only to means of communication programmed by the establishment. Thus education increased the efficiency of the system but did not question it. Now education includes practice in the art of critical thinking. Previously, culture, including its political and economic manifestations, was assumed to be a "given"—certainly not something to be enriched or changed by the lowly peasant. The process of "conscientization" now makes the peasant aware that culture is not divinely ordained but a human product. And as a human product, it is subject to change by human beings formulating more humane goals.

If the implications for education are already apparent, can we expect similarly far-reaching implications for the theory and practice of psychotherapy and pastoral counseling? What changes would result if human existence were seen not as a process of adaptation to a preordained order but as the interaction of a subject with his or her environment in the light of an alternative force? Admittedly, the motif of the kingdom has not been prominent in the approaches of most of those who have sought to do therapy or counseling from a Christian point of view and out of Christian presuppositions. There are several reasons for this, the most obvious being that the kingdom is a social rather than an individual category, and the preoccupation of much of psychotherapy has been with the individual. Within the helping professions voices are being raised to ask whether the traditional approach to healing has been too centered on the self as individual and has not taken sufficiently into account the social context within which illness occurs. Is it possible that the counseling profession has unwittingly been influenced by the pietistic heritage that has dominated both Catholicism and Protestantism over the past two centuries, which has focused on the salvation of the individual soul and has been scarcely aware of the social fabric and its conditioning power?[7] Certainly influences other than pietism have also

---

6. Paulo Freire, *Pedagogy of the Oppressed* (New York: Seabury Press, 1970).

7. George V. Pixley argues that the kingdom of God, in contrast with its original

been at work in shaping this individualism—Enlightenment rationalism, the influence of the frontier, the logic of capitalism, and so forth—but pietism has been so pervasive and so successful precisely because of its hand-in-glove congruence with these other cultural factors.

One way to redress the balance would be to take a cue from the theologies of liberation and hope and begin with the kingdom, working our way back to creation. This is, in fact, the road we will take in the remainder of this chapter. Along the way we may discover that it is necessary to speak of the kingdom and of creation in one breath, as we find in the one the clues to the real nature of the other. And we may also discover that it is necessary to rethink the corporate as well as the individual aspects of the human condition.

THE KINGDOM AND THE SELF

When early Christians were called into discipleship, it was not so much to prepare for life in another world as to prepare for the coming of another world into this one. The kingdom was viewed quite concretely as divine intervention to bring about a new order that would defeat the forces of sin and corruption and usher in an era of God's rule over all flesh.

We cannot ignore the fact, therefore, that it is not the saved individual that stands at the heart of the gospel but a redeemed social order. In the kingdom the individual is saved as a participant in the reconciling power of positive relationships with God and others. This presupposes, however, that the present order of things is negative, that social relations have broken down and that kingdom power is missing, obscured, or ignored in our common life. If the kingdom is the answer to a problem and the kingdom is social, then the nature of the problem must also be social and not just individual. If this be the case, where then does the individual fit in?

In order to answer these questions, let us take a closer look at Jesus' call to repentance, a call that was intimately connected with his announcement of the kingdom. The call to repentance was addressed not just to the nation but to individuals. It thus can provide us an avenue for seeing how the sense of individuality and individual destiny emerged

---

meaning in Jesus' message and Palestinian Christianity, becomes inevitably individualized and privatized as it moves into the urban heterogeneity and rootlessness of the Roman Empire. *God's Kingdom* (Maryknoll, N.Y.: Orbis, 1981), 88–100.

in Christianity without in any way abrogating the social nature of God's saving work.

"The time is fulfilled, and the kingdom of God has come near; repent, and believe in the good news" (Mark 1:15). This is the first account we have of Jesus' preaching. The message seems straightforward enough, but we have difficulty hearing it in its original sense. For us "repentance" does not seem to go together with rejoicing and good news; it has to do with sorrow, guilt, and remorse. It is important for us to see, therefore, that what Jesus offers is in the first instance not condemnation but promise. *Repent*, in the Jewish sense in which Jesus is using it, means fundamentally "to turn."[8] And in the context of Jesus' message it means to turn toward the new source of power that is appearing on the horizon. This is why it is good news, "gospel." To be sure, it also means turning away from, and breaking with, the old powers of the present age. What is innovative in Jesus' preaching is not what he calls persons to turn from, however, but what he calls them to turn toward—toward the divine mercy and love that elicits and enables the turning. God turns toward human beings through Jesus' healing and saving activity, and God's mercy makes possible our turning. It is good news because God, in this activity, is restoring the covenant with God's people—not the covenant law as interpreted by the religious authorities in Jesus' time—but what Jesus instead takes to be the original, gracious character of the covenant relation between God and human beings. Therefore, the dawning of the kingdom brings a recovery of God's original intention for creation.

To "turn" involves both thought and action. Thus salvation can never be reduced simply to a new self-understanding within the individual. It is insight into the destiny of the self as part of creation, the part that because of its development is enabled to participate consciously with the Creator by playing a responsible role in the realization of the divine intention for the whole of creation. Repentance is effective as it becomes not just insight but action: vocation, calling, work. And action is most effective as it becomes communal, participatory. Insight is constantly

---

8. Neither the English nor the Greek words, *repent* and *metanoein*, in their literal meaning, reproduce accurately the sense of the Aramaic that Jesus used, which could only have meant "to turn around," (Johannes Behm, in Gerhard Kittel, ed., *Theological Dictionary of the New Testament* [Grand Rapids: Wm. B. Eerdmans, 1976], 4:999–1000). *Repent* is literally "being remorseful, having pain," while *metanoein* is to change one's mind. Thus the Latin *convertere* and the German *umkehren* reproduce more accurately the force of the Hebrew and Aramaic.

deepened and reshaped as the self is at work in new situations, informed by the inexhaustible depth and resources of the divine intention and the vision of a common task. To speak of the divine intention, however, is to speak of creation and covenant, and this carries us back to a renewed consideration of these biblical motifs.

CREATION AND COVENANT

Covenant is the special Jewish understanding of the way in which God and human beings are related and, as such, provides clues to Jesus' own understanding of human nature, which he presupposed in his call to the kingdom. A covenant is an agreement entered into by two parties that binds them to each other and to the obligations that they assume under the agreement. Covenants come in many varieties in the ancient world, and the technical distinctions need not concern us here. The biblical covenants with Moses, Abraham, Noah, and Adam, despite their diversity, share the common note that God chooses to be bound in faithfulness to human beings and thereby lends their lives stability and dependability in the midst of threatening and unpredictable circumstances. They, for their part, bind themselves to God and covenant values and obligations that transcend their self-interest. The moral character of the Mosaic covenant meant that the self-interests of those who controlled political, economic, and religious power were no longer absolute; everyone, regardless of station, was answerable to a higher authority who relativized and restricted the power of rulers and institutions by a superior law of justice. God's justice became the plumbline by which to judge and expose political and even religious ideologies. According to George Mendenhall, this was "a development of utmost importance for the history of religion, for it places moral obligations above political and economic interests in the scale of religious values. The continued legitimate existence of any political and economic institutions was thus conditional upon obedience to the ethical norms stipulated in advance by the deity."[9]

This notion of covenant is seen in the creation itself by the authors of Genesis 1–3, and these chapters provide the most succinct statement of Hebrew anthropology. Human beings are singled out from the rest of creation to bear special responsibility for the order of the world under

---

9. George E. Mendenhall, in *Interpreter's Dictionary of the Bible* (Nashville: Abingdon, 1962), 1:719.

its Creator. This call to responsibility implies a creature "capable of being addressed"[10] or, perhaps better, the call supposes "response-ability" on the part of the called. It is creative, therefore, in the sense that it calls into existence that which did not exist prior to it and could not exist apart from it. Humans are defined as those creatures who have their special quality of life not through a unique substance—they are "dust" like the rest of nature—but through the divine call to care for the world in which they have been placed. In the biblical sense the "self" is not something self-contained but is activated in and through its relationships and responsibilities. The word that in the Old Testament is most commonly translated as "self" is *nephesh*, literally "breath," the life force that is received by the self from the Creator (Gen 2:7). Hence the self is constantly dependent for its life principle on relations beyond itself. The God of justice faithfully keeps covenant with those who keep covenant with God. Thus the covenant concept ensures fundamental human dignity and defines the structures of human existence in a relational way. From the Jewish standpoint it relativized authoritarian claims in this world at the same time as it recognized the legitimate claims of the Creator, the natural world, and fellow human beings upon that creature whose very existence is formed in the event of response and answerability.

The "image of God," as developed in Genesis 1, is not something indelible that we human beings "have"; it is not a possession any more than the covenant is a possession. It is a relation that for its actuality is dependent upon a continuing partnership that extends into the future, a relation with the one who is always ahead of us, calling us to new possibilities and responsibilities. An illustration from Sri Lankan theologian D. T. Niles clarifies this:

> The image of a king's head on a coin is part of the coin and cannot be separated from it. Even if the king dies, the image remains on the coin. But there is another kind of image. On a still and cloudless night we may see the image of the moon in the water of a lake. So long as the water is unruffled by wind, and the moon not covered by cloud, the image will shine out clear and beautiful. But if a cloud comes between the moon and earth the image will disappear, or if the water is ruffled by wind the image will be scattered and distorted. Thus the image of the moon in the water does not belong to the water in the same way the image of the

---

10. Emil Brunner, *The Divine-Human Encounter* (London: SCM Press, 1944), 51-64.

king on the coin belongs to the coin. The image depends upon a certain relation between the moon and the water. If this relation is broken, the image is distorted or lost.[11]

Hence the image of God in human beings could perhaps best be described in terms of the "ontology of the not yet." Jesus' call to the kingdom has the effect of locating creation and covenant in the future in the sense that they enter human existence as new possibilities made available in the dawning power of the kingdom. And the kingdom brings "re-creation" and covenant renewal. To be sure, the term *covenant* does not appear as frequently in the New Testament as in the Old, with the exception of the Epistle to the Hebrews.[12] Nevertheless the basic character of the covenant relationship is written into the heart of the New Testament, and its substance is reiterated every time the community gathers to celebrate "the new covenant in my blood" (Luke 22:20; 1 Cor 11:25). It is not surprising, therefore, that the collection of writings about Jesus and his movement became known as the New Covenant *(testamentum)*.

If such a positive understanding of human nature and covenant is found in the Old Testament, however, what is genuinely new in the New? What distinctive accents emerge with Christianity? By Jesus' time the understanding of the covenant had in many respects become moribund, and the only way it could be recovered was not by looking to the past, which the religious authorities had sewed up in their interpretations, but to the eschatological future and the new covenant that was to be the sign of God's sovereignty over all the earth (see Jer 31:31). It is this new future that Jesus announces, a future in which grace replaces the law as the basis of a relationship between God and humankind—without diminishing the call to justice and responsibility. This is the result of Jesus' reinterpretation of the kingdom as a gift, not conditional upon the perfect fulfillment of the law but received out of God's overflowing love and desire to reconcile. Hence those who stood most in need of mercy were the first to grasp the good news of the kingdom, and the oppressed

---

11. In Lesslie Newbigin, *Sin and Salvation* (Philadelphia: Westminster Press, 1956), 16–17.

12. Mendenhall suggests that this less-frequent use of the term *covenant* in the New Testament is because in the Jewish context *covenant* meant the Mosaic law that Christians understood to have been superseded through Christ, and in the Roman context *covenant* meant an illegal secret society (Mendenhall, *Interpreter's Dictionary of the Bible*, 722).

and powerless were those who could rejoice most over God's identification with their cause and their defense.

Moreover, the call is personalized and individualized. This is not to say that there is an absolute dichotomy between the old and new covenant communities in this regard. Obviously every individual had covenant responsibilities in Israel; and just as obviously the new covenant creates a people, the body of Christ, and not just individual Christians. Yet undoubtedly individuality and a sense of selfhood intensified with the Christian understanding of faith emerging out of confrontation with the good news of the kingdom and the call to discipleship. In the closed civil and religious communities of the first century, this call to discipleship could be answered only by individuals or small groups such as families or friendship circles. The breakdown of the authority of the religious system under the impact of pluralism had opened up the possibilities for individuals to identify with alternative sources of meaning and to form conscious subcultures. Thus the emergence of the modern self as individual is at least in part traceable to the milieu that surrounds the birth of Christianity. The Jewish God, through the cross of his Son, overcame both Jewish traditional legalism and Hellenistic cosmic principalities and powers, making release possible from those forces of religion, culture, and the cosmos that previously had been considered determinative in the fate of the individual (Col 2:13–15). Each person was invited into a covenantal relationship with the God whose Spirit is present through the love manifested toward every human being by the Son on the cross. Because this love was given without regard to traditional barriers of race and class, to participate in such love was to be enlisted in the cause of justice, which gives honor to each person not on the basis of merit but on the basis of the divine initiative that affirms the existence of each and calls into covenant even those who, by the world's standards, are of little account (Jas 2:1–5).

The primary community to which one belonged was no longer defined by the natural and cultural ties of clan and nation but, in a development that was quite new in human experience, became a matter of choice as one decided to cast one's lot with the Christian community. All of these factors combined to create a situation in which the self was viewed as an agent responsible for his or her own destiny in a way hitherto unimaginable as long as one's personal identity was submerged in a larger social unit.

One could easily overestimate the degree of individuality that came to birth in this process. Certainly most persons saw themselves not as heroic individuals in the way that Romantics of the nineteenth century did. They saw themselves instead as transferring their allegiance from one Lord to another and their social location from one sustaining community to another. To be sure, the tear in the social fabric occasioned by Hellenistic pluralism was later overcome as Christianity itself became dominant and coextensive with society. But the church always kept those earlier generations vivid in its memory through the gospels and letters that were produced and the stories of the martyrs. Hence the subcultural situation remained normative, at least in theory, even though for most of its history Christianity has fallen as predictably as any other religion into the role of guardian of the establishment. The notions of social counterculture and individual decision and responsibility were nonetheless so deeply etched in Christianity's sources that they proved again and again to be the inspiration for questioning the established order.

As the expectation for a radical transformation of this world waned, however, and as the church appropriated to itself more and more of the prerogatives of the divine kingdom, the notion of an alternative future for this world lessened and faith was diverted from hope for the future to hope for heaven. The *saint* then emerged as the answer to the routinization of Christian culture. The saint is one who by God's grace stands above the imprisonment of this world and its conventions because he or she already dwells in another world. The goal was heaven, which one reached only by the most strenuous individual commitment. The result was a shift from the kingdom model of the holy community to an elitist model of the holy individual. The results of this are still with us, seen for instance in the fact that the terms *call* and *vocation* are commonly reserved for those with clerical status, as if the whole people of God were not called. (Of course, the clergy in their obedience signify the obedience of the whole church. But the sign too easily becomes the substitute for a more universal covenantal responsibility exercised by the entire community.) The recovery of the eschatological orientation of the Bible provides an antidote to this tendency to divide Christians into the spiritual elite and the common "sheep." The Bible points toward a future for all human beings in a transformed world. Moreover, individual decisions and personal efforts are seen as contributing to social and not just individual spiritual goals. The call comes to "seek first the kingdom of God and his righteousness," and all other human concerns and priorities will fall into place. This is not to negate traditional spiritual blessings. They will find their proper location precisely in conjunction with, not in opposition to, material concerns for the well-being of humankind.

THE FALL AND ORIGINAL SIN: THE BONDAGE OF THE SELF

In the discussion thus far, have we given sufficient attention to the other traditional biblical motif in the understanding of human nature, the Fall? Is it not a fact that most persons who seek help from priests and therapists are far from seeing themselves as robust images of God, happily exercising their covenantal responsibilities in anticipation of a better day? They feel themselves instead to be the victims of circumstances beyond their control. They are in bondage to forces and powers about which they feel helpless to do anything. Is there a way of viewing the traditions of the Fall and original sin that can give us insight into both the nature of the problem and the solution without abandoning eschatological hope as a genuine possibility for concrete human existence?

If human beings are created for covenantal relationships and cannot be finally fruitful apart from the kingdom of God, this must mean that they are created incomplete. This to-be-completed state is "good"; as such, it is not a deficient mode of being, for it is precisely what allows human existence to be a lifelong journey. Although conception is the obvious biological starting point, the "creation" of a human being is continuous, and the human being as the image of God is a lifetime in becoming. This incompleteness is the possibility for continuous creation by the Spirit, yet it is also the occasion for insecurity and anxiety. Blessing and curse, so it seems, come from the same structure. Incompleteness necessitates constant change, but change is threatening because it means that the future cannot be predicted or controlled from the present. This insecurity triggers the will to power that sets up situations of conflict that in turn intensify insecurity, raise defenses, escalate the need for control, and lead to the breakdown of the very relationships that support, sustain, and nurture the self in ways that enhance necessary growth. One of the negative manifestations of the human condition, as Augustine recognized, is the *cor curvum in se*, the heart turned in upon itself, which illustrates the "caughtness" character of sin. The heart in its anxiety is deaf to the voices outside itself that seek to affirm it. Or even more tragically in our world, the heart has no memory of positive, affirming voices outside itself and has learned, therefore, to defend itself against further pain by rationalizing its dilemma or, in the more violent form of the same defense, by slaying all comers even before they have a chance to speak.

The traditional doctrine of "original sin" is the classic description of the fact that this condition exists. As an explanation of why it should be, the story of the Fall in Genesis 3 is not very satisfactory. The difficulty of tracing sin back to an actual first cause—if Satan, then who caused Satan to sin?—has led theologians to speak of the *mystery* of evil, for its origins seem lost in an abysmal realm that the mind cannot penetrate. More helpful, it seems to me, is to recognize that the possibility of human evil (and the breakdown of interpersonal and psychic life in general) is given in the very structures of insecurity and change that also make human fulfillment possible. It is the price paid for the potential for positive relations and growth. The alternative to freedom and change would be complete homeostasis, which would mean stagnation, boredom, and the death of existence as we know it. To be sure, constant instability has no meaning if it is not set within the context of an overall purpose and goal. The message of the kingdom provides the goal that gives both a directedness to all human activity and an assurance that the ultimate accomplishment of the goal is not dependent upon the preliminary success of human efforts. Both stability and goal-oriented change are necessary if our efforts are to be purposeful but not anxious and compulsive.

This kind of a universe involves risk. "God does not play dice," quipped Albert Einstein. I believe it is not unfair to say, however, that God does take risks; God accepts the risks involved in a creation that is not static but is moving toward the realization of its possibilities. The genuine independence that the creation has been granted is at once the precondition for partnership and for revolt. It is this fact that is graphically portrayed in the story of the Fall. When the Lord God revisits the Garden "in the cool of the day" (Gen 3:8 RSV), after the man and woman have turned for their fulfillment toward the part of the world under their control—to guarantee their future without having to relate to one who is outside of themselves and beyond their control—it is apparent that a fundamental distortion of relationships has taken place. Tension and insecurity have entered a picture previously characterized by confidence and trust. The one who was not only their Creator but also their Lord and Friend has now become the most obvious threat to their existence. They hide themselves, and in their action lurks the wish that God were not there, the wish that God were not the future to be contended with—in short, the wish that God were dead. In this deceptively simple story we find portrayed all the essentials of the saga of human insecurity and conflict that every psychiatrist and counselor encounters daily in his or her ministry of healing. Adam and Eve appear to be better representatives of ordinary human existence than Prometheus. Most of what we encounter is not grand in scale, not a heroic battle against an irrational fate willed by distant gods. It is a breakdown of communication in the family, perhaps between husband and wife, or a "personality conflict" with the boss, just the kind of situation that is portrayed in the primeval Garden. "Where are you?"... "I was afraid... and I hid myself" (Gen 3:9–10 RSV). The verbatim of Adam and Eve—naked and now self-consciously insecure—could be recorded by any therapist. "Who is at fault?" "Anyone but me." And Paradise is over, never again to be entered until the kingdom.

Note that the usefulness of the doctrine of original sin is not just to provide a description of basic human misery. It serves an often overlooked therapeutic function as well. The story of the Fall recognizes that we bear the consequences of a sinful situation that we did not consciously choose or willfully create. It provides a way of dealing with guilt (therefore not denying the element of human responsibility) while also providing an opening for a nonjudgmental approach. The common way the church has dealt with sin is by assigning guilt. That may be satisfactory for single, isolatable deeds. What we usually are faced with, however, is a complex network of relationships gone awry. And any attempt to assign guilt results predictably in defensive reactions and denials of responsibility—just the opposite of the openness that we are attempting to build. In the doctrine of "original sin," guilt is assigned to Adam. We bear the consequences of his sin; that is, we are allowed to see ourselves as victims of a situation without having to take personal responsibility for its cause. This defuses the situation because the anxiety about losing power and control is not attacked directly. The focus instead can be on what to do about the problem at hand. Our condemnation is not at stake, and so we can begin to assume responsibility for the existing conditions without losing face. Adam is the one to whom guilt can be assigned until we have developed the capacity and resources to face it ourselves. One therapist, in a conscious appropriation of Latin American liberation theology, calls this phase "bondage analysis," which is the clarification of the existing conditions without assigning guilt.

The next stage involves identifying the obstacles that stand in the way of healing. What would it take to remove them? And if they cannot be removed, is there any way to overcome them by another method? Here we must pass from the model of Adam to that of Christ. Adam provides the analysis of how things are; Christ is the one who removes the obstacles to the future by enabling us to trust the future and release our grip on the past. To let go of the past is only possible if the conviction concerning the trustworthiness of the future is powerful enough to sustain us in the midst of objective insecurity. Jesus announced that this power is present and that the first fruits of the kingdom are available wherever his word and promise of divine mercy and love are received as the foretaste of what is to come and in the end will prevail. For Christians, then, the first signs of the coming age are already present through Christ, that is, through his death and resurrection, the new covenant and Christian community he brought into being and the healing forces he has generated in the world. But this is all proleptic and remains obscure to most of humanity. Where is the promised fulfillment for all humankind? Why the delay? As the bumper sticker says, why not "Parousia Now"?

I would like to think it is because God is creating a space in which psychiatrists and psychotherapists, counselors, priests and pastors, teachers and mothers, land reformers and political revolutionaries, can work. In other words, wherever the "dividing walls of hostility" (see Eph 2:14) are being penetrated and new possibilities opened up, the power of the kingdom is at work to enable the whole created order to realize the destiny for which it was called into being. God is still taking risks.

In this chapter we have described some of the changes taking place in theology today and the emergence of new ways of viewing the human condition. It is already evident that the recovery of the revolutionary implications of the biblical motif of the kingdom of God—for so many centuries lost from sight or interpreted in strictly otherworldly terms—is causing a fundamental reorientation in the method and content of theology. This reorientation may be the leaven that will gradually reshape the consciousness and practice of the churches and of those cultures where Christianity continues to exert a major influence.

8

The Earth as the First Sacrament[1]

THE INDISPUTABLE EVIDENCE FOR global warming is now in, and those who dismissed it previously as scientifically unproven and an exaggeration by conservationists are having to reconsider. The effects of climate change, with increasing droughts in some parts of the globe and increasing floods in others, cannot be ignored. Greenhouse gas emissions, those heat-trapping gases produced by industry, power plants, and autos, are melting ice caps at the poles and raising sea levels that threaten life not only on low-lying islands but coastal areas everywhere. The initiatives of the United Nations in the Kyoto Protocol and the Copenhagen and Cancun Climate Conferences seeking significant commitments by the chief producers to reduce greenhouse gasses have been frustrated. What seems to be lacking is grassroots support for climate legislation necessary for political action to take place. Are there biblical and theological resources to convince Christians at the grassroots level to back such efforts? And how does the grace communicated through the sacrament of the Lord's Supper inspire not only our worship but empower us to respond to this major challenge?

In the Genesis stories of creation God establishes a covenant with Adam in the gift to Adam and to humankind of the earth to care for it, "to till it and keep it"(Gen 2:15). Hence we can say that the first sacrament, the *original* sacrament, is the earth. For a sacrament is a material means employed by God to communicate the divine self-gift to

---

1. This chapter will appear in Christiaan Mostert, Gerald O'Collins and Sean Winter, eds., *Immense, Unfathomed, Unconfined: The Grace of God in Creation, Church and Community* (Melbourne: Uniting Academic Press, 2011). Used by permission.

The Earth as the First Sacrament   119

humanity. And God gives God's self to humanity through the earth entrusted to us. A sacrament is supremely exemplified in the Lord's Supper, in which Christ uses material means, bread and wine, in an action in which he gives himself to his disciples and to us who would be his disciples. According to one of the traditional definitions of a sacrament, "a sacrament *effects* what it signifies." It not only points to, or signifies, God's love, but expresses, enacts, and transmits that love so that it has its effects in the hearts and lives of those who receive it. Can this love transform our hearts to care for the earth God has given us?

God's love and care for humanity from the beginning is expressed in both of the Genesis stories of creation. Indeed, as Old Testament scholar Gerhard von Rad points out, the first story in Genesis, which describes humanity as the "image of God," was written in the context of the captivity of the Hebrew people in Babylon, and the authors may have utilized a conscious analogy to the Babylonian custom at the time. When the Babylonian emperor conquered a new territory he set up an image of himself in the capital city of the province and appointed a governor who ruled the province by virtue of the authority vested in the image. The governor could rely on his own judgment in most matters as long as he kept the province loyal to the emperor.[2] If this combination of image and governor was indeed in the minds of those who in the first chapter of Genesis set forth the Hebrew understanding of human life, it stood in stark (and perhaps even polemical) contrast to the official view contained in the Babylonian epic of creation, the *Enuma elish*. In that saga the high god, Marduk, created human beings as slaves for the gods so the gods could take their ease as the original leisure class. Hebrew consciousness, however, originated precisely in the revolt against slavery in Egypt. Their God had called them not into slavery but into a covenant that included, as the image of God, co-responsibility for the earth, a governor *imaging* the Creator's governance over the whole creation.

> God blessed them, and God said to them, "Be fruitful and multiply, and fill the earth and subdue it; and have dominion over the fish of the sea and over the birds of the air and over every living thing that moves upon the earth."
>
> God said, "See, I have given you every plant yielding seed that is upon the face of all the earth, and every tree with seed in its fruit; you shall have them for food. And to . . . everything that has

---

2. Gerhard von Rad, *Genesis* (Philadelphia: Westminster Press, 1961), 58.

the breath of life, I have given every green plant for food. And it was so.

God saw everything that he had made, and indeed, it was very good (Gen 1:28–31).

From this we can say that the earth serves as the very first sacrament, the original material sign to express God's relation to humanity. It serves as the visible and tactile sign of divine grace in a world God entrusts to our care.

Moreover, in placing the earth in our hands, God gives us not just some*thing*. "In, with, under, and through" this gift we are given God's own self as our Divine Parent. To *parent* is to create a life related to oneself yet free, an independent center of thought, will, and action. In giving us the earth, the Father both undergirds us with a parent's love, and affirms us in our capacity to care for a heritage that has been entrusted to us.

In this sacramental gift, therefore, God gives us three interrelations that are basic to human existence. First, our relation to the earth, the source that continues to meet our material needs. Second, our relation as stewards of the earth links us in a special way to God, for we have our calling in continuing answerability to our Creator for the care of creation. Third, through these relations to God and to creation, we receive our relationship to ourselves and our fellow creatures, our identity as co-responsible and mutually answerable both to our own time and to future generations.

John Wesley described human beings as the image of God in a tripartite way: the *natural* image, with the gift of reason, will and freedom; the *political* image, with the vocation to serve as "governor of this lower world"; and the *moral* image, the gift of a relation with the God of "justice, mercy, and truth."[3] All aspects of the image are interrelated, but the political image is the most directly involved in our relation to the environment. As Wesley said, because "God is in all things, we are to see the Creator in the glass of [reflected in] every creature; we should use and look upon nothing as separate from God, which indeed is a kind of practical atheism."[4] If we are to see all creation in God and God in

---

3. John Wesley, Sermon 45, "The New Birth," *The Works of John Wesley*, Bicentennial edition; hereafter *Works*, Albert C. Outler et. al., eds. (Nashville: Abingdon Press, 1984), vol. 2:188. Direct quotations used by permission.

4. *Works*, Sermon 23, "Sermon on the Mount III," 1:516–17.

all creation, then the neglect of our duty to protect the created order is practical atheism, it is our seeing it apart from its existence in God and apart from God's life in it. When we deal with the earth and its resources, and when we deal with our fellow creatures, we are dealing with God. "We are now God's stewards.... [A steward] is not the owner of any of these things but barely entrusted with them by another."[5] We are not the possessors of this earth. We only hold in trust what belongs to the Creator. And we hold it in trust not only for our own generation but for future generations as well.

The implications of this for ecology, for an environmental theology, and for an ethic of responsibility are evident. But just as evident is the fact that we have strayed from the original divine intention. We have separated the gift from the Giver, the sacramental element from the Provider, the inheritance from the Testator, and acted as if the earth were our own to be exploited for our own immediate benefit with no answerability to anyone. The ironic result of this willful absconding with our inheritance is not increased freedom but fateful bondage. For the earth is becoming an ever more threatening environment, with climate change, the loss of the ozone layer, the melting of the polar ice caps, the exhausting of natural resources due to mismanagement and exploitation, the loss of species because of reduction of habitat, the growth of deserts due to competition for water resources; the list goes on and on. As a result, we see the world becoming more and more a threat and a burden rather than a "gift of the Father's unfailing grace." We are overwhelmed and disheartened by the sacrifices it would require of our economic system and our affluent lifestyles to overcome injustices both to the world of nature and to our fellow inhabitants of the earth. Where can we find the will to make these sacrifices?

If the world as we experience it has become more a threat than a promise, a tragic destiny in which we are embroiled but over which we feel we have little control, if it is the domain of principalities and powers, of impersonal economic forces rather than the creation of God, how can it serve as the sacrament of God's unfailing grace? Can the sacrament of the Son, the Lord's Supper, restore the sacrament of the Creator-Father, the earth, to its function as the gift of God to humanity? How can the sacrament represent both this corrupted world and the Redeemer of this world? Are they not antithetical?

5. *Works,* Sermon 51, "The Good Steward," 2:283.

Yet precisely here, in the Eucharist (the meal of thanksgiving), the redemptive work of Christ is made clear. In his hands the sacrament is presented to us as *the earth in its original and redeemed form.* He takes the bread and wine, which are products of the earth and our ordinary world—and therefore related to the complexities of international grain cartels, embargoes, shortages, starvation, alcoholism, and all the other ways God's good gifts have gone awry—and turns them into signs of his kingdom of justice and love. He does this by identifying them with himself—this is my body, this is my blood—and with the kingdom mission from God he embodied, just as he did the paschal bread and wine at the Last Supper. Having joined them with his body and with his life for the kingdom, Jesus hands the bread and wine back to us to make us participants in his mission and his kingdom by sharing its first fruits (*aparche*) that nourish us along the way.

Because this bread and this wine are signs of the *resurrected* Christ, they bring with them the assurance that he cannot finally be defeated. And as overwhelming as the task of stewardship of this earth may seem, it is not meaningless or without ultimate purpose because it joins us to Christ's own redemptive work, bringing order out of chaos. In the end he will prevail! Because this bread and wine are also signs of the *crucified* Christ, we are reminded that responsibility involves suffering and sacrifice. There are no guarantees of progress, no promises of easy victories. Yet the signs communicate to us that profound and persistent love from the cross that sustains us when faced with defeat, assuring us that "neither death, nor life, . . . nor rulers, . . . nor powers, nor height, nor depth, nor anything else in all creation, will be able to separate us from the love of God in Christ Jesus our Lord" (Rom 8:38-39).

It is precisely this love, according to Wesley, that has the power to renew the *moral* image of God in us. And *salvation* is defined by Wesley as the *renewal of the image of God.* The moral image is therefore not something we possess in and of ourselves. It is therefore not like the *natural* image, the capacities for reason, will, and freedom with which we are endowed and that we continue to exercise, if in a distorted and self-serving manner after the Fall. Nor is it like the *political* image, our ability to manage the world, the capacity for which we retain even if we exercise it in an irresponsible and corrupted fashion. For the moral image is neither a capacity within humanity nor a function that can be employed independently of our Maker because it is a relationship in which we receive continuously from our Creator, and through which we mediate further what we receive.

The *moral* image is a *mirror* that reflects the love it receives not only back to God but also into the world. It shares the life of God with a world toward which God is reaching out and seeking to redeem. It is this moral outreach that is written into the very nature of the God-relation in Wesley. Therefore this aspect of the image cannot be called simply "spiritual," for the intention is not just to renew the spirit of the human being but to create an agent that extends the moral energy of the love it receives from the Creator into a world God would reconcile and re-create. To be this kind of agent requires what Wesley calls "spiritual respiration,"

> God's breathing into the soul, and the soul's breathing back what it first receives from God; a continual *action* of God upon the soul, the *re-action* of the soul upon God; and unceasing presence of God, the loving, pardoning God, manifested to the heart, and perceived by faith; and an unceasing return of love, praise and prayer, offering up all the thoughts of our hearts, all the words of our tongues, all the works of our hands, all our body, soul, and spirit to be an holy sacrifice, acceptable unto God in Christ Jesus.[6]

The renewal of the *moral* image is therefore crucial to the renewal of the *natural* and the *political* image, for it is only when the relation with God and the fundamental security it provides is restored to human existence that the reason is freed from its necessity to rationalize and justify self-seeking behavior, and the will is freed to commit itself to carry out the sacrifices that the responsible political image is called to make. Thus genuine freedom requires the restoration of all aspects of the image of God for the practical benefits of human wholeness to be realized. Then we will be free to make the sacrifices and practice the self-denial that our future as the political image would seem to require of us. Then the Lord's Supper can play a crucial role in empowering the kind of response that can make a practical difference. Through the bread and the wine—the earth's products which Jesus identifies with himself and his mission—we receive from the hands of Christ the earth in its

---

6. *Works*, Sermon 19, "The Great Priviledge of Those That Are Born of God," 1:442 (italics added). (The *Oxford English Dictionary* traces its definition of *reaction* to this use by Wesley.)

original and redeemed form. For he is the "firstborn of all creation," the true "image of the invisible God," and "in him all things hold together ... whether on earth or in heaven, by making peace through the blood of his cross" (Col 1:15–20). When we receive from Christ his body and blood with all that this means, therefore, we receive him as the *true image* who renews in us the image of God in all its dimensions. This gift and the grace that accompanies it awaken and empower our role as the political image so that we can be "looking and working for the renewal of the earth given by the Creator-God."[7] We can approach with renewed commitment and dedication the tasks to which we are called, the tasks that are ours under God as "governor of this lower world."[8]

---

7. Norman Young, *Creator, Creation and Faith* (Philadelphia: Westminster Press, 1976), 175.

8. *Works*, Sermon 45, "The New Birth," 2:188.

9

A Contemporary Understanding of the Sacraments[1]

THIS CHAPTER FIRST APPEARED in *Keeping the Faith*,[2] edited by Geoffrey Wainwright, and celebrating the one hundredth anniversary of the publication of *Lux Mundi*[3], a volume produced by eleven Oxford dons in 1889 to address what was understood to be the main threat to the Christian faith in the nineteenth century, namely, "materialism." The original authors were all Anglicans, but the anniversary volume was ecumenical, indicating the growing sense of interdependence of the churches today. The intention was nevertheless the same as in the initial volume, to affirm the basic Christian truths.

In his chapter on the sacraments in *Lux Mundi*, Francis Paget, who was later to be bishop of Oxford, viewed the sacraments not only as central to worship but as the "unsurpassed expression" of that doctrine that is central to Christian faith itself: the Incarnation.[4] Just as in the historical figure of Jesus the divine has appeared in human flesh, visible to the eye and understandable to the ear, so in the sacraments the Incarnation continues to be the model of divine-human communication. The Savior makes himself available through water, bread, and wine: physical and

---

1. Originally published as "The Sacraments" in *Keeping the Faith: Essays to Mark the Centenary of* Lux Mundi, edited by Geoffrey Wainwright (Philadelphia: Fortress Press, 1988), 209–23. Used by permission.

2. Geoffrey Wainwright, ed., *Keeping the Faith* (Philadelphia: Fortress Press, 1988).

3. Charles Gore, ed., *Lux Mundi: A Series of Studies in the Religion of the Incarnation* (London: John Murray, 1913).

4. Francis Paget, "Sacraments" in ibid., 296–317.

material—visible, tangible, tasteable—yet transmitting a reality that includes and transcends the physical as such.

What undergirded the *Lux Mundi* enterprise—and made it so appealing to many of its readers—was the conviction that a religion grounded in the doctrine of the Incarnation could successfully confront the main intellectual challenge of the time, materialism, and Paget was convinced that the sacraments could speak to this challenge most directly. He viewed materialism not as a dire threat to genuine Christianity but as a stimulus that forced an awareness of resources of the faith hitherto unapparent. Paget regarded a "false spiritualism," which rejects the body and the material world, as the chief misunderstanding of Christianity in the popular mind of his time. And materialism, he claimed, "has done a valuable service in correcting the exaggeration of a one-sided spiritualism."[5] From the Incarnation flows the "sacramental principle," which sees the physical universe not as disjoined from or antithetical to the spiritual but rather views the two as interpenetrating: the physical and material are infused with the transcendent and spiritual, and the spiritual communicates itself through the this-worldly and material. "Sensible objects, agents and acts [become] the means or instruments of Divine energies." The saving and sanctifying transcendent power is "conveyed by means . . . taken from this world, and addressed to human senses."[6]

According to Paget, the fact that Judaism served as the seedbed of Christianity reinforced this affirmation of the material world, for Judaism was a nation and a people with a history "replete with forecasts of the consecration of material things, . . . encouraged to look for the blessings of Divine goodness through sensible means." There was no need to "dislodge the sacramental principle out of the minds of those among whom our Lord came." The purpose was not to destroy but to fulfill this Jewish heritage through the

> embodiment of grace in ordinances: the designation of visible agents, acts, and substances, to be the instruments of Divine virtue—this principle is so intimately and essentially woven into the

---

5. Ibid., 299. Cf. Robert W. Jenson's observation that most non-Christian religions, at their more sophisticated levels, tend toward non-embodied representations of the divine (*Visible Words* [Philadelphia: Fortress Press, 1978], 29–30).

6. Paget, "Sacraments," 297.

texture of Christianity that it cannot be got out without destroying the whole fabric.[7]

If materialism posed a major challenge to the ingenuity and resources of the Christian faith at the end of the nineteenth century, what is a comparable challenge today? To be sure, materialism has by no means disappeared as a threat in our time. Yet reductionist materialism, which seemed so potent in the nineteenth century, has been largely discredited by philosophical materialists themselves, many of whom in the meantime have come to recognize the inexhaustible nature of values traditionally called "spiritual" and the limitations of reductionism. Moreover, for Paget the issue was posed in the framework of the perennial mind/matter problem, or spirit/body dichotomy. And a solution was sought on the intellectual level in terms of satisfactory metaphysical relations. In our time the issue is more practical, for the form that the threat of materialism takes today is the acute problem of the *ecological crisis,* which is a problem not just for the intellect and consciousness but for the environment, for health, for economics and the whole material base. This is a crisis brought about by systems that have made the production and distribution of material goods and the increase of material wealth their chief aim but in the process are destroying and exhausting the material resources upon which all life and future generations depend. Can the doctrine of the sacraments say something to "materialism" in this form? Obviously there are many other issues in the life of society and of the church to which the sacraments can speak, but for purposes of illustration we will address ourselves primarily to this one in the conviction that, if it can be shown how the sacraments illumine an issue that is among the most pressing of modern life, it will demonstrate today what *Lux Mundi* sought to do for its time. Its purpose was "to present positively the central ideas and principles of religion, in the light of contemporary thought and current problems," and thus to engage in "the real development of theology." For it defined theology as

> the process in which the Church, standing firm in her old truths, enters into the apprehension of the new social and intellectual movements of each age: and because "the truth makes her free" is able to assimilate all new material, to welcome and give its place

---

7. Ibid., 304.

to all new knowledge, [and] to throw herself into the sanctification of each new social order.[8]

This "sanctification of the social order" requires the transformation and modification of the individuals and institutions that comprise it.

One positive contribution that dialectical materialism in its contemporary form of "critical theory" has made to theological reflection is to call attention to the responsibility of thought to modify behavior. To paraphrase Marx, as long as theology simply "interprets the world," its effects on systems and structures will be minimal. "The point is to change it." Religion reduced to the private sphere and predilections of the individual cannot serve as the agent of change that *Lux Mundi* seeks when it calls upon the church to "throw herself into the sanctification of each new social order." Ideas that do not lead to change in structures and behavior have the effect of reinforcing the status quo. Sacramental worship at its best, however, is always a praxis, a way of being and thinking about God, self, community, and world that is acted out and reflected upon in a process that leads to an ever new and more profound understanding of reality as well as intervention in it. This is what the "sanctification" of both the individual and society today involves. Thus, in what follows, the praxis element will never be far from our considerations.

KINGDOM AND SACRAMENT

If there has been a characteristic paradigm shift in theology from the end of the nineteenth century to the present, it is the shift from Incarnation to *kingdom* as the organizing motif. This is by no means a denial of the central role that Christology plays in all Christian thought. It is, rather, the attempt to do justice to what scholars agree was at the center of Jesus' own ministry. His healings, his exorcisms, his commandments, his parables—even his supper with his disciples—anticipate the kingdom. They are signs and first fruits that appear wherever Jesus' words, as agent of the kingdom, are truly heard, judgment and forgiveness are received, and God's intended order of justice and love is reestablished. The repentance *(metanoia)* for which Jesus calls is a turning away from the world as it is now constituted and toward the future as constituted by the One who is addressed in the "kingdom prayer" with the petition, "Thy kingdom come, thy will be done on earth as it is in heaven." This

---

8. Charles Gore, *Lux Mundi*, Preface, viii.

is the context in which Jesus' words to Pilate in the Johannine account must be understood, "My kingdom is not from this world" (John 18:36). The "world" to which he refers is the present age, presided over by the likes of Pilate, Herod, and Caiaphas, which will be superseded by the age to come presided over by God's own agent of justice, the Son of man. Although the new age will be a radical transformation of the present, in neither the Old nor the New Testament is it envisioned as a volatilization of this present material world into a realm of pure spirit. It is precisely *this* world that is the object of God's redeeming activity, for it is this world that is God's creation which God will not abandon! Under the sign of the rainbow it is to be transformed and restored, not annihilated. Therefore, the sacraments are to be understood as *signs of the kingdom* within this cosmic drama and overarching purpose.[9] Indeed, material evidences and actions—food, drink, clothing, housing, visitation—become the clearest indication of participation (or nonparticipation) in the power of the kingdom (Matt 25:31–46).

In a section entitled "The Eucharist as Meal of the Kingdom," the ecumenical document *Baptism, Eucharist and Ministry,* claims that "the eucharist opens up the vision of the divine rule which has been promised as the final renewal of creation and is a foretaste of it."[10] According to Yves Congar, sacrament cannot be understood apart from this notion of the renewal of creation. But he joins this with the doctrine of the Incarnation by saying that, with the Incarnation of the Son into the life of this world, "God had irrevocably decided" for renewal:

> Seen in this light, the notion of sacrament assumes dynamic value; it is related to the world and its history. It becomes the concrete historical expression of God's design for salvation in this world, the sign and instrument through which God works out his decision to intervene with his grace in mankind and in creation in order to make them achieve the end for which he had destined them from the beginning.[11]

---

9. See an earlier version of the argument here presented, Theodore Runyon, "The World as Original Sacrament," *Worship* 54, no. 6 (November 1980): 495–511. Cf. also Alexander Schmemann, *For the Life of the World*. rev. ed. (Crestwood, N.Y.: St. Vladimir's Seminary Press, 1973), and idem, *The Eucharist: Sacrament of the Kingdom* (Crestwood, N.Y.: St. Vladimir's Seminary Press, 1988).

10. *Baptism, Eucharist and Ministry* (Geneva: World Council of Churches, 1982), 14.

11. Yves Congar, "The Notion of 'Major' or 'Principal' Sacraments" in *The Sacraments in General*, Edward Schillebeeckx and Boniface Willems, eds., vol. 31 of

Moreover, in this renewal no sharp line is drawn between the human and natural worlds, for their futures intertwine,[12] as the prophet envisions the future:

> With righteousness [God] shall judge the poor,
>   and decide with equity for the meek of the earth;
>
> ....
>
> The wolf shall live with the lamb,
>   the leopard shall lie down with the kid,
> the calf and the lion and the fatling together,
>   and a little child shall lead them.
>
> ....
>
> They will not hurt or destroy
>   on all my holy mountain;
> for the earth will be full of the knowledge of the Lord
>   as the waters cover the sea. (Isa 11:4, 6, 9)

Indeed, as St. Paul later describes it, the creation itself will benefit from the redemption of humanity through Christ (just as the world of nature now suffers under the burden of human corruption): "For the creation waits with eager longing for the revealing of the children of God; . . . in hope that the creation itself will be set free from its bondage to decay and will obtain the freedom of the glory of the children of God" (Rom 8:19, 21).

As Jesus assembles his followers for a final meal, he enacts a parable that in summary fashion dramatizes his own life as a servant of the kingdom, a kingdom whose first signs according to his preaching are the forgiveness of sins and God's love poured out for the reconciliation of all who are open to the good news of divine mercy. As they begin the meal, he says to them, "I have eagerly desired to eat this Passover with you before I suffer; for I tell you I will not eat it until it is fulfilled in the kingdom of God" (Luke 22:15–16). As he passes the cup he says, "[F]rom now on I will not drink of the fruit of the vine until the kingdom of God comes" (v. 18). With these words and actions Jesus transforms the paschal meal, the Jewish meal of remembrance that celebrates the

---

Concilium (New York: Paulist Press, 1968), 28.

12. See *Lumen Gentium*, chap. 7, par. 48, in *Vatican Council II*, Austin Flannery, ed. (Collegeville, Minn.: Liturgical Press, 1975), 407.

faithfulness of God in the past, into an eschatological feast, the foretaste of the age to come.[13]

What is this kingdom for which Jesus risks everything? And how can bread and wine serve as indications of its coming and at the same time be identified with Jesus' own life and mission?

In the hands of Jesus, the bread and the wine, symbols of the old order and the previous covenant, become signs of the new covenant of grace that is the hallmark of Jesus' interpretation of the kingdom. To receive them is to receive the very substance of his life given for the kingdom as he understood it. To participate in that life is to receive eschatological food and drink, the new creation in its promissory form, the earnest *(arrabōn)* of that which is to come. "The Eucharist is the meal at which the messiah feeds His people as a sign of the feasting in the coming kingdom."[14] To receive bread and wine from Christ is therefore to receive the power of the kingdom, which was the driving force in his existence as he embodied and lived out the intention of God. This is why, according to Paul, one cannot "eat the bread" (i.e., partake in who Christ was in his body, his very being) and "drink the cup" (i.e., partake in that for which he poured out his life's blood) and not eat and drink the kingdom of God. To participate in the sacramental power of the new age and yet to operate habitually in terms of the selfishness, injustice, and insensitivity of the old order, as Paul saw some of the Corinthian Christians doing, is to partake "in an unworthy manner" and to invite judgment and dire consequences (see 1 Cor 11:20–32).

FROM KINGDOM TO CREATION: THE ECOLOGICAL SETTING

Once we have grasped the eschatological quality of the sacrament as revealed in Christ, we are in a position to look back from the *eschaton* to the *proton*, from kingdom to creation, and to look at the creation with new eyes. Turning to the first chapters of Genesis, we discover that the ancient Hebrew stories of origins open up the character of our relationship to the world afresh. Indeed, it could be said that in the hands of the Creator, the world itself serves as the *first sacrament,* the first and most basic use of the material to communicate and facilitate the divine-human

---

13. See Alasdair I. C. Heron. *Table and Tradition* (Philadelphia: Westminster Press, 1984), 54, 152.

14. Geoffrey Wainwright. *Eucharist and Eschatology* (New York: Oxford University Press. 1981), 94.

relationship. Christ's own giving of freedom through bread and wine to humankind is prefigured in the Creator's bestowal of freedom to the creatures as God entrusts to male and female the care and protection of the earth and calls upon them to use it in ways consistent with the divine intentions. God called them into a suzerainty covenant, into co-responsibility for the earth.[15]

> God blessed them, and God said to them, "Be fruitful and multiply, and fill the earth and subdue it; and have dominion over the fish of the sea and over the birds of the air and over every living thing that moves upon the earth." God said, "See, I have given you every plant yielding seed that is upon the face of all the earth, and every tree with seed in its fruit; you shall have them for food. And to . . . everything that has the breath of life, I have given every green plant for food." And it was so. And God saw everything that he had made, and indeed, it was very good. (Gen 1:28–31)

The gift to humanity of the earth entrusted to our care, to "till it and keep it" (Gen 2:15) is therefore God's most fundamental sacramental act.

The implications of this sacramental relationship to God and the world for a theology of ecology and an ethic of responsibility are obvious. But just as obvious, as seen in the ecological crisis, is the fact that humankind is far gone from the original covenantal relation. We have separated the gift from the Giver and acted as if the earth were our own with no answerability to the Creator, our fellow inhabitants of the planet, or to future generations. The ironic result of this willful absconding with our inheritance has been not increased freedom but fateful bondage. The world is becoming an ever more intolerable burden, an ominous fate and threat, our own white whale from which, like Captain Ahab, we cannot disentangle ourselves, though it carry us with it to destruction. This apocalyptic turn of events impresses itself upon the imagination of the present generation and makes it very difficult to see the world in its basic sacramental reality. How can we envision it as the "gift of the Father's unfailing grace"? It would be easy to accuse the church of shortchanging humankind at this point. Too often the church has been unaware of the larger meaning and cosmic implications of the sacrament, and has fostered a timid, truncated, pious understanding, content to settle for religious practices in a sacred corner of the world where it controls

---

15. Cf. Walther Eichrodt, *Theology of the Old Testament* (Philadelphia: Westminster Press, 1967), 2, 127.

the sacramental keys to heaven—yet it has lost the keys of the kingdom and its world-transforming power. But such accusations would serve no useful purpose. As the authors of *Lux Mundi* recognized, often a new situation and new challenges are necessary for the church to discover its own treasures. They were writing at the very beginning of a recovery of the eschatological, world-historical dimension of Christianity. The nineteenth century had begun to suspect that the original Jewishness of the Christian message had been obscured by layers of Hellenistic and Neoplatonic interpretation that had transformed Jesus' message of the kingdom into an otherworldly realm. Paget was aware of the importance of the recovery of Jewishness for sacramental theology. Nevertheless, his interpretation of the kingdom was still conceived in terms of an idealist "realm of souls," those nurtured by the sacraments to look beyond this world for salvation. The natural world and its preservation did not enter the picture because there was not yet an awareness of impending crisis.

How can the redemptive mission of Christ extend not just to humanity but to the rest of creation as well? How can God's purpose "set forth in Christ, as a plan for the fullness of time, [serve] to gather up all things in him, things in heaven and things on earth" (Eph 1:9–10)? The corruption that has entered history through human irresponsibility now affects the whole planet. Can God's grace in Christ have an effect equally basic? The starting point for this fundamental transformation is to be found in the sacramental event itself.

We receive the sacrament from Christ's own hands. He takes the bread and wine, products of our ordinary world, and identifies them with himself, his mission and his message. He makes them part of his own identity—his body, his blood—given for all humanity and for God's kingdom and rule over all of life. When he hands them to us and we receive them, he extends through us the kingdom mission for which he gave his life. We become agents of the love his body and blood express reaching out into the world he is seeking to redeem and bring back to the Creator-Father.

When we receive the bread and wine we receive the resurrected Christ, the Presence who cannot be defeated. God's kingdom of justice, mercy and peace, will in the end triumph. His resurrection is the sure sign of that triumph. At the same time, his body and blood are signs that this road into the future will include crucifixion. Being stewards of God's world means there will be struggles and defeats along the way. All the entrenched forces will resist responsible stewardship. Yet St. Paul, who preceded us on the journey of faith, assures us that "neither death, nor life, . . . nor things present, nor things to come, nor powers, nor height, nor depth, nor anything else in all creation, will be able to separate us from the love of God in Christ Jesus our Lord" (Rom 8:38–39).

BAPTISM

If the eucharist is the sacrament that nourishes us along the way by making us participants in Christ's redeeming and renewing work in the world, baptism is the rite that inaugurates this identification with Christ and his body, the church. Baptism "unites the one baptized with Christ and with his people."[16] It places the person in a new context by incorporating him or her into the ongoing history of Christ's kingdom mission.

Baptism, like eucharist, is thus best understood within its original biblical, eschatological setting. It identifies the one baptized with the new age which Christ is bringing. As Geoffrey Wainwright observes:

> For the Christian community, meaning is in the making: life is oriented towards God's ultimate purpose, and history-making is the way to the attainment of that purpose both for individuals and humanity as a whole; the most characteristic Christian rituals [eucharist and baptism] are therefore predominantly transformative in character;[17]

Although in baptism today attention is directed primarily to the individual being baptized, it is probably accurate to say that in biblical times, in the awareness of both the congregation and the one being baptized, the larger context was more prominent. They viewed the event, first of all, as occurring at a crucial moment in *world history* as part of God's intervention and saving acts; and second, as an event in the life of the *church*, to which God is adding daily in order that it might be the body of Christ at work in the world; third, the *individual* is consequently understood as identifying with, and being incorporated into, this larger picture—washed, cleansed, and made part of God's new history in Christ Jesus and sealed for the age to come by the Spirit (Eph 1:3–14). Let us look more closely at these three aspects of baptism.

---

16. *Baptism, Eucharist and Ministry*, 2.

17. Geoffrey Wainwright, *Doxology* (New York: Oxford University Press, 1980), 121.

First, according to Mark's account, Jesus' original and fundamental message was, "The time is fulfilled, and the kingdom of God has come near; repent, and believe in the good news" (Mark 1:15). Jesus understood his own ministry within *the cosmic framework of events* that would reestablish God's order and reign over the world. This reign would not be arbitrarily imposed, however, for God seeks those who serve not out of compulsion "but in the new life of the Spirit" (Rom 7:6), who obey not out of fear or self-interest but in the genuine partnership of inner conviction, gratitude, and love, which God's grace alone makes possible. Thus the kingdom is heralded both by Jesus and the early church with the freeing declaration of God's radical mercy and love, even toward the "ungodly" (Rom 5:6). Thus the events that accompany the dawning of the new age are acts of forgiveness that usher in the age of reconciliation (2 Cor 5:17–21) and cut through the vicious circles of sin, guilt, judgment, and recrimination that have only added to the world's misery. Baptism occurs in the setting of these new possibilities that God has opened up, accompanied by the urgent call to respond to the good news: "See, now is the acceptable time; see, now is the day of salvation" (2 Cor 6:2).

Second, there is a keen awareness that God has taken the initiative in Christ Jesus to create a community, the *church*, instrumental to the kingdom in word and deed. This community is called variously the people of a new covenant (Heb 8), the renewed Israel (Gal 6), the body of Christ (Rom 12; 1 Cor 12; Eph 4), and the fellowship of the Holy Spirit (1 Cor 12; Eph 4) The Spirit was universally recognized as the inaugurator of the age to come (Acts 2:17–21). The church is therefore God's creation, understood as preceding the individual and providing the environment in which the power of the kingdom is extended. God saves by creating a people of the covenant. "You are a chosen race, a royal priesthood, a holy nation, God's own people" (1 Pet 2:9). Here as in the whole Hebrew tradition salvation is unthinkable apart from community. This people is where God's rule is first recognized and where, through worship, proclamation, nurture, and service, the new reality begins to penetrate the old eon.

This priority of the communal is the continuing truth to which the practice of infant baptism legitimately bears witness. Just as God's activity in history precedes the individual ("while we were still weak, at the right time . . ." Rom 5:6), so the saving community precedes the individual believer and the individual finds his or her identity within the calling of the church. Understood in this way, *all* baptism is (qualitatively) "infant" baptism, regardless of the maturity of the person, for all enter into the community as "babes in Christ," needing the training, nurture, and sustenance of the community if they are to grow in the awareness, understanding, and performance of their role as members of the body of Christ.

At the same time, an identity and a vocation are granted the *individual*. In baptism the individual person is commissioned, made a disciple, and given a mission. The "people of God" is created for a purpose, in order to "proclaim the mighty acts of him who called you out of darkness into his marvelous light. Once you were not a people, but now you are God's people; once you had not received mercy, but now you have received mercy" (1 Pet 2:9–10). The awareness of mercy and the consciousness of reconciling love are events that take place in the hearts and lives of persons—or they do not occur. As important as groups and movements, structures, and institutions are for the realization of goals, discipleship requires committed individuals. Therefore *all* baptism is (qualitatively) "adult" baptism, regardless of the age at which it takes place, because it has as its aim *responsible discipleship* in the world. It creates active agents of the kingdom, those who have themselves tasted the grace and mercy of God and whose lives are dedicated to extending that power. This aim is clearly stated in the practice of baptizing those who have come to the "age of responsibility," but it is also recognized in the practice of *confirmation,* especially where this is understood as the confirming by the individual and the community of the vocation given with baptism. This vocation is closely tied to loyalty to Christ. "In that the name of Jesus Christ is named over the neophyte, he is committed to Jesus as Lord, belongs to him, and owes him obedience."[18] The World Council of Churches' *Baptism, Eucharist and Ministry,* and its accompanying Commentary, recognizes the complementarity of the baptismal practices traditionally termed "adult" (or "believers") baptism and "infant" baptism. "Both forms of baptism require a similar and responsible attitude towards Christian nurture,"[19] and both view baptism as laying the foundation in divine grace for lifelong commitment and service. This mutual recognition, that different baptismal practices are

---

18. Eduard Lohse, as quoted by Jenson, *Visible Words,* 130.
19. *Baptism, Eucharist and Ministry,* 5.

in fact complementary and preserve the larger meaning of baptism as cosmic, communal, and personal, is one of the real accomplishments of the ecumenical movement and represents a genuine advance over the situation at the time *Lux Mundi* was written.

In the context of the ecological crisis, however, it is also important to see baptism and its confirmation as renewing of the *image of God*, taking up anew the responsibility to care for the world entrusted to humanity (Gen 1 and 2). Every child entering the world is burdened with the accumulated sins of previous generations. Each could claim, "I am not responsible for what generations before me have done to poison the atmosphere of the planet, both physically and morally." The waters of baptism, by enacting God's grace and new beginnings, cleanse us from the necessity to make excuses and to justify and defend ourselves in the face of the situation of ecological deterioration in which we find ourselves. The point is not to assign blame but to open up the possibility for freely accepted responsibility in the present for the future. Baptism accomplishes this by renewing in us the vocation of the image of God. This is the history-making function of baptism and the way in which the praxis of the church can serve to transform the praxis of the world. Such an understanding of baptism contrasts of course with the popular view—especially in old Christendom where baptism was virtually automatic—that allowed baptism to serve in a merely sociocultural way as consecration of the status quo. Such a distortion appears as a travesty in the light of the eschatological and transformative intention of the rite. It tames and trivializes baptism and robs it of its ability to mediate God's renewing power. Part of the church's responsibility today, therefore, is to shock traditional Christian societies into an awareness of the revolutionary import of celebrations that have become all too conformist and harmless. In the developing world and non-Christian cultures the intended role of baptism and the eucharist can often be seen more clearly, where a lively church functions as the leaven of hope in society.

UNITY

It is ironic that the sacraments, which are the sign of the unity of the church in Christ, have been the occasion for some of the most bitter divisions. At the time of the writing of the *Lux Mundi,* for example, the sacraments had contributed to factionalism among Anglicans. In one sense, this is a testimony to the sacraments' historic importance and meaningfulness; for individuals, churches, and nations do not quarrel over what to them is unimportant. Nevertheless, these conflicts have proved a scandal to the non-Christian world, and the ecumenical movement has rightly set about not only to repair the damage but to build a new positive consensus based on solid biblical and historical grounds, which can enable the sacraments to serve as the basis for unity and common mission rather than as the occasion for strife.

An encouraging example of this new trend is the document, already referred to, *Baptism, Eucharist and Ministry*, a product of the World Council of Churches' Faith and Order Commission. Often termed the "Lima Document" after the city in which it was finalized, it spells out substantial areas of agreement among Protestants, Orthodox, and Roman Catholics. This process of convergence has already resulted in mutual recognition of baptism among many bodies, and in table and pulpit fellowship among some, and it may eventually flower into fuller communion across lines that continue to divide the body of Christ. Moreover, the conviction is becoming increasingly widespread that sacramental fellowship *(communicatio in sacris)*, practiced *before* full doctrinal agreement can be achieved, could be a strong impetus toward genuine unity. The sacraments would then be allowed to exercise the healing power that all parties agree they possess.

The tension that continues regarding intercommunion is but an example of the creative tension that is the mark of the eschatological nature of the church and of the salvation it brings to the world. In one sense, the new has already arrived. We recognize the power of Christ and God's Spirit where the church is alive and faithful. As Christians we live partly in the old order, partly in the new, tasting just enough of the first fruits to yearn for more. But this is our destiny and our calling, to be heralds of the new creation in the midst of the old, nurtured and strengthened with identity and purpose by the sacraments.

Part III

Religious Experience

10

Orthopathy and Criteria for Religious Experience[1]

RELIGIOUS EXPERIENCE IS NO longer the taboo topic that it was during the Barthian era when any discussion of the affective side of the Christian life could be put down as succumbing to subjectivism or *(horribile dictu!)* Schleiermacherianism. After all, is not religious experience inevitably individual, private, and unverifiable? Little wonder that theologians sought some more objective grounds for making the case for divine reality. For when the spotlight is turned on religious experience, are we not confronted with all kinds of extravagant claims and bizarre behavior?

Yet, we cannot deny that religious experience is a sought-after commodity in today's religion market. From Angels to Zoroastrianism there seems to be a hunger and a yearning for palpable contact with a transcendent and otherworldly reality. This raises the question: Do theologians and churches have some responsibility to suggest standards by which to judge the adequacy and authenticity of claims to religious experience? Just as *orthodoxy* sets guidelines and standards for right doctrine, and *orthopraxy* sets standards for right practice, is there a need for an "orthopathy" (right feelings, affections and in the larger sense experience) that can offer norms and guidelines for right religious experience? And

---

1. Originally published as "Orthopathy: Wesleyan Criteria for Religious Experience" in *"Heart Religion" in the Methodist Tradition and Related Movements*, ed. Richard B. Steele, (Lanham, Md.: The Scarecrow Press, 2001), 291–305. Used by permission, Richard B. Steele.

if this is an important undertaking, what better resource to draw on than John Wesley, who is often cited as the one who applied Lockean epistemology—the principle that knowledge is gained through experience—to religion? He asserted that the knowledge of God is not just believing the right things (orthodoxy), or doing the right things (orthopraxy), but involves an experience of the reality of God that is the product, not of the subjective imagination, but of the divine Spirit, "The Spirit itself beareth witness with our spirit, that we are the children of God" (Rom 8:16). This text was for Wesley clear evidence that the grace of God is "perceptible," that God's affirming action can actually be sensed by a person and register on his or her consciousness. This experience, he asserted, is "one of the peculiar privileges of the children of God," and one that is also encouraged and reinforced by a community in which others, moreover, testify to this kind of experience. If the experience dimension is neglected, "there is grave danger lest our religion degenerate into mere formality," into saying the right creeds and obeying the right rules but with no *sense* of the reality and presence of God. On the other hand, he cautioned, "if we allow [experience], but do not understand what we allow, we are liable to run into all the wildness of enthusiasm."[2]

It was necessary for Wesley to clarify his position because the Methodist movement had been attacked as smacking of "enthusiasm" by such formidable authorities as the bishops of London, Exeter, Lichfield, and Coventry, and the archbishop of York.[3] Wesley was well aware of the dangers of enthusiasm because he himself had warmly criticized the so-called "French prophets," Camisards or apocalyptic Huguenots, who had fled the intense persecutions of Protestants in southern France but had brought with them to England dire predictions of the wrath to come and the imminent end of the world.[4] They threw the crowds who gathered to hear them into a frenzy, which Wesley could not countenance as genuine fruits of the Spirit.

At the same time, he is convinced that the "testimony of the Spirit" is indeed perceptible, and by this he means: "An inward impression of

---

2. John Wesley, *The Works of John Wesley*, Bicentennial edition; hereafter *Works* or *Works* (Bicentennial), Albert Outler et al., eds. (Nashville: Abingdon Press, 1984), Sermon 11, "The Witness of the Spirit II," 285. Direct quotations used by permission.

3. *Works*, 1:267, See Albert Outler's "Introductory Comment" to Sermons 10–11, "The Witness of the Spirit. Discourses I and II."

4. *Works*, 1:293, Sermon 11.

the soul, whereby the Spirit of God immediately and directly witnesses to my spirit that I am a child of God, that 'Jesus Christ hath loved me, and given himself for me;' that all my sins, are blotted out, and that I, even I, am reconciled to God."[5]

One of Wesley's critics, Thomas Church, argued that God is not known "by any sensible feelings or impulses whatsoever." Rather, divine approval is won by "doing what God commands." Wesley could have attacked Church's position as a reliance upon justification by works. Instead, he questions Church's explicit rejection of any experiential knowledge of God and asks:

> Do you, then, exclude all sensible impulses? Do you reject inward feelings *toto genere?* Then you reject both the love of God and of our neighbor; for if these cannot be inwardly felt, nothing can. You reject all joy in the Holy Ghost; for if we cannot be sensible of this, it is no joy at all. You reject the peace of God, which, if it be not felt in the innermost soul, is a dream, a notion, an empty name.[6]

In Thomas Church and the Anglican bishops Wesley faced two interpretations of Christianity, both of which discounted the feelings that accompany religious experience, but on different grounds. Thomas Church, like many of the Deists, understood religion primarily as a code of moral conduct. Adherence to the rules therefore justified the Christian and secured the divine blessing. And he feared that Wesley's relying upon the faith relation alone as the grounds for justification would lead to antinomianism.

The bishops, on the other hand, suspected that any emphasis on experience would tend to undermine the church's claim to be *the* mediator of divine grace. They continued to rely on the medieval mentality in which grace is metaphysically mediated through the church, whether human beings are conscious of it or not. If grace is made a matter of individual experience, they feared that grace would be hopelessly subjectivized. Baptism, for example, could no longer be administered without the person baptized consciously experiencing the grace transmitted, and the practical result would be the abandoning of infant baptism.

---

5. Ibid., 1:287. Wesley is quoting (and slightly modifying) a passage from Sermon 10, "The Witness of the Spirit I," 1:274.

6. *Works,* 9:16, "An Answer to the Rev. Mr. Church's Remarks."

Now Wesley had no difficulty with the metaphysical reality of the grace mediated in infant baptism. Indeed, in the sermon, "The New Birth," while he decries the tendency of adults to assume their baptism as infants guarantees their salvation, he nevertheless defends infant baptism, saying:

> [I]t is certain our Church supposes that all who are baptized in their infancy are at the same time born again. And it is allowed that the whole office for the baptism of infants proceeds upon this supposition. Nor is it an objection of any weight against this that we cannot comprehend how this work can be wrought in infants: for neither can we comprehend *how* it is wrought in a person of riper years.[7]

It is clear that for Wesley not all of the action of God is perceptible, as his own doctrine of *prevenient grace* testifies. God's grace is at work even before we are conscious of it. And in that respect infant baptism is a declaration and a celebration of God's prevenient grace that undergirds all of our lives.

Nevertheless, with *justifying* grace there is a move into a *conscious* relationship. Whether occasioned by a sudden breakthrough or more gradual in its development, it includes a *sense* and awareness of the reality and presence of God that cannot be denied. It is this awakening of the "spiritual senses" that Wesley regards as the *sine qua non* of new birth. Yet Wesley warns against any mechanistic explanation of *how* this happens. Recalling Jesus' conversation with Nicodemus, Wesley comments,

> "The wind bloweth where it listeth.". . . [T]hou art absolutely assured beyond a doubt that it doth blow; "but thou canst not tell whence it cometh, neither whither it goeth." . . . "So is everyone that is born of the Spirit." Thou mayest be as absolutely assured of the fact as of the blowing of the wind; but the precise manner how it is done, how the Holy Spirit works this in the soul, neither thou or the wisest of the children of men is able to explain.[8]

Nevertheless, a felt awareness of God is necessary for the reality of God to register upon a human being's consciousness.

Here it is helpful to remember the influence on Wesley of John Locke's theory of knowledge. To provide an epistemological foundation

---

7. *Works*, 2:197, Sermon 45, "The New Birth."
8. Ibid., 2:191.

for the empirical sciences that were emerging into their own in the seventeenth and eighteenth centuries, Locke added *experience* to the traditionally accepted sources of knowledge: Scripture, tradition and reason. The physical senses—sight, hearing, taste, touch, and smell—were to provide the data by means of empirical experimentation on which the reason could then reflect and provide accurate knowledge of the physical world. For Locke, the five senses mediate sensations to the mind, but then reason must sort out these sensations and reflect on them in order to constitute genuine experience. "Experience" was thus a combination of *sensation* plus *reflection*. This combination was the basis of all scientific experimentation. And experience had to be taken seriously in order to arrive at genuine knowledge.

Now Wesley found this method useful and prescribed Locke's *Essay on Human Understanding* for the curriculum of the Kingswood School and even reprinted extensive excerpts from it in the *Arminian Magazine*.[9] Like Locke, he assumed experience was not just sensed but was a combination of feeling plus interpretation, using the reason within the context of a supportive community of experience. This is why Wesley insisted "religion and reason go hand in hand, and . . . to renounce reason is to renounce religion"[10] For interpretation reflects on the "whence" the feeling comes and includes the witness of Scripture and tradition as well as critique and correction by the faith community.

Yet Wesley had to modify the Lockean method in *two* basic ways in order to do justice to religious knowledge. It was obvious that the *physical* senses could not produce information on the world of the Spirit. Wesley was convinced, however, that human beings are equipped by their Creator with "spiritual senses" that are able to register spiritual reality in a way analogous to the way the physical senses register the physical world. Thus we have "eyes to see" and "ears to hear" in the realm of the spirit. These spiritual senses have been corrupted by the Fall, however, with the result that we are blind and deaf to spiritual reality. They need to be brought to life, awakened from the habits of indifference and neglect. The "impenetrable veil" that stands between the spiritual senses and spiritual reality must be torn away. And this is exactly what happens in the "new birth." Sensitivity to the divine is reborn; awareness of the Other is renewed. Then in the life of the believer the "'eyes of his

---

9. *Arminian Magazine*, vols. 5–7 (1782–1784).
10. *Works*, 9:382, "A Letter to the Rev. Dr. Rutherforth" (28 March, 1768).

understanding are opened,' and 'he sees the light of the glory of God,' his glorious love, 'in the face of Jesus Christ.'"[11]

But this points to a second way in which it was necessary for Wesley to modify Lockean empiricism in order to do justice to spiritual knowledge. Locke assumed that the knower is unaffected by the data that is gathered. This bracketing out of the person of the scientist is necessary in order to ensure the objectivity of the experience derived from experiments. (Today we know that this objectivity is never as complete as it seems, especially when scientists operate at the subatomic level.) But *spiritual* perception unavoidably involves the knower. He or she is transformed by what is known. "For if any man be in Christ he is a new creature," says St. Paul, "the old has passed away, behold the new has come" (2 Cor 5:17). And Wesley's favorite Eastern Father, Macarius, describes this as the birth of new senses: "For our Lord Jesus Christ came . . . to work a new mind, a new soul, and new eyes, new ears, a new spiritual tongue; yes, to make them that believe in him new men, that he might pour into them the new wine, which is his Spirit."[12] Yet this involvement of the knower in the process of knowing is precisely what prevents Wesley's approach from lapsing into subjectivism. In this regard he retains the structure of Lockean epistemology, which grants reality external to the self priority in the knowing process. Whoever would learn the truth must first be open to the input the sense data supply. Reason's task is to receive what is "out there." Thus experience is determined by a source external to the self, though for Wesley we are inevitably taken up into a relationship with that source, for the transforming power is the power of divine love. That which is known takes the initiative. And because it takes the initiative, it helps to avoid the charge of subjectivism that plagues most discussions of religious experience.

MARKS OF ORTHOPATHY

Now we are in a position to spell out criteria for identifying religious experience that is orthopathic.[13] *First,* in order to be "right" it must have its source in God, it must *transcend subjectivism.* As Jürgen Moltmann

---

11. Ibid., *Works,* 2:192, Sermon 45.

12. Wesley's edition of Macarius' *Homilies* in *The Christian Library* (New York: T. Blanshard, 1819), 1:121.

13. I have suggested these in chapter 5 of my book, *The New Creation: John Wesley's Theology Today* (Nashville: Abingdon Press, 1998).

has said, "The modern concept of experience . . . threatens to transform experience into the experience of the self."[14] Nineteenth-century Romanticism and Pietism tended to reduce experience to feelings within the individual.[15] Only you can feel the way you do, and therefore experience was reduced to the gut level of the individual. If with Wesley we go behind this nineteenth-century approach back to the eighteenth century, and to the empirical method propounded by Locke, we see that the structure of Lockean epistemology avoided this subjectivism because in the knowing process it gives *priority* to the world external to the self to disclose itself through evidence registering upon the senses. Wesley presupposes that same structure. With Locke he rejects Cartesianism. And he rejects the innate knowledge of God in both natural theology and mysticism.

> If indeed God had stamped (as some have maintained) an idea of himself on every human soul, we must certainly have understood something of . . . his attributes; for we cannot suppose he would have impressed upon us either a false or imperfect idea of himself. But the truth is, no man ever did, or does now find any such idea stamped upon his soul. The little that we know of God (except what we receive by the inspiration of the Holy One) we do not gather from an inward impression but gradually acquire from without.[16]

The priority belongs to God. Our knowledge of God comes only through God's act of self-disclosure through the Spirit. Our experience of God comes to us from beyond ourselves, though it engages us at the center of our being, which was for Wesley the heart.

This trans-subjective element in orthopathy is an important corrective to the subjectivist danger in both orthodoxy and orthopraxy. For orthodoxy's right truth about God may be nothing more than notions held in the head of the subject if it lacks the vital relation to the Spirit that makes faith an actual participation in the life of God. As one of the

---

14. Jürgen Moltmann, *The Trinity and the Kingdom* (Minneapolis: Fortress Press, 1993), 109.

15. See, e.g., such standard surveys as Karl Barth, *Protestant Thought: From Rousseau to Ritschl*, trans. Brian Cozens (New York: Harper & Row, 1959); Claude Welch, *Protestant Thought in the Nineteenth Century*, 2 vols. (New Haven: Yale University Press, 1972–1985); and Ninian Smart et al., eds., *Nineteenth Century Religious Thought in the West*, 3 vols. (Cambridge: Cambridge University Press, 1985).

16. *Works*, 2:570, Sermon 69, "The Imperfection of Human Knowledge."

authors included by Wesley in his *Christian Library,* Joseph Hall, puts it: "There is nothing more easy than to say divinity by rote; . . . but to hear God speak it to the soul, and to feel the power of religion in ourselves, and to express it out of the truth of experience within, is both rare and hard."[17] As for orthopraxy, it can do good works, but if those works lack the partnership with the divine Spirit in their creation, they are simply our own subjective product and are in that sense not genuinely "good," that is, not the product of synergism.

Genuine experience of God is therefore not my experience alone, it is the experience of the Other into whose life I am taken by grace. It is a *shared* reality. In experiencing God we become part of *God's* experience. This is the *koinonia* of which the Eastern Fathers spoke. And this experience of the Other is at odds with the privatistic notion of experience that has characterized popular Western thought. The language of experience, if it is private, is narcissistic; if it stems from the Other, it is *witness* and *testimony*. Witness engenders experience in those who hear and receive the testimony. This is how right experience, orthopathy, breaks through the limits of subjectivism.

The *second* mark of orthopathic experience is that it is *transforming*. This is implied in the second modification Wesley made in Locke's method. Whereas for Locke the observer is basically unaffected by the data-collecting experience, for Wesley religious experience is a kind of knowing that impacts the person who receives it, for the paradigmatic religious experience is the impression made on the mind and heart by the love of God. As Martin Buber observes, one "does not pass from the moment of supreme meeting the same being as he entered into it."[18] God's love cannot be received with cool and detached objectivity, for the recipient is engaged, captured, and changed by the divine self-disclosure, and a new relationship is formed.

Certainly, Count Nicolaus von Zinzendorf, leader of the Moravians, shared with Wesley this conviction concerning the power of the love of God. But he set it within a different soteriological context, one that he thought was true to his Lutheran heritage. From a Lutheran point of

---

17. Joseph Hall, *Meditations and Vows,* in John Wesley, ed., *Christian Library,* 4:109. Hall (1574–1656), was an Anglican divine who became bishop of Exeter in 1627 and Norwich in 1641. Despite his Puritan leanings, Hall remained loyal to the Establishment and was therefore ejected from his episcopal residence in 1647 during the Cromwell era. He lived in poverty until his death.

18. Martin Buber, *I and Thou* (Edinburgh: T. & T. Clark, 1937), 109.

view the declaration by God that the sinner is righteous is the fundamental content of salvation. This declaration is based, not on the merits of the sinner, but on the merits of Christ, whose righteousness is imputed to the sinner. The graciousness of God expressed in Christ calls forth faith, a trusting response to this love of God. With this imputed or forensic righteousness, Wesley could fully agree. Indeed, that is what broke through to him at Aldersgate. But he sets that experience within the larger context familiar to him from the Eastern Fathers and characteristic of his own Anglican tradition. What is God's aim in forgiving our sin and imputing righteousness to us? It is not simply to forgive us but to restore us to the *image of God*, which Albert Outler terms "the axial theme of Wesley's soteriology."[19] This means, according to Wesley, that God wants not just to impute righteousness but to *impart* it, that is, for us to live out the righteousness of Christ in our lives, and in this sense to image or reflect God through transformed lives in the world. Zinzendorf feared that this emphasis on a righteous life would undermine the Lutheran reliance on faith *alone*. And in the conversation at Gray's Inn Walks in London, Zinzendorf insisted that

> Christian perfection is entirely imputed, not inherent. We are perfect in Christ, never perfect in ourselves. . . . Holiness does not belong to the believer. He is not more holy if more loving, or less holy if less loving. . . . From the moment one is justified, he is entirely sanctified [with the imputed sanctity of Christ]. Thereafter till death he is neither more holy nor less holy.[20]

Wesley would agree that "holiness does not *belong* to the believer." This is because God is the transformer of our lives, not we ourselves, so that our holiness is always in cooperation with God's Spirit, who is the source of holiness. But God desires to renew the image of God in us so that we not only benefit from the righteousness of Christ imputed to us but "let the same mind be in [us] that was in Christ Jesus" (Phil 2:5). The purpose of Christ is not just forgiveness, important as that is, but *change* in the creature. An awareness of God's affirmation of us in Christ frees us for a similar affirmation by us of our fellow human beings. In orthopathic experience, the experience produces us. It not only modifies us in our being and behavior but makes us partners with God in God's

---

19. *Works,* 2:185, See n.70 to Sermon 44, "Original Sin."

20. Albert Outler, ed., *John Wesley* (New York: Oxford University Press, 1964), 369-70.

transformation of the world. Therefore, only where genuine transformation occurs is experience *right*.

The *third* mark of orthopathic experience is that it is *social*. What is received is not ours to hoard but to share in order that "whatever grace you have received of God may through you be communicated to others."[21] Wesley's oft-quoted thesis from his Fourth Discourse on the Sermon on the Mount summarizes his position: "I shall endeavor to show that Christianity is essentially a social religion, and that to turn it into a solitary religion is indeed to destroy it." And he adds, "By Christianity I mean that method of worshiping God that is here revealed to man by Jesus Christ. When I say this is essentially a social religion, I mean not only that it cannot subsist so well, but that it cannot subsist at all without society, without living and conversing with other men."[22] This sermon was written in reaction to certain Moravians who were of a quietist bent and believed that only by withdrawal from society and "stillness" could one come to genuine faith. Wesley does not deny the importance of retreat from the daily round:

> We have need daily to retire from the world, at least morning and evening, to converse with God, to commune more freely with our Father which is in secret. Nor indeed can a man of experience condemn even longer seasons of religious retirement, so [long as] they do not imply any neglect of the worldly employ wherein the providence of God has placed us. Yet such retirement must not swallow up all our time; this would be to destroy, not advance, true religion.[23]

But Christ in the Sermon on the Mount has placed us in the world as "salt" and as "light," and we cannot carry out these functions in isolation. Neither can we be "peacemakers" without associating with those who are in conflict. Wesley also disagreed with the neglect by the quietists of the means of grace, the worship and sacraments of the church. And their advocacy of withdrawal was a real threat to his conviction that the Methodist movement, with its societies and class meetings and "conferencing," was the most effective way of spreading the gospel in the world. Wesley quotes a member of a class meeting as saying:

---

21. *Works*, 1:537, Sermon 24, "Sermon on the Mount, IV."
22. Ibid., 1:533–34.
23. Ibid., 1:534.

> That part of our economy, the private weekly meetings for prayer, examination, and particular exhortation, has been the greatest means of deepening and confirming every blessing that was received by the word preached, and of diffusing it to others, who could not attend the public ministry; whereas, without this religious connexion and intercourse, the most ardent attempts by mere preaching, have proved of no lasting use.[24]

To be sure, Wesley was not spelling out a full-fledged Social Gospel as it was to emerge in the twentieth century. But he did provide a theological justification for such a development The love *to* us from the world's Savior flows *through* us to the world's creatures, especially those who are in need and distress. Orthopathy demands orthopraxy as right experience is expressed in right service.

Fourth, orthopathic faith is *rational.* Not just feeling is constitutive of experience. Reflection and interpretation are equally constitutive, as we saw in the influence of Locke's method on Wesley. For the feeling is aroused by a message that communicates God's grace, and the reason is necessary for receiving and understanding that message. Wesley does not put as much distance between feeling and rationality as was common with the Deists in his day, for reason is somatic, it is connected with the body. "An embodied spirit cannot form one thought but by the mediation of its bodily organs. For *thinking* is not (as many suppose) the act of a pure spirit, but the act of *a spirit connected with a body, and playing upon a set of material keys.*"[25] Moreover, experience requires and invites "testing the spirits" to see "whether they are of God" (1 John 4:1), for it is always open to comparison with, and correction by, the faith experiences of others, whether from Scriptures, or historical Christianity, or the present-day community. This was clear in Wesley's principle of "conference," the conferring together of Christians that took place in the societies, the class meetings, and in his regular gatherings of the lay preachers. In a fast-growing and volatile movement, the rational element was necessary to check irrational excesses and "enthusiasm."

Orthopathic faith therefore welcomes the cooperation of orthodoxy, right doctrine, in its rational task. For the sources of orthodoxy are

---

24. John Wesley, *The Works of the Rev. John Wesley,* Jackson edition; hereafter *Works* (Jackson), Thomas Jackson, ed. (Grand Rapids: Zondervan Publishing House, 1872), XI: 433. *A Plain Account of Christian Perfection,* §25, Answer to Question 37.

25. *Works* (Bicentennial), 2: 405f., Sermon 57, "On the Fall of Man," (italics added).

in fact the faith experiences of the Old and New Covenant communities (that provide the biblical norms) and the faith experiences of the church through the ages (i.e., tradition, which provides the historical norms) in terms of which the adequacy of experience today is to be judged. Reason must therefore organize and clarify the principles that undergird Christian proclamation. And orthopathic faith is the kind that is open to reason and willing to be corrected and reshaped in its self-understanding by normative experience and by the community of faith.

Fifth, orthopathic faith is *sacramental*. The rational dimension in experience is complemented by the feeling dimension. The role of feeling for Wesley can perhaps best be described with the use of a sacramental analogy. A sacrament employs this worldly and material means to communicate transcendent reality. As we have seen, both reason and feelings are material as well as spiritual, and are used by God to communicate grace and register that grace in our consciousness. Feelings are sacramental because, like the bread and the wine, they are part of the physical and material world; but "in, with, under, and through" the feelings comes a message from beyond themselves. Any message that affects us at the very center of our being will be attended by feelings. In fact, these feelings are often the memorable part of an experience. To recall an experience is to recall the feelings concomitant to it that, in turn, recall the meaning at the core of it.

The sacramental model can also explain how experience and its role can be distorted. A sacrament can be distorted in two ways: by making it of *absolute* importance or by making it of *no* importance, that is, in the words of Wesley's excerpts from the seventeenth-century Anglican theologian, Daniel Brevint, "either to make [of the sacrament] a false God, or an empty ceremony."[26] When made of no importance, "an empty ceremony," it is approached with no expectation and no awareness of its transcendent purpose. As a result, no communication of transcendent reality is possible. There are no eyes to see, no ears to hear, and thus no significant experience. This is the typical rationalist and memorialist Protestant error. But a sacrament can also be distorted by raising it to absolute importance, "a false God," when it replaces what it symbolizes rather than standing in a relative relationship to it and mediating its reality. This was the typical pre-Vatican II Roman Catholic error in

---

26. J. Ernest Rattenbury, *The Eucharistic Hymns of John and Charles Wesley* (London: Epworth Press, 1948), 145.

transubstantiation and Corpus Christi adorations, as they were popularly understood and practiced. Thus, where experience and the feeling element are judged to be irrelevant to faith, the result is an abstract, rationalistic belief structure (Wesley called it "dead orthodoxy") that fails to engage whole persons. Where the feeling element is made absolute however, and turned into a new law or requirement that describes how the Spirit must act, then faith is reduced to a prescribed feeling. What can be true only as a relation is collapsed into a subjective emotion. Any critical appeal that would go beyond feelings to their source, as that source is revealed through Scripture, tradition, and the larger experience of the faith community, is disallowed. Thus, there can be no corrective. The result is that feelings are no longer finite mediations but are the functional equivalent of God. They are then no longer sacramental but the Absolute itself. And this is idolatry.

But these dangers should not obscure the positive role of feeling as a *consciousness* of the reality of God. Only as we are incorporated into God's renewing activity are we able to speak out of the experience of God as our Creator. Apart from this participation, we can talk only abstractly, pointing to a tradition established by others. Participation in the vitality of a living tradition leads to testimony that, according to Wesley, is the means most often used by the Spirit to reach out to others and incorporate them into that same vitality. Orthopathy guards the legitimacy of the feeling dimension of religion by critiquing the distortions of it.

Sixth, orthopathic faith is *teleological*. It is experience that is not limited to a single moment in time, as powerful as that moment may be. It is directional; it is on its way toward a goal. It is this criterion that is perhaps the most distinctively Wesleyan. In one sense it is an extension of the second mark of orthopathic faith, that it is transforming, but it sets that transformation into a larger context and gives it a direction. For Wesley the goal is set by Jesus. "Be perfect, therefore, even as your heavenly Father is perfect" (Matt 5:48). The aim is therefore toward "Christian perfection." But what is perfection? Interpreters of Wesley have disagreed about what he intended. Albert Outler suggests that perfection has been misunderstood not only by his opponents but by his friends and followers because they have read it from the Western Latin translation as *perfectus* (an achieved state of perfection), rather than as *teleiotes* (perfecting perfection) in the Eastern tradition, "a never ending aspiration for all of love's fulness."[27] But this would seem to point in a direction rather than providing the achievable goal that Wesley appeared to think necessary to motivate the quest.

What is the nature of this goal? It has two branches that are inseparable yet distinct: to be entirely without sin (the "negative branch"), and to be made perfect in love (the "positive branch"). The two branches are correlated, for if love increases to fill the whole, asks Wesley, what room is left for sin? Yet it is the negative branch that raised the most skepticism. To counter this skepticism, Wesley sought to define carefully what he meant by the sin that can be conquered and overcome. "Sin, properly so called, . . . is a voluntary transgression of a known law." And he adds, "I believe there is no such perfection in this life as excludes . . . involuntary transgressions which I apprehend to be naturally consequent on the ignorance and mistakes inseparable from mortality. Therefore, *sinless perfection* is a phrase I never use." Because of involuntary transgressions no one "can stand before infinite justice without a Mediator." Therefore, everyone, including those who fulfill the criterion of scriptural perfection, namely, "pure love filling the heart, and governing all the words and actions," "needs the atoning blood," needs the forgiveness that Christ alone can offer.[28] Pure love does not exclude ignorance and mistakes, but it does mean that one's life is guided and directed in every respect by the relationship to God, which results not only in constant communion with God but "loving our neighbors as ourselves." Yet love may lead to mistakes in judgment. "This very temper, unsuspicious, ready to believe and hope the best of all men, may occasion our thinking some men better than they really are. Here then is a manifest mistake, accidentally flowing from pure love."[29]

It is clear, therefore, that the goal is not *absolute* perfection but such a relationship with both God and our fellows that is consistent on a finite level with "the mind that was in Christ Jesus." This then is the aim, the directedness, that ought to characterize any religious experience that is orthopathic. The goal is the renewal of the image of God, the ability to receive from God, and to reflect back to God and neighbor, God's transforming love permeating every aspect of our existence. This goal

---

27. *Works*, 2:98-9. See Albert Outler's "Introductory Comment" to Sermon 40, "Christian Perfection."

28. *Works* (Jackson), XI: 396, 401.

29. Ibid., XI: 397.

is what Wesley could not give up, in spite of the many criticisms that were raised against his doctrine of sanctification, and especially *entire* sanctification. Eliminate the goal and you eliminate the journey toward that goal, which is why Wesley, when forced, could fall back on a very pragmatic argument for his doctrine: "For suppose we were mistaken, suppose no such blessing [as entire sanctification] ever was or can be attained; yet we lose nothing. Nay, that very expectation quickens us in using all the talents which God has given us; yea, in improving them all, so that when our Lord cometh he will 'receive his own with increase.'"[30] The *truth* of a doctrine, for Wesley as for the Johannine tradition, lies in the doing of it, in the practical results it brings to people's lives who make it their own. Thus the rightness of religious experience is to be found in the kind of lives it engenders, as tested by the scriptural norms.

These six criteria of orthopathy assist in evaluating the legitimacy of claims to religious experience, while at the same time recognizing the importance of the experiential dimension for genuine faith and discipleship. Orthopathy makes its contribution to ecumenical theology by adding the religious experience dimension to orthodoxy and orthopraxy. It puts orthodoxy in the context of a living faith relation, and orthopraxy in the context of a synergy in which the Holy Spirit is the co-producer of our activity. And it combines all three in what Gal 5:6 calls "faith working by love," for, as Wesley says, faith energized by God's love "is the length and breadth and depth and height of Christian perfection."[31]

---

30. *Works* (Bicentennial), 2:167, Sermon 43, "The Scripture Way of Salvation."
31. *Works* (Jackson), XIV:321, Preface to *Hymns and Sacred Poems* (1739).

11

What the Spirit Is Saying to the Churches[1]

"Let anyone who has an ear hear what the Spirit is saying to the churches." Seven times this call sounds forth from the second and third chapters of the last book of the Bible (Rev 2:7, 11, 17, 29; 3:6, 13, 22). And sandwiched between this recurrent refrain are words of hope, of judgment, and of promise, which the author addresses to seven early Christian congregations strung along the trade routes from Ephesus to Pergamos, from Philadelphia to Laodicea. Yet how does the spirit speak, and how are we to hear?

The Spirit is a member of the Trinity, but few doctrines have caused more head scratching and puzzlement for the average layperson than the doctrine of the Trinity. "Three in one and one in three" sounds like mystical mathematics the real import of which lies buried somewhere back in church history. The necessity for the doctrine becomes evident only when over a period of time one or another member of the Trinity, the Creator-Father, the Son, or the Holy Spirit, is neglected and the life of the church begins to suffer as a result.

For all its shortcomings, the charismatic movement is making a major contribution by renewing interest in the Spirit, that aspect of the Trinity that has received the least attention during the past generation. In theology much has been made of the *Word*, whether understood as the Second Person of the Trinity, Jesus Christ, or as the Scriptures and

1. Excepts from the Introduction to Theodore Runyon, *What the Spirit Is Saying to the Churches* (New York: Hawthorn Books, Inc., 1975), 3–15. Permission granted by Candler School of Theology, Emory University. Originally presented in lectures for Ministers' Week, Candler School of Theology, 1974.

preaching that testify to him. That emphasis remains valid as a reminder that the good news is not our own product. It comes to us from outside ourselves and is never reducible to our thoughts, insights, and feelings.

But there is another word as well, the word implied in classical theology's references to the *testimonium internum,* the inner witness, the word that is the promptings of the Spirit. John Wesley points to the same phenomenon when he speaks of the "two witnesses," the one *external,* the other *internal,* that testify to one reality.[2] The inner word is not different in content from the Word of God's love in Christ that comes to us from outside ourselves. Rather, it is formed simultaneously by the Spirit of Christ active within us. God does not just work outside of us but works by the creative Spirit, enabling us at the very core of our being to say "Amen" to God's Word of love addressed to us. Indeed, that is what the birth of faith is all about. Faith happens when the Word said to us sparks to life a word waiting to be born within us, a word that is truly ourselves, which yearns to express our real selves, yet which usually remains inchoate, unformed, and unexpressed. This is the situation to which St. Paul refers when he speaks of our inability to communicate what is deepest in us and the Spirit's intercession in our behalf (Rom 8:26). There is a presence and a power at work within to assist us to shape a word that is truly ourselves, which at the same time receives itself from the Word that transcends us.

Faith is made possible in the moment when the Word from without (the declaration of the love of God in Christ that affirms us) unites with a word from within (our response as the Spirit kindles it) and a new creature is born. "[I]t is that very Spirit bearing witness with our spirit that we are children of God" (Rom 8:16). The word from without (Christ) provides the form and structure, the norms of our new existence. But the word from within—the word that is "I, yet not I," but God's grace and Spirit in me (see 1 Cor 15:10)—completes the circuit and enables the power of new birth to surge through life, bringing integrity to the person and fellowship with God and others. "God's love has been poured into our hearts through the Holy Spirit that has been given to us" (Rom 5:5). The unity and simultaneity of the two words, Christ and the Spirit, give rise to genuine Trinitarian faith. And it is the testimony of the inner

---

2. John Wesley, *Works* Bicentennial edition, Albert Outler et al., eds. (Nashville: Abingdon Press, 1984), Sermon 11,"The Witness of the Spirit II," vol. 1:288. Direct quotations used by permission.

word that makes the gospel not simply a truth laid on us but the authentic expression of our own selves.

By this time it should be obvious that such faith is not a mindless assent to some ancient dogma but active participation in the creative, healing, unifying power of God now. For some, speaking in tongues will be the natural overflow of this event. Others will find quite sufficient the deepened sense of the reality of God and the kind of wholeness lent to their lives. But for everyone the source of the new life is God, whose Spirit works in concert with the Son to assure us that we are claimed and redeemed.

If this is an accurate description of the dynamics of faith, it is clear why, whenever the confirming witness of the Spirit is neglected, the inner plausibility of faith gradually erodes until only the outward form remains. Integrity is lost when the concrete demands of Christ and his kingdom are not matched by the inward "Amen" of the Spirit. Inertia keeps institutions and programs going for a while, but they tend to become lifeless and hollow, even though they continue to use all the right words. At the same time, integrity can also be lost when the words welling up from within do not allow themselves to be formed and shaped by the Word that is Christ, so as to make a difference in the world he came to claim for God. Unless they are put at the service of the Son and his love, tongues will soon cease and prophecy will pass away (see 1 Cor 13:8). For we are "created in Christ Jesus for good works, which God prepared beforehand to be our way of life" (Eph 2:10). Where these works are not forthcoming the power of the Spirit is frittered away and made of no effect.

What does this say about the *task of the church*? It means that the church has the responsibility to initiate new consciousness-raising efforts to make persons aware of the power of God at work within them. Because God values and respects our human freedom, the presence of the Spirit may be ignored or overlooked or buried beneath years of insensitivity and indifference. Hence the first task is making persons aware of that which is "closer . . . than breathing, and nearer than hands and feet."[3] This imagery of the presence of the Spirit in our midst is disturbing to some. To put it bluntly, we don't want God that close! The fact of this presence cannot be changed, for God is present whether we wish it

---

3. Alfred Tennyson, "The Higher Pantheism," *Poems of Tennyson* (Boston: Ginn & Company, 1903), 209.

or not. What we can do is to balance this picture by pointing to the external Word, the historical revelation in the Son, where we see that Jesus never imposes himself on anyone. He meticulously honors the right of people to turn away from him as well as toward him because his reign is not something that can be imposed but must be freely willed by anyone who would be his follower. This is why the promptings of the Spirit must be so subtle. They dare not overwhelm the human will, but seek simply to move it to trust.

This trust is directed not only toward the Word of God's love that comes to us in Christ, but toward one's own self as well, toward the self the Spirit joins as "the Spirit witnesses with our spirit."[4] Indeed, the foundation for Christian self-affirmation is laid in the event of faith. To trust God is to be enabled to trust oneself at the very core of one's being. To be sure, we humans do not live at the core all the time, or even most of the time. Nevertheless, once we have been grasped by God's affirmation of us, we have experienced love at the very heart of things, an affirmation of our existence, a love that cannot be denied and that will not let us go. And the power of that love begins to make all things in this fragmented world whole again.

The Word from without and the word from within together give rise to Trinitarian faith and sustain the individual as well as the church in service to God in the world. If that message gets through we may have confidence that "what the Spirit is saying to the churches" is being heard and acted upon.

---

4. Wesley, *Works*, 1:288.

12

Testing the Spirits[1]

WHEN CONFIDENCE IN NORMS, systems, and institutions wanes; when traditional external authorities no longer have the power to organize life, to give it shape and structure, form and focus; the human need for order in life does not disappear. If anything, it becomes more intense. Increased confusion in the world external to us sharpens our awareness of the necessity for something that will make sense of life.

If outward authorities cannot speak with convincing certainty, inevitably we turn in the only other direction available, we turn *inward*, and search for certainty there. We yearn for some personal experience that can serve as a "peak experience," a moment of undeniable reality, a lodestar around which the other things in life can be located, sorted out, and held together in a meaningful whole.

It is helpful to me, therefore, to see the charismatic movement and its manifestations—especially the intensely personal experience of speaking in tongues (*glossolalia*)—as part of a larger cultural phenomenon, the search for peak experiences. This search has many other expressions as well—the youth counterculture, the sexual revolution, experiments in psychic phenomena, Eastern religions, and drugs, all of which promise vivid experiences. Therefore, although pentecostalism has been with us a long time, the present moment in American history is unusually open and receptive to what pentecostalism has to offer.

---

1. Originally published as "Testing the Spirits" in Theodore Runyon, ed., *What the Spirit Is Saying to the Churches* (New York: Hawthorn Books, Inc., 1975), 105–24. Used by permission, Candler School of Theology, Emory University.

If we recognize this fact about our cultural situation, then we must recognize at the same time that the most useless thing we could do would be to decry the increase of glossolalia and pray that it would soon go away. Confusion in our culture is, if anything, increasing. As a result, intense person religious experiences will continue in the foreseeable future to meet intensely felt needs in the general population. What then should be our attitude toward the phenomenon?

Perhaps the apostle Paul can help us, since speaking in tongues was not uncommon in the congregations he served. According to his own testimony, Paul himself spoke in tongues. He provides us therefore with an insider's approach rather than just an observer's opinion. Moreover, glossolalia had become a matter of strife in the church at Corinth, just as it is controversial in many congregations today. The discussion of tongues focuses in 1 Cor 12–14, and it is to those chapters we turn for help in sorting out the issues.

At least some of the party championing tongues in the Corinthian congregation were convinced that this gift indicated they had achieved the highest level of spirituality. In ecstatic moments they knew they were speaking the language of heaven and were already dwelling in heavenly places. In worship they joined the heavenly Christ and left this world and all its cares far below. In their eyes those who did not have this ability to speak in tongues were on a lower level of spirituality and were not as blessed by God.

Paul was not at all happy with this potentially damaging situation. This attitude of higher spirituality could split the church down the middle, turning Christian against Christian. Indeed the schism was already beginning. What could he say to them? What advice could he give that would reconcile the disputing parties and be true to the essential gospel? Should he simply confront the people speaking in tongues and declare their position unequivocally wrong?

No, he did not condemn the tongues speakers because he agreed with them that glossolalia signifies the presence of spiritual power. He was not against speaking in tongues as such. How could he be? He did it himself. And with his usual modesty he informed the Corinthians that he was more expert at it than they (see 1 Cor 14:18). He went so far as to say, "I want all of you to speak in tongues" (14:5), and later admonished the congregation not to forbid the practice (14:39). So it was not tongues as such that he opposed.

Was his concern based on practical considerations? A little enthusiasm is a good thing, but too much gets people upset; therefore, it is time to pull in the reins and get the excitable members settled down—was that his motivation? No, I don't think his primary concern was getting everyone calmed down so they could pull together to raise next year's budget—important as that may have been for First Church, Corinth.

The real problem at Corinth was not pragmatic but theological. The Corinthian Christians had the enthusiasm but, as Paul says in 1 Cor 12:1, that enthusiasm was "uninformed": "Now concerning spiritual gifts, brothers and sisters, I do not want you to be uninformed." They had not worked through the important question of how tongues fit into the larger framework of genuine Christian faith. They had done what all humans are wont to do: they took the most exciting, invigorating thing that had ever happened to them—a peak experience of undeniable reality—and gave it absolute status. This experience became the highest category in their theology; it became the standard by which they measured everything else. When they worshiped, did the worship promote speaking in tongues? If there was preaching, did the preaching break into tongues and encourage others to do likewise? When they sang, when they prayed, did glossolalia result? The experience was the big thing. And they never stopped to ask the question Paul found so obvious: what is the theological content of the experience? *Who* is the Spirit that inspires? Is just any intense experience valid? Is just any spirit that grasps us authentic? Or, to borrow the question from John's Epistle, do we have to "test the spirits to see whether they are from God" (1 John 4:1)? Are some ecstatic experiences just so much emotionalism without any real substance? Worse yet, can they be a tragic distortion of the substance of Christian faith?

Today, many are ready to grasp any kind of intense personal experience, regardless of its content, as an authority around which to organize life, as the maypole around which to dance. Are not pastors required to press the tough theological question, not to condemn those who are theologically uninformed, but to enable them to put their vivid religious experience into a more comprehensive context, under a larger umbrella, at the service of a more ultimate truth? Thus the experience is seen not as an end in itself, but as related to a more fundamental reality.

This is the course Paul followed in dealing with the Corinthians, and it should be instructive to us. He first helped them to see the inevitable consequences of the position they had been taking, and then gave them some criteria by which they could develop a more adequate faith.

From the third verse of chapter 12 we can almost reconstruct what had gone on in that Corinthian congregation. Some were having wonderful tongues-speaking experiences. They felt high and lifted up, speaking the language of the angels, praising God and sitting with Christ in the heavenly spheres. We can conjecture that they were challenged by other members of the congregation who asked: "What about the earthly Jesus, what about the Jesus subject to all of the struggles of this life, and suffered and died? Is not he the one in whom God revealed himself to us and redeemed us?" And perhaps the enthusiasts replied, "The Christ with whom we commune in the language of heaven has left that Jesus far behind. The human Jesus has become transmuted into the glorified Christ. He has shed all the limitations of that earthly body of Jesus. Our Christ is glorious and exalted. In this new experience we can dispense with the earthbound Jesus. That Jesus be anathema!"

In his counter argument Paul repeats just that last phrase, which is literally, "Let Jesus be cursed!"(12:3) We are hard put to understand how any Christian in his right mind could say that. But when we see the phrase in its original context it does not seem quite so blatant. It reflects a persistent and familiar strain of thought—usually called "gnosticism" or "docetism"—that finds the essence of Christianity not in God's radical identification with this world in Jesus but as a way of escape from this world and its woes provided by God. Christ is important because of his heavenly powers, not his earthly mission.

But Paul comes down hard against that understanding, not by denying Christ's transcendent power, which he can assert with unequaled eloquence, nor by denying that the Corinthians have had spiritual experiences. He asks them instead to take a second, critical look at those experiences, "You know that while you were still heathen you had all kinds of exotic religious experiences—yet they were false" (see 12:2). Is the Spirit manifested in God's commitment to redeem this world and humankind in Jesus of Nazareth, a salvation that arouses not just the hope of heaven but also results in the transformation of relationships here and now? (Here Paul in some ways anticipated what the Western church later was to insist upon in defining the doctrine of the Trinity, that "the Holy Spirit proceeds from the Father *and the Son*" [*filioque*]).

The Holy Spirit is not a disembodied freelancer. The form and shape of the Spirit is revealed in Jesus of Nazareth. Thenceforth the Spirit is not to be understood apart from the life and mission, suffering and death, resurrection and exaltation of that same Jesus of Nazareth. That Jesus, therefore, is the basic criterion and norm by which a charismatic can determine the validity of his or her experience, according to Paul. Does the wonderful experience testify to the Spirit operative in the earthly Jesus—to his compassion for the neighbor, for the downtrodden and dispossessed of this world? Or does it tend to praise Christ only in his glory and leave behind the concerns of Jesus' earthly life and the kind of compassion he calls for?

"No one speaking by the Spirit of God," says Paul in the third verse, can ignore or reject that earthly Jesus. For the Spirit inspires us to say *that* Jesus, that earthly Jesus, is the one whom God has made Lord, sovereign Lord over everything and everyone. And in the process his real humanity is not denied, it is vested with universal significance as the eternal revelation of God in human flesh! Gnosticism is so impressed by heavenly language and heavenly experiences that it dissolves the commitment of God to this world in Jesus Christ. It undoes the Incarnation, the "infleshness" of the revelation. When that is done, the distinctiveness of Christianity is dissolved, and it becomes just another mystery religion, of which there were already too many in the first century, just as there are too many today.

Paul could well have used the words of the author of 1 John who later, faced with a similar kind of Gnostic heresy, advised to church to which he wrote, "Test the spirits to see whether they are of God" (1 John 4:1). The test he suggested was to ask whether the spiritual experience is consistent with the truth that "Jesus Christ has come in the flesh" (v. 2). According to John, the chief mark of Jesus' earthly career was the love of God he showed forth, the love that sought not to be served but to serve, not to be ministered to but to minister. Therefore, outgoing love that results in concrete deeds of service is the characteristic of one touched by his Spirit. Does one claim he loves God, asks John, yet hates his brother? He is a liar (v. 20). Does one claim to be in the light but despises other persons? He is in the darkness still (2:9).

For John this is a serious matter because what is involved is not just a lack of the true Spirit of God but actually the presence of the spirit of the antichrist (4:3). The spirit of the antichrist is deceitful because it is able to inspire all of the same psychological manifestations as the Holy Spirit, yet the results are opposite to those inspired by the Spirit of Jesus. The person becomes preoccupied with his or her experiences and authority; the person becomes argumentative, dogmatic, and generally a hindrance to the life of the congregation—all the time maintaining superior religiosity.

Paul is equally concerned about spelling out more detailed tests of the spirits, and he spends the next three chapters showing in specific terms the marks of the Spirit of Jesus. He describes the work of the Spirit to give *grace to serve others* (chapter 12), *strength to love others* (chapter 13), and *power to edify and build up others* (chapter 14). Let us look at these criteria for the hints they give us.

First, the grace to serve others. At the beginning of chapter 12, Paul makes a decisive point, which unfortunately is lost on those of us who do not know New Testament Greek, for Paul makes a change in terminology that we are not likely to catch in our English translations. Paul was fond of coining his own words or employing little-used words and giving them his own special meaning.[2] *Agape* is one of those words. *Charisma* is another. And it is charisma with which we are concerned here. Seldom used prior to Paul, the word appears only twice in the Septuagint, the Greek translation of the Old Testament. And its use there seems to be more as a literary device to intensify the root word, *charis*, or "grace," than to portray the meaning Paul gives it. And thereby hangs a tale. The Corinthians already had a word for gifts of the Spirit, a word generally used in the Hellenistic world to describe religious ecstasy of the kind experienced in speaking in tongues. That word was *pneumatika*. He does not want them to be misinformed or ignorant about these gifts. Reminding them that when they practiced pagan religions, they got carried away by all kinds of experience, all kinds of *pneumatika*, he goes on to note that Christian faith is different. And to show the difference, Paul switches terminology on them. When referring to spiritual powers in the fourth verse, he employs his own word, *charismata*, or "grace-filled powers." Our English versions simply translate the word as "gifts," but that translation obscures for us the very distinction Paul was keen to make.

---

2. Lucien Cerfaux, *The Christian in Pauline Theology* (New York: Seabury, 1967), 250: "It is through Paul that the technical word, *charisma*, was introduced into religious language."

For Paul this was not just a matter of literary style. He was not simply using another word for the same thing. By substituting a new word he was giving the experience a new and different quality and content. And the terms *charisma* and *charismatic* were to become Paul's distinctive way of defining spiritual gifts, a terminology he carried over into his letter to the Romans as well.[3]

A charismatic is not just a pneumatic. A pneumatic—and they abounded in that Hellenistic world seething with cults and exotic religions—is anyone who has a religious experience in which he or she believes another power, a spiritual power, has taken over his or her life. A charismatic, on the other hand, says Paul, is one who has received gifts of *charis*, gifts of grace, gifts by which to serve others. *Charis* is God's powerful outgoing mercy, blessing, and love, given its complete divine and human expression in Jesus of Nazareth. *Charisma* is that same power now flowing into the lives of Jesus' followers, so that they might share in his mission to humankind as instruments to extend God's grace and active service that first shone forth in him.

In the rest of the chapter, Paul spells out the ways in which this can happen concretely, combining the imagery concerning the Spirit with the familiar imagery concerning the body of Christ. "[T]here are varieties of service, but the same Lord; and there are varieties of activities, but it is the same God who activates all of them in everyone" (12:5-6). And each of these services is important. There is none higher and none lower because all are necessary to enable the Spirit of Christ to function through his body, which is the church in service in and to the world.

(How amazed Paul would be to hear his word *charisma* used today to describe the ability of a showman or manipulator to stir emotions, excite passions, sway a crowd, or whip people into an emotional frenzy. Frank Sinatra had charisma, Elvis Presley had charisma, Adolf Hitler had charisma! What irony, what proof of the human ability to distort the best and to transform it into its opposite! This word that Paul used to test the spirits to see whether they express the Spirit of Jesus, is used by us today in utter ignorance of its original ethical content and purpose. All the more important that we recover the original sense of what it means to be a charismatic and make that meaning clear to our own time.)

---

3. The case I am making here was first made by New Testament scholar Ernst Käsemann in a seminar in 1957 and published in his *Commentary on Romans*, translated by Goeffrey W. Bromiley (Grand Rapids: William B. Eerdmans, 1980), 333-35.

As we have seen in Paul's writing, the first mark of the true charismatic is that the Spirit received gives the grace to *serve* others.

In the famous thirteenth chapter Paul adds a *second* test: the Spirit we receive enables us to *show God's love to others.* This chapter is set in the midst of the discussion of tongues. Whether it was originally composed for this context, or whether it was composed by Paul or borrowed from another source, are matters on which scholars disagree. Nevertheless, Paul's intention is clear. He wants to make sure we understand what a spiritual blessing in Christianity really is. Therefore he begins with, "If I speak in the tongues of mortals and of angels," if I can exercise glossolalia remarkably, "*but do not have love,*" I am just a lot of noise—"a noisy gong or a clanging cymbal" (13:1). Nothing could be more straightforward and clear than that. But note again that the intention is not to deny the experience of tongues as such, but to place glossolalia in the service of something at the heart of Christianity.

By *love* the apostle here means more than vague feeling of good will toward people. He means acts of compassion—charity in the best sense of the word. Indeed, this may be the reason the King James Version translators chose the word "charity" to translate *agape* in this chapter. Elsewhere they more frequently use "love" to render *agape.* Yet here they may have been attempting to approximate the ethical overtones of the context in Paul's letter. Add to this what may have seemed to them a cognate relation between charis and charity and you can understand why they decided on a word that to our ears has a somewhat quaint ring. Even though the cognate is probably a false one, the intuition of the translators was correct. The love, the charity that is the mark of the true charismatic in chapter 13 follows from the nature of the *charis* described in chapter 12.

In the next chapter Paul develops his *third* criterion for testing the spirits. Does the spiritual experience *build up* the community, he asks, does it edify others, or is it of primary benefit only to the one who has it? Here Paul is thinking of the mission of the church beyond its own walls. And what he says applies to all of our churches, whether we practice tongues or not.

Do we speak only an insider's language, one that is understood by those who have grown up in the church but that seems alien to those outside or estranged from it? If so, we might as well be talking in tongues. While Paul admits there is a language of ecstasy and, indeed, speaks it himself, yet he says, "In church I would rather speak five words with my mind, in order to instruct others also, than ten thousand words in a tongue" (14:19). Why? Not because he is against tongues, but because he thinks the main purpose of the language used in church ought to be to communicate. If an outsider, someone untutored in insider language, happens into your assembly and can't understand what you are talking about, Paul says, that person will simply go away, convinced that you are crazy or at least irrelevant (v. 23).

The church's language is supposed to communicate in such a way as to get through to others and build them up, give them a structure for their confused lives—not just cause more confusion. This is a criterion to which we must all subject ourselves. So often when we say we are going to hold a revival or a preaching mission, we do not mean a *mission* at all. A mission would require that we go to others where they are and communicate with them in terms they can understand. What we generally do instead is to get the good church folk together and talk to one another every night for a week in "churchese." And at the end of the week we announce that the Spirit has blessed us. But if we really had the Spirit, says New Testament scholar Eduard Schweizer, we would stop talking only to one another and start communicating with the world. In the New Testament the church is not given the Spirit for its own enjoyment, he points out, but so that it might be empowered to fulfill its mission to the world.[4] Spirit without mission is unthinkable, because the Spirit is the Spirit of God's communication of grace and love to the world, to outsider and insider alike. And the church exists as God's instrument to reach those outside its walls. So on fire with that mission and calling is Paul that he would rather say five words that make sense to the outsider than ten thousand that can be understood only by those within.

There we have Paul's criteria for testing the spirits. The fundamental one is, of course, this: does what we do and what we say reflect the influence of the Spirit that acted concretely through Jesus of Nazareth? Or are we secret Gnostics? Not that we say outright, as did some at Corinth, "Jesus be anathema." But do we undermine his Incarnation in more subtle ways, like the spirit of the antichrist to which John refers, which manifests all the external marks of religious practice and even enthusiasm, but on the inside is preoccupied with self, and thus in fundamental

---

4. Cf. A. Kittel and G. Friedrich, *Theological Dictionary of the New Testament*, vol. 6 (Grand Rapids: Eerdmans, 1968), 412-13.

contradiction to the Spirit of Jesus? Is the earthly Jesus Lord of our lives, and does he extend his kind of Lordship through us? That is, are we true charismatics, are we agents of his *grace*, do we concretely extend his *love*, and are we part of his mission to *build up* the community and the world? If we want to be a charismatics in the biblical sense, if we want to take both the Holy Spirit and the Bible seriously, we must be willing to apply Paul's criteria to ourselves, to work through these three chapters of Paul's letter to the church at Corinth and understand the implications.

Now we cannot avoid an issue that many who have had the pentecostal experience would want to raise. They would ask, is there not something in the very nature of glossolalia that resists setting up norms, criteria, and standards by which authenticity can be measured? Is it not the virtue of tongues that they break through the rationalism and uptightness that characterize Protestantism today? Do they not unleash a new sense of freedom that might be quenched if standards and norms were introduced? We are told by the youth revolt, the counter-culture, and the drug scene that people today are seeking intense, meaningful experiences anywhere they can get them. Is it better for them to get those experiences at a rock festival than in church? Is it not better for them to get high on Jesus than on pot? Experience the intense individual ecstasy first. And then later, if one stays with the church, they will learn that there are other implications of a social nature that a Christian has to take seriously too?

I am sympathetic toward this concern because I am well aware that a false intellectualism can dry up the springs of an inadequately grounded enthusiasm. But I find myself asking, need these be separable realities? Can we encourage people to start out as Corinthian Gnostics and then expect them to move over into Pauline Christianity as they become more mature? Can we start them out on a gospel that has little or nothing to do with the concrete world outside their immediate circle of interest and then, once they have experienced what we identify as salvation, tell them, that was only point A, now you have to move on to point B? No wonder that, to so many of our good church people, social concern looks like something tacked on, something they did not sign up for in the first place, something alien to their basic religious experience.

Rather than separating personal experience and social responsibility into A and B, we must find a way to proclaim a gospel that keeps them together; not a message that quenches ecstasy, but one that from the beginning identifies that ecstasy with the Spirit of Christ, the one who comes to make all free! Is this not indeed the only way we can be true to Paul's admonition to recognize no other spirit than the Spirit that proceeds from Jesus of Nazareth, the one who announced the coming of the kingdom and proclaimed God's standards of justice for his time and for ours? In the true charismatic experience the evangelical and the social are locked into one indissoluble unity. This is seen by Christian conservatives and social activists alike. A manifesto signed by conservative leaders declared:

> We confess we have not acknowledged the complete claim of God upon our lives.
> ....
> We acknowledge that God requires justice. But we have not proclaimed or demonstrated his justice to an unjust American society. . . . Further, we have failed to condemn the exploitation of racism at home and abroad by our economic system.
> ....
> We must attack the materialism of our culture and the maldistribution of the nation's wealth and services. . . . Before God and a billion hungry neighbors, we must rethink our values regarding our present standard of living. . . .
> . . . [W]e must challenge the misplaced trust of the nation in economic and military might. . . . We must resist the temptation to make the nation and its institutions objects of near-religious loyalty.[5]

Yes, the Spirit is at work in our world today—a much more socially relevant Spirit than the Corinthian Gnostics would have us believe, for this is the Spirit of Jesus come in the flesh to proclaim the kingdom of God and God's righteousness. And where God's message is at the heart of the church, tongues will find their proper place.

---

5. "Chicago Declaration of Evangelical Social Concern," see *Chicago Sun-Times*, December 1, 1973. See http://www.evangelicalsforsocialaction.org/document.doc?id=107, accessed September 6, 2011.

PART IV

What Can Wesleyan Theology
Contribute Today?

13

The Wesleyan Distinctive

The New Creation[1]

IS IT APPROPRIATE TO speak of "Wesleyan distinctives"?[2] Does this give the impression that we are about to sound the trumpets and attempt to prove the superiority of Wesleyan theology to all other alternatives? My own commitment to ecumenism is too deep and too long-standing for that kind of chauvinism. However, I am well aware that ecumenical theology is not produced in a vacuum, nor does it originate out of whole cloth. It emerges from the creative confrontation of various historic traditions in interaction with the present needs of the church and the world. And this is possible only if the traditions are conscious of their heritage and seek to share it.

Therefore I ask, is there a distinctive contribution the Wesleyan tradition has to make to ecumenical theology and to the whole church? This is indeed my contention, and this is why I believe we as Wesleyans have a responsibility to *retrieve* our tradition.

"Retrieval of tradition" is a rich notion first clarified by Martin Heidegger, and then utilized by Karl Rahner, and more recently by David Tracy. "Human historicity is such," claims Heidegger, "that when we go back to a text [or a tradition] we unavoidably bring to it out of our

---

1. Originally published as "The New Creation: A Wesleyan Distinctive" in *Wesleyan Theological Journal* 31:2 (Fall 1996), 5–19. Used by permission of Barry L. Callen, editor.

2. I am aware that most dictionaries do not allow *distinctive* to be used as a noun, but I was pleased to find this nounal use endorsed by the Oxford English Dictionary, which defines a *distinctive* as "a distinguishing mark or quality, a characteristic."

cultural milieu questions that force the text to yield answers not heard before. Something genuinely new comes to light. Granted that this occurs within human subjectivity, it is not subjectivistic because it arises out of the *sensus plenior* of the text [or tradition] itself."[3] The angle of our questions causes the light to reflect off the facets of the tradition in a new way. Retrieval is therefore not an attempt to repeat the past or to honor the past for its own sake, but to allow the past to confront us in the present as it provides a key to unlock a richer future. It is with this in mind that we approach the Wesleyan tradition, a tradition that we are convinced has resources that can benefit the whole church.

In pointing to the Wesleyan distinctives, however, we must remind ourselves that Wesley himself was an amazingly ecumenical product. No less than five distinct traditions inform his thinking: Puritanism, Anglicanism, Lutheranism by way of Moravian Pietism, Roman Catholicism, and Eastern Orthodoxy by way of the Eastern Fathers. What marks his approach, however, are the themes he draws from these sources, how he critiques them, and how he combines them.

One of the most basic Wesleyan distinctives is the *new creation*, the very real transformation in the creature and the world that salvation brings about. The note of hope and expected transformation virtually sings its way through many of the sermons produced by Wesley during the final years of his long life. Listen to this passage from his 1783 sermon, "The General Spread of the Gospel":

> [God] is already renewing the face of the earth: And we have strong reason to hope that the work he hath begun, he will carry on unto the day of the Lord Jesus; that he will never intermit this blessed work of his Spirit, until he has fulfilled all his promises; until he hath put a period to sin, and misery, and infirmity, and death; and re-established universal holiness and happiness, and caused all the inhabitants of the earth to sing together, "Hallelujah, the Lord God omnipotent reigneth!"[4]

In their latter days reformers often grow weary, disillusioned by the setbacks that erase the memories of early victories and the first flush of success. Wesley had reason enough to question the future of his

---

3. William J. Hill, *The Search for the Absent God* (New York: Crossroad, 1992), 171.

4. *John Wesley's Works*, Bicentennial edition; hereafter *Works* or *Works* (Bicentennial), Albert Outler et al., eds. (Nashville: Abingdon, 1984), vol. 2:499. Direct quotations used by permission.

movement. He had seen his followers divide and separate over issues that seemed to him of secondary importance; the increase in numbers of Methodists brought with it increased opposition from the church he loved and to which he was deeply loyal; the sobriety and frugality of Methodists had led to their accumulation of material wealth, causing him to fear that within the movement lay the seeds of its own destruction. Yet through all the negative signs on the horizon this note of hope and sure confidence persists. In what is this hope grounded? What were its theological and experiential underpinnings? And is it a hope both accessible and viable not only in Wesley's time but today?

THE RENEWAL OF THE IMAGE OF GOD

The new creation is cosmic in its overall dimensions and its implications, but for Wesley it is focused in the renewal of persons. "Ye know that the great end of religion is to renew our hearts in the image of God."[5] This *renewing of the image* is what Albert Outler calls "the axial theme of Wesley's soteriology."[6] The renewing of the face of the earth begins, therefore, with the renewing of its human inhabitants. This is the pattern is followed by the Eastern Fathers whom Wesley admired, linking cosmic redemption to human salvation. And this is the renewal that Wesley sees beginning in the hearts and lives of those touched by his movement.

The distinctive that sets Wesleyanism apart from the predominant Protestant heritage, however, is Wesley's insistence that the renewal of the image involves the creature in actual transformation—in no less than *re*-creation. In "The Scripture Way of Salvation," Wesley describes it as a "real" as well as a "relative" change in the believer, the actual renewal of the image.

Of course the image of God has traditionally been identified with those unique abilities or capacities within human beings that have set them apart from other creatures. Thus the Deists of Wesley's day identified the image with *reason*, and soon after Wesley the philosopher Immanuel Kant identified it with *conscience*.[7] Reason and conscience were viewed as capacities resident within human beings that can provide

---

5. Ibid., 2:185.
6. Ibid., 2:185n.
7. Immanuel Kant, *Lectures on Ethics* (New York: Harper Torchbook, 1963), 133.

access to the divine.[8] Wesley, by contrast, sees the image more *relationally*, not as something we possess but we receive and exercise out of a relationship to the Creator.

In an early sermon he describes human beings as receiving the love of God and then *reflecting* that love toward all other creatures, but especially toward those likewise called to bear "the image of their Creator."[9] This is not image as a human capability or inherent possession, but as a living relationship made possible by divine uncreated grace. In this he shared the understanding of image found in the tradition of the Eastern Fathers. They used the metaphor of humanity as a "mirror," called not only to mirror God in their own lives but to *reflect* the grace that they received into the world, and thus to mediate the life of God to the rest of creation.[10] It follows that the image is not understood as an independent agent operating out of its own capacities—a mirror does not possess the image it reflects—but as an agent that must constantly receive from God what it transmits further. It images its Maker in its words and deeds.

Therefore, the image of God as Wesley understands it might best be described as a vocation or calling to which human beings are called, the fulfillment of which constitutes their true destiny. Because it is not innate, the image can be lost or forfeited or betrayed. It resides not so much in the creature as in the way the creature lives out his or her relation to the Creator, using whatever gifts and capacities have been received to be in communion with and to reflect God in the world. In order that the creature might do so freely and out of a heart responsive to the Creator, the human being was "endued not only with sense and understanding but also with a will . . . with liberty, a power of directing his own affections and actions, a capacity of determining himself, or of choosing good or evil."[11]

The tragedy of the human situation is that human beings have misused this freedom. They have revolted against their Creator, distorting

---

8. See *Works*, 2:570-1. With his commitment to a Lockean epistemology, Wesley consistently rejected natural theology, a knowledge of God inherent within the creature. Note Albert Outler's strange interpretation of Wesley as a Platonist, in spite of the evidence to the contrary in the passage itself (n. 14).

9. Ibid., 4:295.

10. John Meyendorff, *A Study of Gregory Palamas* (London: Faith Press, 1964), 120.

11. John Wesley, *The Works of the Rev. John Wesley*, Jackson edition; hereafter *Works* (Jackson), Thomas Jackson, ed. (Grand Rapids: Zondervan Publishing House, 1872), Sermon 57, "The Fall of Man," para. 1.

the image relationship for which they were created. "By rebelling against God [Adam] destroyed himself, lost the favour and the image of God, and entailed sin, with its attendant pain, on himself and all his posterity."[12] By turning from God to seek "happiness independent of God," he threw "not only himself but likewise the whole creation, which was intimately connected with him, into disorder, misery, death."[13] A cosmic and interrelated Fall, if it is to be reversed, requires a cosmic and interrelated re-creation.

In referring to the Fall, Wesley assumes he is describing a historical event and its far-reaching consequences. At a deeper level, however, he is describing the fundamental nature of the human predicament, the fact that a creature given freedom in order to be in a positive relation to the Creator has misused that freedom to turn away and construct a self-sufficient world.

Yet God does not abandon this creature to the consequences of disobedience. To the question, "'Did not God foresee that Adam would abuse his liberty? And did he not know the baneful consequences that this must naturally have on all his posterity?" Wesley takes the classic *felix culpa* position: God permitted this disobedience because the divine remedy for it would far exceed in blessedness the harmful consequences of the fall. For humanity has "gained by the fall of Adam a capacity of attaining more holiness and happiness on earth than it would have been possible for [humanity] to attain if Adam had not fallen. For if Adam had not fallen, Christ had not died." Wesley goes on to say:

> Unless all the partakers of human nature had received that deadly wound in Adam it would not have been needful for the Son of God to take our nature upon him. Do you not see that this was the very ground of his coming into the world? . . . Was it not to remedy this very thing that "the Word was made flesh"? That "as in Adam all die, even so in Christ shall all be made alive"? . . . So there would have been no room for that amazing display of the Son of God's love to mankind . . . .There could have been no such thing as faith in the Son of God, "as loving us and giving himself for us." There could have been no faith in the Spirit of God, as renewing the image of God in our hearts.[14]

---

12. *Works* (Bicentennial), 2:452.
13. Ibid., 2:399.
14. Ibid., 2:425.

Note the Trinitarian character of this intervention by the Creator. Through Christ *and the Spirit* the possibility of restoring and renewing that relationship for which we were created is opened up again.

It is important to emphasize this Trinitarian nature of the renewal, because it is here that Wesley differentiates himself from the characteristic Lutheran emphasis on Christ alone, and it is here that he introduces his distinction between the *real* and the *relative* change that takes place in the believer's relationship to God. Both types of change are absolutely crucial. The relative change occurs with justification. It is important to note, however, that when Wesley calls the change that comes with justification "relative," it is not because it is less significant. He intends "relative" to be understood in its literal sense, as *relational*,[15] referring to the change in the nature of the relationship between the sinner and God that Christ effects. He takes our place, sacrificing himself for us and satisfying divine justice. God accepts this sacrifice, pardoning us and accepting us once again as God's own children, transforming alienation into reconciliation. In justifying us God sets us in a new relationship that is basic to everything that follows. This is the *first* point that must be made. Justification as a new relationship provides the continuing foundation for the Christian life. This is what Wesley learned from Luther through the Moravians. Justification provides the foundation necessary for genuine sanctification. This is why it is important to recognize that the position taken earlier in some holiness circles that justification is a preliminary stage to be left behind as one goes on to perfection, was a fundamental misunderstanding of Wesley. Justification provides the necessary substructure of God's grace for everything else that is built upon it. This base is never outgrown or transcended. When Wesley says "justification implies only a relative . . . change,"[16] he is not questioning the importance of justification, which he describes as God's work in Christ "*for* us." He is—in contrast to those positions that emphasized only justification—making the case for the equal importance of God's work "*in* us" through the Spirit. It is this work of the Spirit that carries Christ's work forward toward its intended goal, the new creation.

---

15. Mildred Bangs Wynkoop deserves the credit for opening up the undeniably relational character of Wesley's theology in *A Theology of Love* (Kansas City: Beacon Hill Press, 1972).

16. *Works*, 1:431.

SANCTIFICATION

Given that the relative change is essential, the point regarding the *real* change must be made with equal force. The foundation of justification is laid in order *to build upon it*. This is the point that has been obscured in Protestantism whenever justification or conversion have been viewed as completing salvation. And this is the distinctive for which Wesleyans must make a clear case. Justification is intended not as the end but as the beginning of the salvation process. The relative change lays the foundation for a *real* change in the creature, and it is this change that brings about the renewal of the image of God. This change begins with the new birth, which inaugurates sanctification. Justification, says Wesley, "restores us to the favour," sanctification "to the image of God." The one takes away the guilt of sin, the other the power of sin.[17] By contrast, for Luther there is no goal higher than justification. In his "Lectures on Romans," Luther says,

> The whole life of the new people, the believing people, the spiritual people, is this: with the sigh of the heart, the cry of the deed, the toil of the body to ask, seek, and pray only for justification ever and ever again until the hour of death.[18]

Lutheran theologian, Gerhard Ford, defines sanctification as nothing more than "the art of getting used to... justification."[19] But Wesleyans are convinced that God is not content simply to forgive and reconcile the sinner. God's intention is to create a new creature. Therefore, to be content with justification alone is to truncate the divine action and frustrate the divine goal. A full doctrine of sanctification is necessary. Anything less will fall short of what Wesley calls the promise of "the great salvation."

Wesleyans are united, therefore, in insisting that salvation includes the transformation of the creature. And many would extend this not only to the individual but to society. They find a peculiar affinity between Wesley's doctrine of sanctification and movements for social change. When Christian perfection becomes the goal on the individual

---

17. Ibid., 1:432.

18. Martin Luther, "Lectures on Romans," *The Library of Christian Classics* (Philadelphia: Westminster Press, 1961), XV: 128.

19. In Donald L. Alexander, *Christian Spirituality* (Downer's Grove, Ill.: InterVarsity Press, 1988), 13.

level, a fundamental hope is engendered that the future can surpass the present. Concomitantly, a holy dissatisfaction is aroused with regard to any present state of affairs—a dissatisfaction that supplies the critical edge necessary to keep the process of individual transformation moving. Moreover, this holy dissatisfaction is readily transferable from the realm of the individual to that of society, where it provides a persistent motivation for reform in the light of "a more perfect way" that transcends any status quo.[20] And so, Wesleyans are united on both the possibility and the necessity for transformation.

But Wesleyans divide when it comes to the interpretation of the *goal* of that process, *entire* sanctification. Just how complete can the transformation of the creature be? How new is the new creation? Wesley himself drew back from any notion of absolute perfection. He begins both of his sermons on Christian perfection with disclaimers. And in "A Plain Account," after the introduction, he adds a section on "In what sense Christians are not . . . perfect."[21] Finite creatures do not, with entire sanctification, suddenly become non-finite.

> The highest perfection which man can attain while the soul dwells in the body does not exclude ignorance and error, and a thousand other infirmities. Now from wrong judgments wrong words and actions will often necessarily flow. . . . Nor can I be freed from a liableness to such a mistake while I remain in a corruptible body.[22]

What then is the perfection that *is* possible in this world?

INTENTION

A case could be made that Wesley's concern was mainly for perfection of *intention*. If the intention is right, this is what really counts. "Intention" was a theme important to him from his 1725 self-dedication onward. He recounts the influence of Jeremy Taylor's *Holy Living*, and reports, "In reading several parts of this book, I was exceedingly affected; that part in particular which relates to purity of intention. Instantly I resolved to

---

20. Cf. Theodore Runyon, ed., *Sanctification and Liberation* (Nashville: Abingdon Press, 1981), 10.
21. *Works* (Jackson) XI:374.
22. *Works* (Bicentennial), 3:73.

dedicate all my life to God, all my thoughts, and words, and actions."[23] And in his tract, "The Character of a Methodist," he describes a person whose "one intention at all times and in all places is, not to please himself, but Him whom his soul loveth. He hath a single eye; and because his eye is single, his whole body is full of light.'"[24]

Purity of intention does allow for an interpretation of Christian perfection within the limits of human finitude. Yet, we all know what the road to hell is paved with. This is not a sufficient reason, however, to discount purity of intention as an adequate rendering, especially when we recognize that Wesley understood intention as "right tempers" and a "right disposition," a value-orientation of one's life that he could view, not as simply subjective, but as a work of the Holy Spirit in the person. Nevertheless, this interpretation of Christian perfection does not seem adequate because it does not do justice to the trans-individual, to the social nature of sanctification. The renewed image is a witness in society and accomplishes the purposes God has for it in that context. This is why Wesley insists that "Christianity is essentially a social religion, and that to turn it into a solitary religion is indeed to destroy it . . . . I mean not only that it cannot subsist so well, but that it cannot subsist at all without society, without living and conversing with other men."[25]

To be sure, Wesley was here reacting to "quietist" elements among the Moravians and to William Law. But his point concerning the social context of perfection is well taken. "Ye are the salt of the earth,'" he says in his Fourth Discourse on the Sermon on the Mount.

> It is your very nature to season whatever is round about you. It is the nature of the divine savour which is in you to spread to whatsoever you touch; to diffuse itself on every side, to all those among whom you are. This is the great reason why the providence of God has so mingled you together with other men, that whatever grace you have received of God may through you be communicated to others.[26]

---

23. *Works* (Jackson), XI: 366.
24. Ibid., XI:372.
25. *Works* (Bicentennial), 1:533–34.
26. Ibid., 1:537.

IMAGE OF GOD

If "purity of intention" is not an adequate rendering of Christian perfection, where should we go to find an alternative? My suggestion is to look again at Wesley's axial theme, the renewal of the image of God. One of his favorite Scripture passages was Col 3:10: "Ye have put off the old man with his deeds; and have put on the new man, which is renewed in knowledge after the image of him that created him." When we look carefully at how Wesley defines this renewal of the image, however, we find that he allows considerable flexibility. Renewal *begins* with *regeneration*. This new birth quickens the "spiritual senses," the basic sensors the image needs in order to respond to and reflect the Creator. These senses, operating in a fashion analogous to the way the physical senses operate in Locke's empiricism, register impressions made on them by spiritual reality. Just as we have five physical senses through which we collect data from the physical world, we must have spiritual senses capable of receiving sense impressions from the spiritual world. However, the spiritual senses have been dulled by the Fall and by sin and neglect, and must be quickened or reawakened if they are to provide access to the realm of the Spirit.

Macarius describes this quickening in the *Homilies* that Wesley edited for his *Christian Library*:

> "For if any man be in Christ, he is a new creature" [2 Cor 5:17]. For our Lord Jesus Christ came for this very reason, that he might change, and renew, and create afresh this soul that had been perverted by vile affections, tempering it with his own Divine Spirit. He came to work a new mind, a new soul, and new eyes, new ears, a new spiritual tongue; yea, to make them that believe in him new men, that he might pour into them the new wine, which is his Spirit.[27]

Wesley could speak of the image being renewed, therefore, with this regeneration that inaugurates the process of sanctification. Regeneration of spiritual sensitivity opens up the communication between God and human beings that marks the continuing process of sanctification. However, Wesley could also speak of the recovery of the image as the *telos*, the goal, of the process of sanctification. As Outler puts it, "The restoration of our corrupted and disabled 'image' to its pristine capacity is, indeed, the goal

---

27. John Wesley, editor, *The Christian Library*, vol. I (London: Houlston & Stoneman, 1845), 123.

of Wesley's *ordo salutis*."[28] In this sense, the renewal of the image functions in a way similar to the Eastern Fathers' doctrine of *theosis* that, whether it describes the beginning of the journey of faith or its culmination, is effective participation in divine reality that both guides the believer at every step along the way and culminates the journey.

The recovery of the image also makes clear the social dimension of sanctification for Wesley, which was not as evident in perfection of intention. When asked to summarize his doctrine of perfection, Wesley frequently quotes Galatians 5:6. "'Faith working by love,'" he says, "is the length and breadth and depth and height of Christian perfection."[29] And he never tires of reminding us that perfection is nothing greater and nothing less than "loving God with all our heart, and our neighbor as ourselves." Loving God involves "giving God all our heart; . . . devoting, not a part, but all our soul, body, and substance to God." Loving neighbor involves having that "mind which was in Christ, enabling us to walk as Christ walked," sharing his spirit in self-giving to others[30] Again, he summarizes "the whole of scriptural perfection" as "pure love filling the heart, and governing all the words and actions."[31]

But how is such love possible? How can self-centered human beings aspire to this kind of dedication, this kind of service? This question Wesley answers by a literal translation of the Gal 5:6 text when he asks, "Is thy faith *energoumene di agapes*—filled with the energy of love?"[32] On the basis of human efforts alone, this kind of self-giving love is impossible. But the source of the energy is the love of God received through the life-giving Spirit.

> We must love God before we can be holy at all; this being the root of all holiness. Now we cannot love God till we know he loves us: "We love him, because he first loved us." And we cannot know his pardoning love to us till his Spirit witnesses it to our spirit.[33] There is no love of God but from a sense of his loving us.[34]

---

28. *Works*, 1:118n.
29. *Works* (Jackson), XIV:321.
30. Ibid., XI:444.
31. Ibid., XI:401; cf. 394.
32. *Works* (Bicentennial), 2:88. This translation of *energein* (usually translated "to work"), as "energy" is probably the result of the Eastern Fathers' similar use of the term.
33. Ibid., 1:274.
34. Ibid., 1:191.

THE PERFECTION OF GOD'S LOVE

The starting point, therefore, of a re-appropriation of the doctrine of Christian perfection would be, it seems to me, the *perfection of God's love* that we receive from Christ through the Spirit. In the first instance, therefore, in rethinking the doctrine we need to focus not on a concern about our own perfection, but on the perfection of that which we receive. God's love is perfect. There is no more ultimate, more complete, more holy, more self-giving love than that which is directed toward us from the divine Giver. And this perfect love God shares with those called to be God's image. We receive and participate in perfect love.

However, as the image of God we are called not just to receive but to reflect this perfect love into the world, to share it with our fellow creatures—and to share it *perfectly*, that is, to share it in such a way that it can be received and appropriated by others. Now what does this mean? It means that perfection is not for our own sakes but for the fulfillment of the vocation to which we are called, to image and reflect to others that which we have received from God. This is in accord with Wesley's emphasis on the renewal of the image as a key to God's redemption of the whole world. Obviously, there is no way to reflect and share God's love except by participating in it. This is what Wesley means when he observes, "There is no love of God but from a sense of his loving us."[35] Love cannot be appropriated as an abstract idea; it must be participated in. It must be allowed to work its transforming power in the heart, at the center of human identity, where its affirmation is received and responded to.

This affirmation from our Creator is also the source of our love to our fellow creatures. In an early sermon Wesley disagrees with the Cambridge Platonist, John Norris, because Norris gives God exclusive rights to our love, claiming that God should be "not only the principal, but the only object of our love." Wesley counters, quoting Psalm 104:31:

> "The Lord rejoiceth in his works;" and consequently man, made after his likeness, not only may, but ought to imitate him therein, and with pleasure to own that "they are very good." Nay, the love of God constraineth those in whose hearts it is shed abroad to love what bears his image. And we cannot suppose any love forbidden by God which necessarily flows from this love of him. . . . The contrary opinion, that we are forbid to love any creature in any degree,

---

35. Ibid.

supposes the all-knowing God to command our love of himself, and yet to prohibit the immediate necessary effect of it.³⁶

This necessary effect is due to the nature of God's love that, when we receive it, opens us to all our neighbors. We are

> so to love God, who hath thus loved you, . . . that ye are constrained to love all men as yourselves; with a love not only ever burning in your hearts, but flaming out in all your actions and conversations, making your whole life one "labor of love," one continued obedience to those commands, "Be ye merciful, as God is merciful;" "Be ye holy, as I the Lord am holy;" "Be ye perfect, as your Father which is in heaven is perfect."³⁷

Such a love forbids us from limiting our love to those with whom we have common interests or the same social class. Instead we are to regard

> every man as our neighbor who needs our assistance. Let us renounce that bigotry and party-zeal which would contract our hearts into an insensibility for all the human race but a small number whose sentiments and practices are so much our own, that our love to them is but self-love reflected. With an honest openness of mind, let us always remember the kindred between man and man; and cultivate that happy instinct whereby, in the original constitution of our nature, God has strongly bound us to each other.³⁸

Moreover, this same love must be extended to our enemies, says Wesley, and not only to *our* enemies, a task difficult enough, but to those we deem to be "the enemies of God."³⁹ Why? Because God loves them, and the heart of God yearns to overcome their distance from him. Hence, for those who are conduits of God's love, there is no separating themselves from sinners, because it is precisely sinners that divine love is seeking out.

Thus far the emphasis has been on the affirmative role of God's perfect love in sanctification. But is there not also a "negative branch" to sanctification, the negation of sin? This is undoubtedly true, but it is also implicit in the positive force of that love that we are to reflect into the world. The affirmation that wills the good of the other and readily

---

36. Ibid., 4:334.

37. Ibid., 1:428.

38. John Wesley, *Explanatory Notes on the New Testament*, (London: Epworth Press, 1952), vol. I, Luke 10:37.

39. *Works*, 2:89.

sacrifices for the other, abhors whatever is destructive of persons or society or the good creation. God's perfect love is therefore a *critical principle*. It does not hesitate to fight injustice and falsehood wherever they are found. And it forms and informs the Christian conscience with sensitivity to issues in heaven's war against the forces of evil. Thus the negative function of love, the prophetic and critical principle, does not compete with the positive principle of the steady increase of love in sanctification because both are part of the divine battle to reclaim the world and to enlist humanity in that struggle.

The greatest strength of the Wesleyan doctrine lies in its ability to mobilize the believer to seek a future that surpasses the present. It turns the Christian life into a project constantly open to new possibilities. As we have seen, it is not blind to the negative forces. However, it does not take them as the inevitable consequences of original sin in human existence but precisely as that which can be overcome. It was this goal-orientation that Wesley did not want to give up to the critics of entire sanctification. If the conditions of life are fixed and sin is permanent, the future is robbed of the kind of hope Wesley is convinced is found in the New Testament.

In this Wesley is backed by the Eastern Fathers. A Lutheran commentator, criticizing the traditional Lutheran position, points out that the Eastern Fathers

> speak as easily as Paul [in Rom 6] about free will and about the Christian's possibility of not sinning.... In this respect, many of these Eastern fathers could be more biblical than the fathers of the West. We must see once more that for the Christian sin has been extinguished, destroyed, forgiven.[40]

SUMMARY

Allow me to summarize the four main points I have sought to make above:

1. The perfection of God's love is, I believe, the most viable starting point of any reinterpretation of the doctrine of perfection today. This guards against the preoccupation with self that has hobbled some past

---

40. Quoted in Dietrich Ritschl, *Memory and Hope* (New York: Macmillan, 1967), 134.

interpretations. And it keeps us constantly open to the only source of genuine sanctification, the love and grace of our Creator-Redeemer.

2. The "renewal of the image of God" was for Wesley a favorite way of characterizing sanctification, and lends itself to describing both the individual and social dimensions important to Wesley. Human beings renewed in the image not only become a new creation, they reflect into the world the perfect love that they receive.

3. The renewal of the image also does justice to the relation between justification, as Christ's work *for* us, and sanctification, as the Spirit's work *in* us. Both undergird this renewal and make it Trinitarian.

4. The renewal of the image also helps us to explain how sanctification is a process that begins with the renewal in regeneration but continues toward fullness of perfection, with ever increasing possibilities to reflect the perfection of divine love, driving out sin and renewing the creature and the world.

Therefore, the Wesleyan doctrine of sanctification is worth retrieving and rethinking, not for the glory of the Wesleyans, but for the contribution it can make to ecumenical theology and to the life of the church today.

14

Wesleyan Roots of Pastoral Care and Counseling[1]

IS THERE A DISTINCTIVELY Wesleyan approach to pastoral care and counseling—a characteristic theological grounding that may prove useful to those seeking resources in the founder of Methodism for their own practice of pastoral care? It is my contention that John Wesley offers resources for developing a theology of pastoral care surprisingly relevant to today's needs.

Every theology of pastoral care presupposes an anthropology; assumptions about who human beings are, their high calling, and their limitations, their capabilities and foibles. And a Wesleyan starting point for counseling is no exception. Humans are created in the image of God. This is Wesley's foundational anthropological assertion. Their Creator intends for humans to stand in a role and relationship for which they are equipped with special gifts and the accompanying responsibilities. In defining the image of God, Wesley differentiates between the *natural* image. the *political* image and the *moral* image.[2] Under the natural image he includes the gifts of *reason, will,* and *freedom.* These are the basic capacities necessary for humans to be in conscious relationship with their Creator. With regard to human reason, Wesley's view was functional and

---

1. Originally published as "Wesleyan Roots of Pastoral Care and Counseling" in *Quarterly Review* vol. 25, no. 4:353–65, Winter 2005. Used by permission of the General Board of Higher Education and Ministry, The United Methodist Church.

2. John Wesley, *The Works of John Wesley*, Bicentennial edition; hereafter *Works* or *Works* (Bicentennial), Albert C. Outler, ed. (Nashville: Abingdon, 1985), vol. 2:474f. Direct quotations used by permission.

pragmatic, geared to the world that was emerging at the beginning of the eighteenth century through Locke and empiricism rather than the intuitional capabilities that had been ascribed to reason by Descartes, the Cambridge Platonists, and the Deists. Reason receives sense data and grasps how things work together. It discerns order and relationships that make possible right judgments. The gift of will enables humans to exercise agency, sort out priorities, make commitments, and execute responsibilities. The gift of freedom gives to reason and will the power to choose the good and resist evil. These were Enlightenment values, which Wesley shared.

The *political* image reflects the way in which humanity "images" on the finite level God's ordering of the universe. In Genesis humanity is described as having "dominion over the fish of the sea and over the birds of the air and over every living thing that moves upon the earth" (1:28). Humanity thus has a place of special responsibility for the care of the earth and its creatures. Wesley notes, "So . . . man was God's vicegerent [manager] upon earth, the prince and governor of this lower world: and all the blessings of God flowed through him to the inferior creatures."[3] We are the stewards of a world entrusted to us.

The *moral* image is the most strategic mark of the human imaging of God, for it is the one on which the other two depend. It consists of a relationship in which the creature receives continuously from the Creator and mediates further what is received. "'God is love': accordingly man at his creation was full of love, which was the sole principle of all his tempers, thoughts, words and actions. God is full of justice, mercy and truth: so man as he came from the hands of the Creator."[4] The image in its relation to its Source images and transmits further those qualities it receives from beyond itself. This relationship Wesley terms "spiritual respiration":

> God's breathing into the soul, and the soul's breathing back what it first receives from God; a continual action of God upon the soul, the re-action of the soul upon God; an unceasing presence of God, the loving pardoning God, manifested to the heart, and perceived by faith; and an unceasing return of love, praise, and prayer, offering up all the thoughts of our hearts, all the words of

---

3. Ibid., 2:440.
4. Ibid., 2:188.

our tongues, all the works of our hands, all our body, soul, and spirit, to be an holy sacrifice unto God in Christ Jesus.[5]

What Wesley is describing is *theosis* as it is understood in the Eastern Church—God's participation in our lives by the power of the Spirit and our participation by the same Spirit in the life of God. What is necessary for participation, however, is "the absolute necessity of this re-action of the soul (whatsoever it be called) in order to the continuance of the divine life therein. For it plainly appears God does not continue to act upon the soul unless the soul re-acts upon God."[6] It is clear to Wesley that humans have failed to "re-act," faithfully to image God as participants in the divine life.

The result is that the components in the natural image have become distorted. They have been turned in a direction opposite from the purpose for which they were given, so that our reason is now used to excuse and rationalize, our will is turned to serve egocentric purposes, and our freedom becomes bondage as we pursue false goals that, once chosen, do not allow us to choose what we know to be better. In the familiar words of Paul, "I can will what is right, but I cannot do it. For I do not do the good I want, but the evil I do not want is what I do" (Rom 7:18b–19). Thus we retain the characteristics of reason, will, and freedom; but they no longer function in the way intended, and often we are unable to do anything about it.

The political image is also distorted. As the steward, we have not been faithful in the care of the world placed in our hands. We think not of future generations but only of our present needs and desires. The earth suffers from our exploitation. While we retain our role of "prince and governor," we mismanage that over which we have been made stewards and exploit it to satisfy our selfish, excessive consumption.

If the natural image and political image have become distorted, it is the moral image that has broken down most completely; for we have lost the ability to transmit to others the justice, mercy, truth, and love that we have received from our Maker. We no longer re-act to God's action. We have become desensitized to grace that flows from the divine Source. Therefore, we do not fulfill our calling of sharing that grace with others.

---

5. Ibid., 1:442.
6. Ibid.

It is not surprising, therefore, that Wesley's doctrine of salvation focuses on the fundamental human need for the *renewal of the image of God*. This is his most frequent way to describe salvation. "You know that the end of religion is to renew our hearts in the image of God, . . . [and] all that stops short of this . . . is no other than a poor farce and a mere mockery of God."[7] Therefore, it is God's intention to "create us anew" in the "image of God, wherein we were first created:"[8] This renewal is the goal of pastoral care and counseling insofar as it is consciously grounded in the Wesleyan tradition. How does this renewal take place?

Wesley sets out for us a kind of template of the factors involved that mark the developmental stages in the journey of faith. Undergirding this soteriology is the conviction that salvation is not a one-time event but an ongoing process of divine grace operative in human experience that Wesley describes in terms broader than those often assumed by his contemporaries. "What is salvation?" he asks. It is "not what is frequently understood by that word, the going to heaven, eternal happiness. . . . It is not a blessing which lies on the other side of death, or (as we usually speak) in the other world." Referring to Eph 2:8, he comments,

> The very words of the text itself put this beyond all question. 'Ye *are* saved.' It is not something at a distance: it is a present thing, a blessing which, through the free mercy of God, ye are now in possession of. . . . So that the salvation which is here spoken of might be extended to the entire work of God, from the first dawning of grace in the soul till it is consummated in glory.[9]

This grace nurtures the person through ever-greater maturation. Basic to this soteriology is therefore the concept of divine grace: the kindness, mercy, blessing, and "outgoingness" of God toward humanity expressed in the life, death, and resurrection of Jesus Christ and activity of the Spirit. Grace is a gift undeserved by humans but overflowing out of generosity of the Creator. It is the means by which God seeks to overcome the estrangement that has distorted the relationships among the creatures, their Maker, and one another. And it is the divine caring that surrounds and sustains everything that has breath. It is this grace that is a chief presupposition of pastoral counseling in a Wesleyan mode,

---

7. Ibid., 2:185.

8. Ibid., 3:77. See Theodore Runyon, *The New Creation: John Wesley's Theology Today* (Nashville: Abingdon, 1998), 8.

9. *Works*, 3:203.

for it can be presupposed even when it is not obvious to the counselor and even when it is not evident to the counselee. The presupposition is that the Spirit is already at work in the life of every person who seeks out counsel. This is the objective presence of grace in any counseling relationship.

Because grace is the Trinitarian God's good will toward us, it is of one piece and cannot be divided, whether it comes from the Father, the Son, or the Spirit. But for purposes of explanation and analysis, Wesley can see grace operating in different ways at different stages in the journey, ways that significantly parallel both the stages of salvation and the stages of counseling. These ways are prevenient grace, justifying grace, and sanctifying grace.

PREVENIENT GRACE

The first stage in the template is prevenient grace. This is, so to say, the porch by which one first approaches the house of faith, health, and wholeness. According to Wesley, this is often the most subtle form of grace. It "the first dawning of grace in the soul."

> the first dawn of light concerning [God's] will, and the first slight, transient conviction of having sinned against him. All these imply some tendency toward life, some degree of salvation, the beginning of a deliverance from a blind. unfeeling heart, quite insensible of God and things of God.[10]

These promptings of prevenient grace may cause a person to seek out counseling, for persons often cannot clearly identify why they have come and have difficulty saying what it is that is troubling them and causing their uneasiness, their "dis-ease." But they sense that a pastoral counselor will be able to assist them in getting to the root of the problem. From Wesley's standpoint they have rightly identified the role of a pastor, for "the religion of Jesus Christ . . . is *therapeia psyches* [soul therapy], God's method of healing a soul which is thus diseased."[11]

This identification of salvation with therapy, or *healing*, is our clue to the fact that Wesley benefitted from the understanding of salvation characteristic of the early Eastern Fathers, whom Wesley with his colleagues in the Holy Club at Oxford studied in the original Greek. His

10. Ibid., 3:203.
11. Ibid., 2:184.

favorites were Macarius and Ephrem Syrus, who could describe sin as an illness and salvation as overcoming illness and bringing about health. Christ is the Great Physician who has come to heal the lame, the blind, and the possessed. This is in contrast to the predominant Western definition of sin as a criminal offense, a breaking of the Law. In the West, the scene is a courtroom and the sinner appears before the Judge, who could rightly condemn the guilty were it not that the Son intervenes. The judgment that should fall on us falls instead on him. He bears the burden of our guilt, pays the price for our crime, and sets us free. Wesley could call upon this tradition as well, and in describing Christ's atoning action he often employs the motifs of substitution, satisfaction, and sacrifice. However, the point is that he explicitly utilized the Eastern tradition and its emphasis upon the healing arts. This may be due to what he describes as his long-term interest in medicine, which he studied at Oxford in preparation for his mission in colonial Georgia, where "I imagined I might be of some service to those who had no Physician among them."[12] He continued his interest in anatomy and medicine, reading extensively in the field. And later, at his London headquarters, the Foundery, he opened a clinic and apothecary for the treatment of the poor, enlisting the help of physicians and pharmacists who volunteered their services. Consulting the medical texts of the time, he published a medical tract in 1745 titled *A Collection of Receipts for the Use of the Poor*. In 1747, Wesley revised the tract to make it a comprehensive self-help book of diagnoses and remedies for some two hundred fifty maladies and published it under the title *Primitive Physick: An Easy and Natural Method of Curing Most Diseases*. The book carefully marked those cures Wesley had tried himself and approved. It was the most popular of Wesley's publications and went through twenty-three editions during his lifetime.[13] Most of the cures have in the meantime proved to be, if not beneficial, then at least harmless.[14]

Prevenient grace is evident in the phenomenon of conscience, says Wesley. "No man living is entirely destitute of what is [commonly] called

---

12. John Wesley, *The Works of the Rev. John Wesley*, Jackson edition; hereafter *Works* (Jackson), Thomas Jackson, ed. (Grand Rapids: Zondervan, 1872), VIII:264.

13. See the discussion in E. Brooks Holifield, *Health and Medicine in the Methodist Tradition* (New York: Crossroad, 1986), 32.

14. See A. Wesley Hill, *John Wesley among the Physicians* (London: Epworth Press, 1958).

'natural conscience.' But this is not natural; it is more properly termed 'preventing [i.e., prevenient] grace.' Every man has a greater or less measure of this."[15] This is testified to by the impulses that strike every human breast.

> Everyone has . . . good desires, although the generality of men stifle them before they can strike deep root or produce any considerable fruit. Everyone has some measure of that light, some faint glimmering ray, which sooner or later . . . enlightens every man that cometh into the world. . . . Everyone feels more or less uneasy when he acts contrary to the light of his own conscience. So that no man sins because he has not grace, but because he does not use the grace he hath.[16]

This implied positive view of conscience helps to clarify the differences between Wesley and the Lutheran and Calvinistic approaches. For Luther, the conscience can condemn; it joins the Law in accusing the sinner before God. The role of grace is to free from the condemnation of conscience. To be sure, Wesley warns against an overly "scrupulous conscience," which he terms "a sore evil" that requires correction by scriptural authority. There are some, he says, "who fear where no fear is, who are continually condemning themselves without cause; imagining some things to be sinful which the Scripture nowhere condemns: and supposing other things to be their duty which the Scripture nowhere enjoins."[17] Yet he accords a more positive role to conscience, perhaps because he detects prevenient grace at work in the lives of the poor who, though untutored and unlettered, testify to the authentic voice of conscience within. This he felt was grounded in Christ, the unknown companion of every human being.

> It is not nature but the Son of God that is "the true light, which enlighteneth every man which cometh into the world." So that we may say to every human creature, "He," not nature, "hath shown thee. O man, what is good." And it is his Spirit who giveth thee an inward check, who causeth thee to feel uneasy, when thou walkest in any instance contrary to the light which he hath given thee.[18]

15. *Works* (Bicentennial), 3:207.
16. Ibid.
17. Ibid., 3:487.
18. Ibid., 3:482.

The contrast with Calvin's approach has to do more with Wesley's emphasis upon human freedom in appropriating grace. Wesley scholar Albert Outler observes that the Calvinists "stressed the Father's elective will," which, before the worlds began, was the first cause of everything that was to follow. The absoluteness of divine sovereignty was therefore the characteristic way in which God's grace was conceived. The immutable divine will is the source of all the gracious benefits for the elect and, because that will is immutable, the grace that results is necessarily viewed as irresistible. Wesley's therapeutic approach shifts the emphasis to the third person of the Trinity. Because it is not an eternal decree but a healing power that is the guiding motif, and because there must be a willing cooperation if grace is to be effective, this grace of the Spirit can be resisted by humans too threatened by the implications of grace for change.[19] While not disagreeing with the Calvinist contention that God is sovereign Lord and therefore able to intervene directly and put things right by fiat, Wesley asserts that this would defeat God's purpose to restore humanity to the image of God, which includes human freedom. The Almighty could, of course,

> act irresistibly, and the thing is done; yea, with just the same ease as when God said, Let there be light: and there was light: But then man would be man no longer; his inmost nature would be changed. He would no longer be a moral agent, any more than the sun or the wind, as he would no longer be endued with liberty, a power of choosing or self-determination. Consequently he would no longer be capable of virtue or vice, of reward or punishment.[20]

Like his mentors among the Eastern Fathers, Wesley understands divine grace as cooperant. It invites into partnership. This partnership cannot be imposed but instead opens up a greater degree of genuine freedom.

> You know how God wrought in your own soul when he first enabled you to say, "The life I now live, I live by faith in the Son of God." . . . He did not take away your understanding, but enlightened and strengthened it. He did not destroy any of your affections; rather they were more vigorous than before. Least of all did he take away your liberty, your power of choosing good or

19. Albert Outler, Introduction to *Works*, 1:81.
20. *Works*, 2:488.

evil; he did not *force* you: but being *assisted* by his grace you, like Mary, *chose* the better part.[21]

Freedom is necessary in order to ensure *synergy*, the cooperative working together of the human and the divine at every step in the process of salvation. Synergy is generally attributed to the Eastern Fathers, although Wesley quotes a Western Father, St. Augustine, to make the point: "He that made us without ourselves, will not save us without ourselves." (Wesley admits, however, that with regard to human freedom Augustine "is generally supposed to favour the contrary doctrine.")[22] Wesley was criticized by his Calvinist opponents for defending synergism, which they considered Pelagian and taking away from the glory of God. It is true that Wesley defended Pelagius and felt he was misrepresented by Augustine; but the version of synergism that he espoused attributed all the initiative to God's grace and was, in the tradition of the Eastern church, perfectly orthodox.[23]

Synergy is an important presupposition of pastoral counseling. The counselor may have his or her assumptions about the diagnosis of the counselee's issues and possible avenues of resolution but knows that his or her solutions, if imposed, are no solution at all. What is required is a mutual process of exploration and discovery freely entered into and contributed to by the counselee.[24] For it is in him or her that understanding and change must take place. The counselor's role is to reinforce the gentle nudgings of the Spirit in prevenient grace.

JUSTIFYING GRACE

The next stage in the process of salvation in Wesley's theological template is justifying grace. If prevenient grace is the porch leading to the house of faith, then justifying grace is the door by which we are brought in. Prevenient grace is God's good will toward all humankind, and we can assume it is operative in the lives of all. "It is found, at least in some small degree, in every child of man, . . . not only in all Christians."[25] Just

---

21. Ibid., 2:489.
22. Ibid., 3:208.
23. José Miguez Bonino, "Sanctification: A Latin American Rereading," in *Faith Born in the Struggle for Life*, Dow Kirkpatrick, ed., (Grand Rapids: Eerdmans, 1988), 21.
24. See Theodore Runyon, *The New Creation*, 22, 31, 55–56.
25. *Works*, 4:163.

as the pastoral counselor must therefore presuppose the operation of prevenient grace in all of his or her clients, justifying grace is analogous to the breakthroughs that occur in the counseling process itself, especially if those breakthroughs bring not just insights for the individual but reconciliation in relationships.

To use the term in a way familiar to us from computer language, *justification* is the way our relationship to God is realigned, rectified, restored, and renewed. This begins with the admission that something has gone wrong; that the gifts and talents we have been given have not proved sufficient or have been distorted; that our reason, will, and freedom have not always served us well and have often led to self-deception, misunderstanding, and bondage. The first step out of this predicament is dissatisfaction and frustration, a desire to be reoriented and to turn things around. Theologically, this is described as *repentance.* Yet this is not something we can accomplish by ourselves. We need an "other" to help us sort things out and come to terms with our situation. This is where the pastor, counselor, or therapist comes in. It is not the therapist's job to make repentance easy; for what is necessary is an utterly realistic look at all the factors involved in our quandary. Wesley describes repentance as a "kind of self-knowledge,"[26] but a knowledge that can best be facilitated by another. "Why is it that it is often easier to confess our sins to God than to a brother?" writes Dietrich Bonhoeffer. "We must ask ourselves whether we have not often been deceiving ourselves with our confession of sin to God, whether we have not rather been confessing our sins to ourselves and also granting ourselves absolution." But when we repent in the presence of another person, we "experience the presence of God in the reality of the other person."[27] The role of the counselor is to be that other person and to mediate divine grace. The counselor accepts the counselee as he or she is. The counselor does not require that the individual first meet any criteria for insight into him- or herself or his or her situation but opens up by warmth and expertise the possibility for candid exchange. Both the interpersonal warmth and the professional expertise are necessary because, to be authentic, grace involves not just acceptance but also the ability to arouse trust so that the counselee can in turn drop defenses. The word of forgiveness, whether

---

26. Ibid., 1:336.
27. Dietrich Bonhoeffer, *Life Together* (New York: Harper & Row, 1954), 115–16.

communicated verbally or nonverbally in attitude, comes from beyond and assures pardon and reconciliation.

Justification is often identified with a sudden breakthrough and with this event of forgiveness and reconciliation. Things fall into place and the clients or parishioners see themselves in a new light. They know themselves to be accepted by that which is infinite. In Wesley's terms, they have experienced "assurance"; they have been affirmed by the ultimate. "If God is for us, who is against us?" (Rom 8:31). Things are now aligned differently than before and the relationship to God is reestablished. Leading up to this realignment, however, is a dialogical process in which the counselor guides toward greater insight. Is the result enlightenment or conversion? On the intellectual level, it could be called enlightenment; but if it is undergirded by the acceptance that communicates divine grace, it brings the counselee into a relation with the divine that can be read as conversion. Usually it is not a one-time conversion, however, because it is often followed by further insights and breakthroughs.

Persons frequently testify to the sense of freedom and release that accompanies these breakthroughs. Therapists may be cautious about such experiences, because they know these can be followed by periods of depression. Wesley was convinced, however, that grace is perceptible—that it can be sensed and experienced so that we become conscious of it. In this he differed from the usual church position that grace is forensic; that is, it is declared and dispensed through the officially authorized administrators of grace—the clergy—in an event that takes place, for example, in the confessional or in the sacraments, whether the recipient is aware of it or not. Wesley felt that God was reaching out precisely in the Eucharist to bring the knowledge of the heart of God to human hearts. And that involves experiential knowledge. Feelings are an important factor in counseling—indeed, often the most memorable factor. Nevertheless, Wesley did not advocate an uncritical attitude toward feelings. He recognized that they could mislead and be misinformed. Therefore, Scripture remains the standard by which feelings are to be judged as to their consistency with the truth of the gospel, and feelings are not in any sense to be taken as absolute in themselves.[28] But the healing power of feelings often contributes to the nurturing process introduced by justification.

28. Cf. Runyon, *New Creation*, 146–67.

SANCTIFYING GRACE

The final piece Wesley offers us in the theological template for use in the ministry of counseling is sanctifying grace. As we have seen, Wesley identifies salvation as a healing process, a *therapeia* that is ongoing. If prevenient grace is the porch and justifying grace the door, then sanctifying grace invites healing into all of the rooms of the house. The healing power generally does not accomplish everything at once but makes its way into the various rooms of a life one by one, bringing the reconciliation that has been discovered in justification to the various aspects of the individual's life and the network of relationships in which he or she is involved. Some are relationships to kindred, others to friends and colleagues, and yet others to the larger society of which we are a part.

As Thomas Oden points out, Jesus had conflicts with the religious authorities because he practiced healing on the Sabbath. They thought the Sabbath should be reserved for religious observances only. When Jesus responded that the Sabbath was made for human beings and not human beings for the Sabbath, he extended the limits of what constituted service to God into the secular arena. "He offered *therapeia* on the Sabbath as a sign of the emerging reign of God, thus intruding upon the holy day with his ministry to sick bodies and souls and erasing the strict boundary between sacred and secular functions."[29] Just as healing was needed for the religious and social structures of Jesus' time, so healing is needed today, especially in the sanctifying of humanity as the political image of God.

The healing process requires nurturing that usually takes time and commitment on the part of both the pastor-counselor and the counselee, for "human freedom is nurtured even amid the conditions of estrangement."[30] Wesley was well aware of this need for a nurturing environment and so he developed within his societies smaller groups—classes and bands—in which members came together weekly for Bible study, prayer, and sharing of the issues they faced in their own lives. They had no professional training in therapy; but often class leaders began the sessions by confessing their own temptations and problems and were adept at drawing out from the ten or twelve persons in the group the issues with which they had been confronted during the previous

---

29. Thomas Oden, *Kerygma and Counseling* (Philadelphia: Westminster, 1966), 150.
30. Ibid., 77.

week—a process not unlike therapy groups today. Wesley was convinced that human beings were social creatures meant to be fulfilled in social relationships and he reacted against those who argued that true piety was cultivated only by withdrawal from society. The quietists and mystics advocated, "To the desert! To the desert! and God will build you up." Wesley countered,

> Directly opposite to this is the gospel of Christ. Solitary religion is not to be found there. "Holy solitaries" is a phrase no more consistent with the gospel holiness than holy adulterers. The gospel of Christ knows of no religion but social, no holiness but social holiness.[31]

The goal of counseling, therefore, is to strengthen persons so that they can play a creative and engaged social role, sharing the healing in which they have participated in all of their social relationships.

> Ye "are the salt of the earth." It is your very nature to season whatever is round about you. It is the nature of the divine savour which is in you to spread to whatsoever you touch; to diffuse itself on every side, to all those among whom you are. This is the great reason why the providence of God has so mingled you together with other men, that whatever grace you have received of God may through you be communicated to others.[32]

Although sanctification includes disciplines of spiritual renewal, it means not withdrawal but active involvement that draws a person out of preoccupation with self into a life of concern for others. "Faith working through love" (Gal 5:6) was Wesley's favorite description of sanctification. And it could well serve as the goal of the empowering that takes place through any pastoral counseling relationship.

This is the template that Wesley suggests can make us open and sensitive to the action of grace at every stage of the counseling process, whether in prevenient, justifying, or sanctifying grace.

---

31. John Wesley, "Preface to Hymns and Sacred Poems (1739)," in *Works* (Jackson), XIV:321.

32. *Works* (Bicentennial), 1:537.

15

German Pietism, Wesley, and English and American Protestantism[1]

Most Methodists are not aware of the profound influence of German pietism in both its Moravian and Hallensian forms upon the founder of Methodism, John Wesley. This influence cannot be overestimated, not only in Wesley's own religious development but also in the rapid spread of Methodism in Britain and on the American frontier. By the mid-nineteenth century half the Protestants in the United States were Methodists. What were these lines of connection with German pietism, and why were they important in shaping not only American but also British Protestantism?

In 1563 the chief doctrines of the Reformation were acknowledged in the Church of England's 39 Articles, including Article 11 on Justification, which reads, "We are accounted righteous before God, only for the merit of our Lord and Saviour Jesus Christ by Faith, and not for our own works or deservings. Wherefore, that we are justified by Faith only, is a most wholesome Doctrine, and very full of comfort" *(Book of Common Prayer).* But *sola fide* did not play the role in the English Reformation that it had in the Lutheran Reformation. And by Wesley's time in the eighteenth Century, "by faith alone" was largely ignored. Through his contacts, first with the Moravians and then with

---

1. Originally published as "German Pietism, Wesley, and English and American Protestantism," in Hans-Jürgen Grabbe, ed., *Halle Pietism, Colonial North America, and the Young United States,* USA Studien, vol. 15 (Stuttgart: Franz Steiner Verlag, 2008), 135–45.

the Hallensians, Wesley encountered this key Lutheran doctrine that through him was to shape not only Methodism but also the evangelical, or "low-church," wing of Anglicanism.

The Moravians actually had roots in pre-Reformation Protestantism going back to Jan Hus (1374–1415), the Bohemian reformer. After 1722, some of the Moravians fleeing persecution found refuge on the estates of Count Nikolaus von Zinzendorf in Saxony. Through his family Zinzendorf had a close relationship to pietism. His godfather was the Pietist leader Philipp Jakob Spener, and his early education was at the Halle Paedagogium.[2] Young Zinzendorf had a keen interest in theology, but his family insisted that he study law at Wittenberg and enter into government service. His pietist background, however, made him sympathetic to the Moravian refugees. He invited them onto his estates, and there they built the refugee town of Herrnhut, where they developed a semi-monastic existence. Their goal, however, was the New World, and Zinzendorf laid plans for colonial settlements in Georgia, Pennsylvania, and the Carolinas.

The Salzburger Lutherans were likewise driven out by the prince-archbishop of Salzburg. And British General James Oglethorpe, with the aid of the Society for Promoting Christian Knowledge and the Society for the Propagation of the Gospel in Foreign Parts, welcomed these refugees to the new colony of Georgia, which was founded by Oglethorpe to give an opportunity for a new start both to religious refugees from the Continent and to persons in debtors prisons in Britain. Oglethorpe enlisted John Wesley, a priest and fellow of Lincoln College, Oxford, and his younger brother, Charles, newly ordained into the priesthood, to accompany him and the colonists to Georgia. In his Journal, John Wesley wrote that there were twenty-six Moravians on board their ship, the *Simmonds*. Actually, there were twenty-five Moravians and one carpenter from Wittenberg.[3]

The voyage, which began in October 1735, lasted until February 1736, and Wesley had opportunity to observe the calmness of the Moravians during the storms at sea that split the sails and snapped the rigging on their ship and threatened to drown them all. Yet the Moravians seemed utterly unperturbed by the dangers and continued to

---

2. Adelaide L. Fries, *The Moravians in Georgia. 1735–1740* (Raleigh, NC: Edwards & Broughton, 1905), 25.

3. Ibid., 107.

sing their hymns through it all. Impressed by their calmness and courage, Wesley began to study German to be able to converse with them, and he spent one hour each day teaching them English. Two hundred Salzburger colonists were on a second ship, the *London Merchant*.

Arriving in Savannah on February 24, where Wesley was to assume his duties as priest to the colonists, he soon met the leader of the Moravian work in North America, August Gottlieb Spangenberg, who later was to serve as Zinzendorf's successor as head of the Moravian movement. Spangenberg had been educated at Jena, and was called for a brief time to the theological faculty in Halle, but left to join the Moravians. When Wesley met him, Spangenberg greeted him with a typical pietist question, "Does the Spirit of God bear witness with your spirit that you are a child of God?" Wesley reports, "I was surprised, and knew not what to answer. He observed it, and asked, 'Do you know Jesus Christ?' I paused, and said, 'I know he is the Saviour of the world.' 'True,' he replied, 'but do you know he has saved you?' I answered, 'I hope he has died to save me.' He only added, 'Do you know yourself?' I said, 'I do.' But I fear they were vain words."[4] This was Wesley's first encounter with pietist directness and insistence upon heart religion.

A few miles from Savannah was the New Ebenezer settlement, where the Salzburger Lutherans were clearing the land and building their community. They were pietists who had more direct relationships to Halle. Their pastors, Martin Boltzius and Christian Gronau, were both from Halle. Wesley soon discovered that there were tensions between these two branches of pietism, Herrnhut and Halle, even though Zinzendorf had connections to both. Gotthilf August Francke, who had taken over the leadership of the Franckesche Stiftungen in Halle after the death of his father, lobbied with the trustees of the Georgia colony against granting the request of the Moravians that they be allowed to settle there. He had already encountered the Moravians' aggressive missionary methods in Europe, and feared that they would be competitors to the Salzburger's mission to the native American Indians. The Moravian leader, Spangenberg, had earlier been dismissed from the Halle faculty because he was suspected of separatist leanings, and now the younger Francke was trying to consolidate the ties of his charity programs to

---

4. John Wesley, *The Works of John Wesley*, Bicentennial edition; herafter *Works* or *Works* (Bicentennial), Albert C. Outler et. al., eds. (Nashville: Abingdon Press, 1984), vol. 18:146. Direct quotations used by permission.

the Lutherans. But Zinzendorf had his friends among the trustees, and the settlement of the Moravians was approved despite Halle's opposition. The Moravians settled close to Savannah, where they could attend Wesley's Anglican services and where Wesley had more constant contact with them. He held devotional services for them in German, just as he did for other immigrant groups in their own languages, the French, the Italians, and also some Spanish Jews. From this we can see that Wesley shared Zinzendorf's enthusiasm for ecumenical cooperation. As Wesley was later to write in his open letter to a Roman Catholic:

> Are you not fully convinced that malice, hatred, revenge, bitterness, whether in us or in you, in our hearts or yours, are an abomination to the Lord? Be our opinions right, or be they wrong, these tempers are undeniably wrong. . . . We ought, without this endless jangling about opinions, to provoke one another to love and to good works. Let the points wherein we differ stand aside; here are enough wherein we agree, enough to be the ground of every Christian temper, and of every Christian action. . . . If we cannot as yet think alike in all things, at least we may love alike.[5]

And so Wesley, when he learned of the tensions between the two groups of German colonists, was eager to help them settle their differences and stop spreading malicious rumors about each other. Wesley arranged a summit meeting between the leaders of the two groups. Spangenberg accompanied Wesley to New Ebenezer in August of 1737, and met with Boltzius and Gronau. The meeting was evidently successful because in the following year Pastor Boltzius discontinued his attacks against the Moravians in his reports back to Halle. The conflicts were in any case resolved when the Moravians departed Georgia in 1741 for Pennsylvania to join the new Herrnhuter colony there.

Meanwhile Wesley also encountered problems in his parish in Savannah. He tried to introduce pre-registration for communion. His parishioners accused him of requiring the Catholic practice of confession before communion. The issue was sharpened when Wesley could not bring himself to marry a woman with whom he had a romantic attachment because of his previous pledge to celibacy. Tired of waiting, she married another suitor. Wesley then refused to serve her communion when she failed to pre-register for it. Whereupon, her husband

---

5. John Wesley, *The Works of the Rev. John Wesley*, Jackson edition, Thomas Jackson, ed. (London: Wesleyan Conference Office, 1872), X:80, 85.

brought a suit for 1,000 pounds against Wesley for defaming his wife's character. Wesley's annual income was 50 pounds. When it appeared that the grand jury was set to convict him, Wesley thought it the better part of wisdom to return to England, which he did on the next ship from Charleston.

Back in England, Wesley was thoroughly discouraged. He felt he had been a failure as a priest in Georgia, though the Georgia trustees in London were well satisfied with his service there. He had put together a first hymnal for the colonists, including several hymns he translated from both Moravian and Salzburger sources. He had started Bible study and prayer groups in the parish, modeled after the religious societies begun in England by Dr. Anton Horneck, a German immigrant who was familiar with the societies formed by Spener and by Francke and introduced this pietist practice into England. And so the trustees were not dissatisfied with Wesley's service to the colony.

However, Wesley knew the Moravian emphasis upon conversion and had also been instructed by the Salzburger pastors concerning Francke's *Bußkampf* (penitential or conversion struggle). He became convinced that he had never been genuinely converted, and so he sought out the Moravians who were in London learning English and awaiting transport to America. One of these was Peter Böhler, who had come under the influence of Spangenberg at the University of Jena and had later joined the Moravians. Böhler was theologically trained and had a good command of Latin so that intensive theological conversations with Wesley were possible. He served for a time as an instructor at the University of Leipzig, and then, when he had been won over to the Moravian cause, served as the tutor of Zinzendorf's son. Böhler took as his task to convince Wesley of the importance of, and biblical basis for, the Lutheran doctrine of "justification by faith alone." Gradually Wesley became intellectually convinced by Böhler's arguments that the doctrine was scripturally sound and not in contradiction to the doctrines of Anglicanism. But he could not claim to have experienced it personally in the way that was normative for the pietists. This left him in a quandary:

> Immediately it struck into my mind, "leave off preaching. How can you preach to others, who have not faith yourself?" I asked Boehler whether he thought I should leave it off or not. He answered, "By no means." I asked, "But what can I preach?" He said;

"Preach faith till you have it, and then, because you have it, you will preach faith."[6]

This he did with a passion, making faith the one subject of the guest sermons he was being invited to preach in London churches. He soon discovered, however, that when he was invited it was because Londoners wanted to hear about his adventures in the New World, not about his theological concerns. And he soon found himself uninvited.

Dispirited, he went one evening, as he reports, "very unwillingly" to what was probably a Moravian society meeting in London's Aldersgate Street.

> One was reading Luther's Preface to the Epistle to the Romans. About a quarter before nine, while [Luther] was describing the change which God works in the heart through faith in Christ, I felt my heart strangely warmed. I felt I did trust in Christ, Christ alone for salvation, and an assurance was given me that he had taken away *my* sins, even *mine,* and saved *me* from the law of sin and death.[7]

The emphasis which Wesley places on the words *me, my,* and *mine,* which he italicizes in the printed version, were of course typically pietistic. But actually they are derived from Luther. For Wesley's brother, Charles, had this same experience of conversion just a few days earlier while studying Luther's Preface to the Epistle to the Galatians where he read, "These words, *who loved me* [2:20], are full of faith. And he that can utter this word *me,* and apply it unto himself with a true and a constant faith," has been grasped by the central message of Paul.

> And this manner of applying is the very true force and power of faith. . . . Read, therefore, with great vehemencie these words, *me,* and *for me,* and so inwardly practise with thy selfe, that thou, with a sure faith, maist conceive and print this *me* in thy heart, and apply it unto thyselfe, not doubting but thou art in the number of those to whom this *me* belongeth.[8]

Thus we see both John and Charles Wesley, through the mediation of Luther, experiencing what Francke described as the evangelical

---

6. *Works* (Bicentennial), 18:228 (March 4–6, 1738).

7. Ibid., 18:249–50 (May 24, 1728).

8. *The Journal of the Rev. Charles Wesley,* Thomas Jackson, ed., 2 vols. (London: John Mason, 1849; reprint, Grand Rapids, Mich.: Baker Book House, 1980), 1:87.

Durchbruch (breakthrough). This alone would guarantee a line of continuity between Lutheran pietism and the movement the Wesleys were about to begin in Britain, Charles as a poet and pre-eminent hymn writer, and John as the organizer of what came to be known as the Methodist revival.

Within three weeks after Aldersgate, and with the encouragement of his Moravian friends, John Wesley decided to visit the Continent, especially the centers of pietist activity about which he had heard so much, Herrnhut and Halle. Accompanied by three friends he set out on a walking journey through Germany. He visited Zinzendorf in Marienborn (near Frankfurt am Main), where Zinzendorf had been exiled for a time due to political difficulties in Saxony. Here he was pleased to learn that not all Moravians were cut from the same mold, as he detected differences of emphasis between what he had learned from Böhler and Zinzendorf's explanation of his own position. He was so impressed by the spirit of the Marienborn community that he wrote back to his brother, Charles, in England a letter of fulsome praise of his hosts. Charles noted on that letter, "A panegyric on Germans."[9]

Wesley then visited Halle, where he had hoped to see Gotthilf August Francke, who had succeeded his father as leader of the Francke charities, but the younger Francke was himself traveling. Wesley was nonetheless impressed by the extensiveness of the institutions and their activities. Already on the ship to Georgia Wesley had read August Hermann Francke's *Nicodemus,* as well as *Pietas Hallensis,* with its description of the development of the institutions and their many human services. The Orphan-house was later to serve as the model for Wesley's own school at Kingswood outside Bristol, which was built to provide an education the equivalent of a university preparatory course to the children of poor miners and the children of Methodist preachers. He was fascinated by Francke's methods of education, which he combined with John Locke's theory of the mind as a *tabula rasa* on which education inscribes knowledge. But unfortunately Wesley was also persuaded by Francke's theories that discouraged play among children. A child who plays, argued Francke, will grow into an adult who plays.

---

9. Martin Schmidt, *John Wesley: A Theological Biography,* Norman P. Goldhawk, trans., 2 vols. (Nashville: Abingdon Press, 1972), 1:279. Originally published as *John Wesley: Leben und Werk* (Zürich: Gotthelf-Verlag, 1966).

From Halle, Wesley made his way to Herrnhut where he was quickly taken into the life of the community. Here he was introduced to the "love feast," a meal of bread and water with Scripture reading, prayer, and testimony, which, unlike the Eucharist, did not require a pastor to celebrate it. This was a practice Wesley adapted to Methodist societies in England. It later became especially important in America because of the lack of ordained clergy. In Herrnhut, Wesley also learned from one of the original founders of the settlement, Christian David, that Moravians did not prescribe a certain kind of experience or feeling as necessary to salvation, something that Wesley had himself questioned in Francke's notion of *Bußkampf*. David said:

> We ought not insist on anything we feel, any more than anything we do, as if it were necessary previous to justification or the remission of sins. . . . It is not this by which you are justified. . . . To think you must be more contrite, more humbled, more grieved, more sensible of the weight of sin, before you can be justified; is to lay your contrition, your grief, your humiliation for the foundation of your being justified. . . . Therefore it hinders your justification; and a hindrance it is which must be removed before you can lay the right foundation.[10]

From David, therefore, Wesley learned that the pietist tendency to rely on feelings was "just another form of justification of self through works."[11] And so he sought, not always successfully, to avoid one of the pitfalls that has plagued pietism throughout its history.

Returning to England, Wesley was prevailed upon by his former colleague in the Holy Club at Oxford, George Whitefield, to take over the field preaching he had begun in Bristol because Whitefield was leaving for a preaching mission in America. Because he had been barred from preaching in the churches of Bristol, Whitefield moved his preaching out of doors. Whereas before he was attracting hundreds to the churches, now he was attracting thousands. And he wanted to leave this mission in good hands. Wesley was loathe to take on this responsibility:

> I could scarce reconcile myself at first to this strange way of preaching in the fields, . . . having been all my life (till very lately) so tenacious of every point relating to decency and order that I should have thought the saving of souls almost a sin if it had not

---

10. *Works*, 18:280 (August 10, 1738).
11. Schmidt, *John Wesley*, 1:294.

been done in a church. Mr. Whitefield being gone, I began expounding our Lord's Sermon on the Mount (one pretty remarkable precedent of field preaching).[12]

To his astonishment, the common people were attracted to this preaching outside the church. The message of justification by faith, to which middle-class parishioners in the churches had turned a deaf ear, in the fields now called forth a joyful response from the miners and industrial workers. But Wesley's approach differed significantly from Whitefield, who had been content, as he would be in his contribution to the American Great Awakening, simply to preach the gospel. Wesley followed the pietist model, however, and those who responded to the preaching he organized into societies committed to meeting together on a regular basis for Bible study, prayers, and to sing the hymns that Charles Wesley composed. His effort was to renew the Church of England by attracting the poor who, especially in urban areas were largely alienated from the church, providing in societies a community of mutual support and spiritual growth. To this he added the Moravian pattern of classes and bands, dividing each society into groups of ten to twelve, each with a lay class leader, for sharing their progress as well as the difficulties they were encountering in their spiritual life.

The rapid growth of the Methodist societies in England was no doubt due to the fact that they were answering not only spiritual hunger but also social needs. Many of the poor in urban areas were former tenant farmers displaced from the rural estates by the enclosure laws that encouraged agricultural production for export rather than for local consumption. Forced off the land, they had no place to go but to the cities, where the industrial revolution was beginning but where there was widespread unemployment, competition for jobs, and depressed wages. The Methodist societies gave them in effect their village life again. Here was a small group of persons they could count on to care about them and to be concerned about their well-being. The penny a week they brought to class meetings grew into a fund from which they could borrow when they fell on hard times, the first credit unions. This meant that Methodists were no longer subject to being thrown into debtors prison. The Foundery, the Methodist headquarters in London, paralleled the Halle institutions as a melting pot of projects and social services. It was

12. *Works*, 19:46 (March 31–April 1, 1739).

"a house of mercy for widows, a school for boys, a dispensary for the sick, a work shop and employment bureau, a loan office and savings bank, a book room, and a church."[13] These projects required management skills and the ability to read and write not widespread among the common people. As John and Barbara Hammond comment in their classic study of the English working class:

> The teaching of reading in the Sunday-schools was an enormous boon to the working classes.... The upper class could learn to speak at Eton: the working class in [the Methodist chapel]. The Methodist Sunday-schools would attract men and women with the gifts of oratory, leadership, organization: they gave scope, experience and training.[14]

Although Wesley kept the Methodist societies related to the Church of England during his lifetime, urging the members to rely on their local Anglican priest for all sacramental services, with Wesley's death in 1791 it was inevitable that the Methodists became independent and began ordaining their own clergy. More than fifty percent of the membership in Methodist societies was made up of Non-conformists, Baptists, Quakers, Independents, and even Roman Catholics. The formation of a separate denomination was probably inevitable, despite Wesley's wishes to the contrary. But the influence of the movement within Anglicanism was considerable, and it was in this way that the Reformation and pietism's emphasis upon personal faith became a continuing factor in evangelical or low-church Anglicanism.

One innovation that proved important in the development of British Methodism and became even more important in America was the circuit system. Societies were organized in circuits with different meeting times, which allowed the full-time preachers to ride around a circuit preaching to the various societies. They were supplemented by local preachers who had regular jobs but who preached on Sundays to their own and neighboring societies. This guaranteed variety in the preaching and ensured continuous lay involvement. This system was transplanted to America and proved invaluable on the frontier. Circuit riders were able to move west with the advancing frontier, organizing

---

13. Oscar Sherwin, *John Wesley: Friend of the People* (New York: Twayne Publishers, 1961), 132.

14. J. L. and Barbara Hammond, *The Town Labourer, 1760–1832: The New Civilization* (London: Longman Green & Co., 1917), 287.

societies in both towns and rural areas wherever they could draw together a few families. In time, as the population increased, these small groups grew into churches.

Although there were a few Methodists in America before the Revolutionary War, the main expansion of the movement came after the war when Anglican clergy for the most part abandoned the former colony to return to England or move to Canada. The Methodists' willingness to use lay preachers meant that it was not necessary to wait for the training and ordination of pastors. In England, Wesley had published a *Christian Library* of fifty volumes for the training of lay preachers. Few in America could afford the fifty volumes, and they were dependent for models on the preaching they heard from others. Also, lay preachers could not perform the sacraments. This lack finally persuaded Wesley to do what up to that point he had refused to do, to ordain pastors for service in America. He tried first to persuade the Bishop of London to ordain these pastors but was refused, which he then decided was providential, for if they had been ordained by British bishops they would have been under their jurisdiction, which would have been impossible in the new nation. Whether Wesley considered his next move a *Notordination* (ordination out of necessity), later to be regularized, is a matter of dispute. But he was convinced by the arguments of church historian Lord Peter King that presbyters and bishops were equivalent in the ancient church. Therefore, as a presbyter he felt justified in ordaining Thomas Coke, who was already an Anglican priest, to serve as a "general superintendent" (the original meaning of "bishop") in America, and authorized him to ordain Francis Asbury, leader of the American Methodists, as superintendent, so that together they could begin ordaining the American lay preachers. It is not surprising that the Americans very quickly referred to Coke and Asbury as bishops. Assisting in Asbury's ordination was Philip William Otterbein, pastor of the German Evangelical Reformed Church in Baltimore, who came from Reformed pietistic circles in Germany. He identified with the Methodists and later helped to found in 1800 the United Brethren Church, a German language church with a name reminiscent of the Moravians but with ties to the Methodists. This church was later joined by another German-language church, the Evangelical Church, to form the Evangelical United Brethren Church, which then merged with the Methodist Church in 1968 to form The United Methodist Church. The three denominations also united in

Germany, and their common theological faculty is now the *Theologische Hochschule der Evangelisch-methodistischen Kirche* in Reutlingen.

SUMMARY

Let me now summarize some of the contributions that German pietism has made to Methodism, both in its British and American versions:

1. The recovery of the Lutheran doctrine and experience of justification by faith, albeit in its pietistic form with the emphasis on the experience of conversion, was to mark not only the Wesleyan revival but the American Methodism that emerged from it. On the American scene this emphasis on conversion and heart religion was reinforced by the development of the camp meetings in the nineteenth century, a tradition shared by most of the other Protestant denominations.

2. From the Halle side came the development of religious societies within the dominant state churches, the *ecclesiola in ecclesia*, which encouraged the growth in piety by mutual accountability and support.

3. From the Herrnhut side came the development of smaller groups, the bands in Moravianism, the classes among the Methodists, for Bible study, extemporaneous prayer and hymn singing.

4. From the Halle side came the emphasis upon practical Christian outreach in social service and institutions for public good, such as schools, colleges, and hospitals.

5. From the Herrnhut side came liturgical innovations such as the love feast, recalling the early Christian agape meal.

6. From both came a recognition of the importance of the laity and lay leadership within the church, and an understanding that the vital life of the church is to be found at the grassroots level.

7. From both came also the role of hymns in the life of a congregation, both for instruction in the faith and for the expression of that faith.

Thus we can see how German pietism, which was from the beginning characterized by an ecumenical spirit, had an influence that spread far beyond its own national borders to bring a renewal of Protestantism that was to reach around the world.

16

Wesley and Liberation Theologies[1]

During the 1970s, liberation theologies moved from the periphery of theological attention to its center. Their insistent questions have instigated a reevaluation not only of traditional understandings of Christianity but of the function and methods of theology. Three types of liberation theology are represented in this chapter: black theology, with its concern for the plight of those oppressed politically and economically because of racial barriers; feminist theology, with its sensitivity to male dominance and the shaping of culture to the detriment and disadvantage of half the human race; and Latin American theology, with its use of Marxist analysis to expose exploitation of developing countries by the privileged groups, classes, and systems that control economic power.

In spite of their obvious differences these theologies share a common *critical* approach. Their task, as they conceive it, is not to rationalize and justify doctrine and church practice but to ask, on the basis of the biblical vision of the kingdom of God and God's righteousness, how Christian theology and practice have been consistent with that vision or have thwarted it. Aware of the extent to which theology has served as an ideology to legitimize unjust social orders in the past, these theologians apply a litmus test to any claim to theological truth: Does it advance the cause of human freedom? With Jürgen Moltmann, they find that *"the new criterion of theology and of faith is to be found in praxis. . . .* Truth

---

1. Originally published as, "Introduction: Wesley and the Theologies of Liberation" in *Sanctification and Liberation: Liberation Theologies in the Light of the Wesleyan Tradition*, edited by Theodore Runyon (Nashville: Abingdon Press, 1981), 9–48.

must be practicable. Unless it contains initiative for the transformation of the world, it becomes a myth of the existing world."[2]

The thesis advanced by some of these theologians is that there is a peculiar affinity between Wesleyan theology—especially Wesley's doctrine of sanctification—and movements for social change. When *Christian perfection* becomes the goal of the individual, a fundamental hope is engendered that the future can surpass the present. Concomitantly, a holy dissatisfaction is aroused with regard to any present state of affairs—a dissatisfaction that supplies the critical edge necessary to keep the process of individual transformation moving. Moreover, this holy dissatisfaction is readily transferable from the realm of the individual to that of society—as was evident in Wesley's own time—where it provides a persistent motivation for reform in the light of "a more perfect way" that transcends any status quo.

Justification by faith, the *leitmotiv* of the Reformation, remained for Wesley a fundamental component of salvation, as we have seen in earlier chapters. But the role of justification is to provide the foundation in grace for the actual transformation of the person that is the divine intention. Justification restores us to God's favor; sanctification, to God's image.[3] Only with sanctification begins the renewal of creation that is explicit in the vision of the kingdom of God. A qualitative change in human existence is the divine objective in the process of reconciliation. From Wesley's standpoint, redemption, therefore, cannot be complete without it. *Entire* sanctification functions on the level of the individual as an eschatological goal, paralleling the kingdom on the social level. Though the realization of this goal is the gift of God's unfailing grace and not the product of human striving, entire sanctification is for Wesley nevertheless a possibility within this world and this life.

It follows that Wesley, unlike most eighteenth-century writers, does not view the kingdom of God as referring exclusively to heaven or to life after death. The first fruits of the kingdom are available now. "A society [is] to be formed . . . to subsist first on earth, and afterward with God in glory. In some places of Scriptures the phrase [kingdom of God] more

---

2. Jürgen Moltmann, *Religion, Revolution and the Future* (New York: Charles Scribner's Sons, 1969), 138, 93–107.

3. *The Works of John Wesley*, Bicentennial edition; hereafter cited as *Works* or *Works* (Bicentennial), Albert Outler et al., eds. (Nashville: Abingdon Press, 1984), Sermon 19, 1:432. Direct quotations used by permission.

particularly denotes the state of it on earth; in others, it signifies only the state of glory; but generally it includes both."[4] Therefore, when we pray "Thy kingdom come, thy will be done in earth as it is in heaven,"

> the meaning is, that all the inhabitants of the earth, even the whole race of mankind, may do the will of their Father which is in heaven, as willingly as the holy angels; that these may do it continually, . . . yes, and that they may do it perfectly—that "the God of peace through the blood of the everlasting covenant, may make them perfect in every good work to do his will, and work in them" all "which is well-pleasing in his sight." In other words, we pray that we and all mankind may do the whole will of God in all things.[5]

"Thy will be done in earth as it is in heaven" is *not* to be understood as it is "by the generality of men" as a phrase expressing only resignation, "a readiness to suffer the will of God, whatsoever it be, concerning us." On the contrary, we pray "not so much for a passive, as for an active, conformity to the will of God."[6]

For Wesley this active conformity includes the responsibility to critique conditions in this world that are not in accord with the divine will. Thomas Madron has detailed Wesley's attacks on the causes of poverty, such as the enclosure laws, which rationalized agriculture, denied the peasants access to common grazing lands, and drove them off the land and into the cities to become the great disenfranchised urban proletariat. Not content simply to *speak* against injustices, Wesley organized various self-help projects, cottage industries, literacy classes, credit unions, medical clinics, and other means of coping with the degrading and impoverishing impact of industrialization and early capitalism.[7]

Wesley's sharpest attacks were directed against the slave trade, which he witnessed firsthand in Carolina (initially the Georgia colony prohibited slavery) and considered the worst abomination found in the Christian world. He cut through the pious rationalizations of the trade offered by his contemporaries—that it was, for instance, an

---

4. John Wesley, *Explanatory Notes upon the New Testament*; hereafter cited as *Notes* (London: Epworth Press, 1952), 22, Matthew 3:2.

5. *Works,* Sermon 26, 1:583.

6. Ibid.

7. Thomas Madron, "John Wesley on Economics," in *Sanctification and Liberation: Liberation Theologies in the Light of the Wesleyan Tradition*, Theodore Runyon, ed. (Nashville: Abingdon Press, 1981), 102–15.

economic necessity. "Better is honest poverty," he wrote, "than all the riches brought in by tears, sweat and blood of our fellow creatures." Or that it brought Africans the benefits of living in so-called civilized lands, to which Wesley retorted that no slave merchant actually operated with such motives. "To get money, not to save lives, is the whole spring of their motions."[8] The profit motive perpetuated the evil for all concerned. He was not impressed by the piety of some slaveholders.

> It is your money that pays the merchant, and through him the captain and the African butchers. You therefore are guilty, yea, principally guilty, of all these frauds, robberies and murders. You are the spring that puts all the rest in motion; they would not stir a step without you; therefore the blood of all these . . . lies upon your head.[9]

The last letter Wesley wrote was to William Wilberforce, who at the time was attempting to win passage of an antislavery bill in Parliament. Wesley did not hesitate to give Wilberforce's cause absolute status and transcendent sanction. "Unless God has raised you up for this very thing you will be worn out by the opposition of men and devils. But if God be for you, who can be against you? . . . Go on, in the name of God and in the power of his might, till even American slavery (the vilest that ever saw the sun) shall vanish away before it."[10]

Black liberation theology has found in Wesley a congenial figure, therefore, whose consistent championing of the rights of black people set an unambiguous standard for the movement he founded. Unfortunately, Wesley's example was not always followed by the movement. The Methodist witness often has been compromised by the socioeconomic structures of slavery and racism. Nevertheless, the abolitionist cause obtained much of its support in nineteenth-century America from the perfectionist orientation called into being by the Wesleyan revivals and frontier preaching. Moreover, the notions of sanctification and holiness proved more compatible with the style of worship and piety of

---

8. John Wesley, *The Works of the Rev. John Wesley*, Jackson edition; hereafter cited as *Works* (Jackson), Thomas Jackson, ed. (Grand Rapids: Zondervan, 1958 [1872]), "Thoughts upon Slavery," XI:74, 72.

9. Ibid., 78.

10. *The Letters of John Wesley*, Telford edition; hereafter cited as *Letters* (London: Epworth Press, 1931), 8:265.

black churches as they developed on American soil than did Calvinism or Anglicanism.

Similarly, feminist theology can point to the openness of both Wesley and the Wesleyans to the contributions of women and to the leadership roles women occupied in the movement, long before they won comparable recognition elsewhere in society. Though scarcely a champion of equal rights in the modern sense, Wesley was capable of passionate prose when arguing for the right of women to exercise ministries such as visitation of the sick.

> But may not women as well as men bear a part of this honorable service? Undoubtedly they may; nay, they ought—it is meet, right and their bounden duty. Herein there is no difference: "there is neither male nor female in Christ Jesus." Indeed it has long passed for a maxim with many that "women are only to be seen; not heard." Accordingly many of them are brought up in such a manner as if they were only designed for agreeable playthings! But is this doing honour to the sex? Or is it real kindness to them? No; it is the deepest unkindness; it is horrid cruelty; it is mere Turkish barbarity. And I know not how any women of sense and spirit can submit to it. Let all you that have it in your power assert the right which the God of nature has given you. Yield not to that vile bondage any longer. You, as well as men, are rational creatures. You, like them, were made in the image of God: you are equally candidates for immortality.[11]

Thus with regard to the first two forms of liberation theology under discussion, the relation of Wesleyan doctrine to human liberation is fairly clear-cut; there is ample historical documentation to suggest a more than coincidental connection between sanctification and social reform. The case is not as clear when we turn to the third type; its criticism of the status quo is grounded not so much in traditional democratic egalitarianism as in Marxism.

THE SPECIAL CHALLENGE OF LATIN AMERICAN THEOLOGY

When we move from black and feminist theologies to Latin American liberationist thought, we move into a new arena. No straight line can be drawn from Wesley through nineteenth-century enlightened liberalism, or through evangelical perfectionism to the political liberation

---

11. *Works*, 3:396.

movements of today. The Wesley whose name lends legitimacy to movements for social reform cannot as readily be called upon to legitimize revolutions. The relationship necessarily becomes more complex and requires a more thorough introduction.

The crux of the problem from the Latin American standpoint is that Wesley was a reformer, but not a revolutionary. His witness may lend itself to increased justice *within* the politico-economic system, but can it endorse radical change? Is there not something in the very notion of sanctification that is meliorist and gradualist, and therefore not appropriate as a model in a situation that calls for more fundamental solutions? Wesley assumes that for the most part, in both church and state, the structures are already in place; what is lacking is the power and the new content of righteousness. This assumption makes him attractive to the liberal reformer, but suspect to the Marxist, for whom liberal reforms may be worse than nothing since they relieve the pressures that otherwise would force the fundamental changes necessary for a new order.

Is it possible to read Wesley in a way that makes sense and that contributes to Christian understanding and action in those parts of the world influenced by the Marxist critique? To spell out the nature of the dilemma, we turn first to the so-called *Halevy thesis* to summarize the issues at stake.

Elie Halevy (1870–1937) was a French historian intrigued by the contrasting developments in England and France at the end of the eighteenth and the beginning of the nineteenth centuries. In the first volume of his monumental six-volume *History of the English People in the Nineteenth Century*, he sought to explain why, with similar conditions of impoverishment and unrest, France went through a bloody revolution, while England moved into the modern period without such violent upheaval.[12] In this and other writings, he concluded that

> England was spared the revolution toward which the contradictions in her polity and economy might otherwise have led her, through the stabilizing influence of evangelical religion, particularly Methodism.... The despair of the working class was the raw material to which Methodist doctrine and discipline gave a shape.[13]

---

12. Elie Halévy, *England in 1815: A History of the English People in the Nineteenth Century*, vol. 1 (London: T. F. Unwin, 1924; New York: Peter Smith, 1949).

13. Elie Halévy, *The Birth of Methodism in England* (Chicago: University of Chicago Press, 1971), 70.

The result was the rise of leaders within the proletariat and petty bourgeoisie who were committed to nonviolence and to the orderly achievement of social reforms in basic loyalty to the government. The influence of Methodism on the trade-union movement in Britain has often been remarked. Labor leaders received their training as class leaders and local preachers, and they adapted the methods of the class meeting and dues collection to the needs of the fledgling trade unions.[14] In his book, *The Methodist Revolution*, Bernard Semmel has updated Halévy and argued, from the standpoint of a social historian, that sociologists should give Wesleyan theology the same careful attention accorded Calvinism by Tawney and Weber, because of Methodism's undeniable social impact.[15]

The Halévy thesis continues to exercise a fascination—not least of all because it is so ambiguous. Does it mean that Wesleyan doctrine and practice instigated profound socioeconomic changes, which in other societies have been accomplished only by prolonged violence and bloody revolution? If so, Wesleyan doctrine conceivably could be touted as the answer to the developing world's search for ideological alternatives to both capitalism and communism.[16] Or does it mean that Methodism's effect was to dampen the fires of revolution by redirecting discontent toward spiritual preoccupations, which would have left the external world unaffected, had it not been for other forces for change at work? Historians of a more critical and Marxist persuasion are inclined toward the latter theory. Their arguments run from the judgment that Methodism simply was not strong enough numerically (150,000 to 200,000 members) by the end of the eighteenth century to wield the kind of influence Halévy attributes to it and that by the time its numbers increased significantly, it had lost most of its identification with the working class and had become bourgeois,[17] to the claim that Methodism was a retrogressive and reactionary force, preoccupied with individual morality and that it drove a wedge between converts and their fellow proletarians—between

14. Cf. Robert F. Wearmouth, *Methodism and the Working-Class Movements of England 1800–1850* (London: Epworth Press, 1937).

15. Bernard Semmel, *The Methodist Revolution* (New York: Basic Books, 1976).

16. This is substantially the claim of the German edition of Garth Lean's *John Wesley, Anglican*, trans. and introduced by Klaus Bockmühler as *John Wesley: Model einer Revolution ohne Gewalt* (Giessen: Brunnen Verlag, 1969).

17. See E. J. Hobsbawm, "Methodism and the Threat of Revolution in Britain," *History Today*, vol. 7 (February 1957), 119–24.

the chapel and the pub. "Energies and emotions which were dangerous to social order . . . were released in the harmless form of sporadic love feasts, watchnights, band meetings or revivalist campaigns."[18] Hence it can be argued that, to the extent that Methodism did affect the working classes, it indoctrinated them in the conservative Toryism of its founder and prevented the kind of radical critique of economic and class structures that could have brought about a new and more just social order.

Wesley's political conservatism cannot be denied. He defended the monarchy, opposed the American colonists in their moves toward independence, and abhorred anarchy in any form. And with good reason. He had faced mobs and lawlessness, and he knew how to value the political structures that guaranteed order and relative freedom of speech. Moreover, he was convinced that under the monarchy and Parliament, in spite of corruptions, Britons enjoyed the greatest degree of freedom found anywhere in Europe. But this same conservatism caused him to oppose the new *laissez-faire* economic policies and to call instead upon the government to return to mercantilist practices, which would assure more just distribution (e.g., setting the price of bread at a level the poor could afford). Oppression lay not in the government as such, but in corruption where it existed—in the buying of votes, for instance, or in an economic policy that accepted unemployment as a matter of course. But the system was presumed to be reformable. True, Wesley's doctrine of universal depravity saw evidence of human folly everywhere, as his treatise "The Doctrine of Original Sin, According to Scripture, Reason and Experience" amply illustrates.[19] But sin can be rooted out; the sanctifying grace of God is given in order that the devil and all his works might be not only renounced but actively opposed and even destroyed.[20]

If we may press the theological analogy, Wesley assumed that the system was "justified"—in its basic lineaments capable of being conformed to the will and purpose of God. What remained was "sanctification," the practice of conformity to that will. Thus the appropriateness of the gradualist, meliorist approach. But what about lands where the regime is neither just nor subject to reform? Is sanctification then not

---

18. E. P. Thompson, *The Making of the English Working Class* (London: Victor Gollancz, 1964), 36.

19. *Works* (Jackson), "The Doctrine of Original Sin According to Scripture, Reason and Experience," IX:191–465.

20. *Works* (Bicentennial), Sermon 62, 2:471–84.

an inappropriate category? Should one demand instead a fundamental "conversion," a break with the past, before sanctification becomes a possibility? Meliorism does not commend itself to those who see radical change as the precondition of any genuine improvement in the lot of the masses. Gradualist reforms are, intentionally or unintentionally, always the ally of the present system. They relieve the worst inequalities and undercut pressure for revolution, thus ensuring that exploitation will continue as before under those who control the wealth and the trade.

What made Wesley appealing to the older liberalism, with its emphasis on humanitarian reform in the context of a democratic, evolving, enlightened capitalism, makes him less than helpful in the eyes of those who see the results of that same capitalism in their own lands, where it has worked hand in glove with local power elites to enrich oligarchies and impoverish the masses. In "A Liberating *Pastoral* for the Rich," Dow Kirkpatrick writes of his own encounter with Latin American realities.[21] He undertakes the difficult task of interpreting to developed-world Christians that, in all its well-intended charity and goodwill, the developed world has not yet grasped the extent to which it is implicated in the developing world's misery and that it has created situations not amenable to the traditional liberal approaches to problem solving. José Míguez Bonino states the issue clearly:

> The liberal ideology under which the liberal project was launched in Latin America, however excellent its intentions may have been, and whatever value it may have had at a point in our history—as a means of breaking the stranglehold of feudal society—proves to be for us *today* an instrument of domination, an ally of neocolonialism and imperialism.[22]

Even the church's missionary efforts are implicated, he charges. "For us in the Third World at least, Methodism as a social force is part of history—and in some ways part of the history of our domination and exploitation."[23]

---

21. Dow Kirkpatrick, "A Liberating *Pastoral* for the Rich," in Theodore Runyon, ed., *Sanctification and Liberation*, 209–23.

22. Miguez Bonino, *Doing Theology in a Revolutionary Situation* (Philadelphia: Fortress Press, 1975), 16.

23. Míguez Bonino, "Wesley's Doctrine of Sanctification from a Liberationist Perspective," in Theodore Runyon, ed., *Sanctification and Liberation*, 60.

If this is the case, the older social liberalism, which produced among other things an impressive body of Wesley scholarship, is no longer able to interpret Wesley convincingly in a world that has been sensitized by the Marxist critique of liberalism. The response to this dilemma, however, may be not to jettison Wesley, but to discover a hermeneutic that opens up his theology in a way that applies to the new situation.

CHALLENGE AND RESPONSE IN WESLEY SCHOLARSHIP

Confrontations such as the one posed by Latin American liberation theology are not to be feared or avoided. Indeed, judging from recent history, research and reflection in the Methodist tradition have been spurred by just such challenges. The two most creative periods of Wesley scholarship in the twentieth century were called forth by cultural and theological changes that provoked questions about the conventional images of Wesley and Methodism. After World War I, the rise of the social gospel confronted scholars with the necessity of demonstrating that Wesley had more to offer than the pietism, revivalism, and individualism popularly associated with his name. The spate of research and publication on the social implications of Methodism—from the series by Wearmouth and Edwards and the studies by Wellman, MacArthur, and Bready, down to the works by Schneeberger and Marquardt—has proved to be a rich lode. It speaks directly to the concerns of black theology and feminist theology. The fact that it cannot, for the most part, answer as directly the Latin American situation by no means discredits its contribution.

When liberalism was challenged in Europe by dialectical theology and in North America by neo-orthodoxy, a new critique of Wesleyanism arose. As neo-Reformation thought became the norm in the Protestant ecumenical movement, the Methodist interest in religious experience was labeled "Schleiermachian," and the doctrine of Christian perfection was viewed as superficial and overly optimistic in the light of the tragedies of World War II and its aftermath. In this period when continental Protestant theology was dominant, Methodists were regarded as not having a theology—at least not one that could contribute significantly to the ecumenical discussion.

Rising to the challenge, studies appeared that reappraised Wesley's thought in continuity with the Reformation tradition beginning with Cell's early study of Calvinist elements in Wesley. This was followed by

Cannon's treatment of the classical soteriological doctrines, Deschner's analysis of Wesley's Christology from a Barthian perspective, and Hildebrandt's examination of Wesley's continuity with Luther. Flew, Sangster, Peters, and Lindstrom all reinterpreted sanctification; and the works of Davies, Outler, Rupp, Williams, and others related Wesley more or less consciously to the mainstream of the Reformation tradition. The role of original sin was rediscovered, and the qualifications with which Wesley hedged Christian perfection were reiterated.

All of which is to say that each generation approaches the study of Wesley—or of any major figure in the past—with the questions and issues that demand attention in that generation's own time. If humanistic Marxism appeared the most viable option to a significant segment of the world's population in the 1970s and 1980s, it is not surprising that the scholars of a world movement like Methodism began to approach Wesley with questions generated by their encounter with Marxism. It can be argued, of course, that in the case of Marxism we are dealing with atheistic thought-forms inimical to any theological discussion. The long-standing Christian/Marxist dialogue would seem to indicate, however, that this is not entirely the case. Latin American liberation theology consciously appropriated Marxist methodology and found it a useful tool for both biblical and historical reflection, much as Thomas Aquinas converted pagan Aristotelianism, which posed no inconsiderable threat in his time, to Christian use.

If the Marxist critical component in Latin American theology tends to discredit the older liberal interpretation of Wesley, it treats the continental Reformation influence in contemporary theology in no more kindly fashion. Latin Americans fault their European Roman Catholic colleagues for allowing protestantizing concerns to dominate their rethinking of Catholicism after Vatican II. The doctrine of justification by faith alone has had fateful historical consequences, they warn. "The disappearance of the notion of *merit* from Protestant theology," says Juan Luis Segundo, ". . . seems to have undermined the possibility of any theology of history."[24] The Catholic doctrine of merit, for all its shortcomings, gave eternal worth to human effort and right intention. But the exclusive emphasis upon justification by faith alone puts human beings in a completely passive position and turns the determination of

---

24. Juan Luis Segundo, *The Liberation of Theology* (Maryknoll, N.Y.: Orbis Books,1976), 142.

history over to the secular powers. Segundo detects vestiges of this heritage even in today's Protestant liberation theologians, such as Moltmann and Alves, and in their Catholic allies, such as Metz, when they view the kingdom of God as so radically different from this world as to negate any human effort to approximate it. This is Luther's "two realms" doctrine *redivivus* in the thin disguise of political theology, Segundo suspects. "The 'revolution' it talks about seems to be more like a Kantian revolution than an historical revolution. It merely revolutionizes the way we formulate our problems."[25] A theology of hope of the European variety, which speaks of a radical future but is unwilling to take responsibility for the concrete and ambiguous steps that lead from here to there, is no theology of hope—at least not of hope for our history. Segundo sees the continuing grip of the Reformation doctrine as the fundamental debilitating element responsible for this impotence. If the theology of hope "remains consistent with itself and its fonts," he claims, "the revolution it speaks about is transformed into faith and hope in something metahistorical and a disgusted turning-away from real-life history." Segundo does not favor a return to the Catholic doctrine of merit in its medieval form. That would reintroduce the legalism from which the Reformation revolted. Rather, he seeks an approach combining the freedom *from*, experienced in justification, with freedom *for* human responsibility.[26] What is needed, say the Latin Americans, is a holistic, critical, transformationist theology, one that understands salvation not only as a process that changes the individual, but as a historical process moving toward a divine goal—one in which the God of the Bible has a stake and takes sides—a process in which human efforts count for something and in which God enlists those efforts and brings them to fulfillment through their incorporation into the divine enterprise.

What happens when we approach Wesley with these Latin American concerns in mind? Because of the limits of space, we can focus on only one example, but one that nonetheless is central enough to demonstrate the usefulness of the method. We shall focus on the role of *work* in the basic anthropologies of Wesley and Marx. In Wesley's case this will inevitably lead to a comparison with Reformation and quietist views on the relation of work to justification and sanctification, which in turn will open up parallels with Marx's criticisms of Feuerbach.

25. Ibid., 145.
26. Ibid., 147, 150.

WESLEY AND MARX ON WORK

What is the role of human work in Wesley's soteriology? This has been a continuing conundrum to those who wish to view Wesley as standing solidly within the Reformation tradition. He maintains that the Methodists espouse and proclaim nothing other than the Reformers' doctrine—justification by faith, without works of the law. At the same time he claims that "one who preaches justification by faith [and] goes no farther than this, [and] does not insist upon . . . all the fruits of faith, upon universal holiness, does not declare the whole counsel of God, and consequently is not a Gospel Minister." Introducing a distinction between "present" and "final" salvation, Wesley declares that "faith alone is the condition of present salvation," but that holiness and obedience are "the ordinary condition of final salvation."[27] As he explains, "Good works . . . cannot be the conditions of justification, because it is impossible to do any good work before we are justified. And yet, notwithstanding, good works may be and are conditions of final salvation."[28]

These and similar statements have led Cell and Peters to conclude that Wesley provides a "synthesis of the Protestant ethic of grace with the Catholic ethic of holiness.[29] Rupp and Williams find this "synthesis" less than helpful and, for their part, cannot believe that Wesley is guilty of adding a Catholic doctrine of works to a Protestant foundation. "The Catholic view of holiness [with its ladder of merit] cannot be molded onto the Protestant view of grace," they object.[30] And if Wesley actually has done this he must perforce have abandoned his essential Protestantism.[31]

But is it not possible that Wesley is operating out of an understanding of the nature and function of works that fits neither a traditional Protestant or a traditional Catholic position? Against the Catholic

---

27. *Works* (Jackson), X:456.

28. *Letters*, 2:189.

29. George C. Cell, *The Rediscovery of John Wesley* (New York: Henry Holt, 1935), 361; John Peters, *Christian Perfection and American Methodism* (Nashville: Abingdon Press, 1956), 21.

30. Gordon Rupp, *Principalities and Powers* (Nashville: Abingdon Press, 1952), 97; Colin Williams, *John Wesley's Theology Today* (Nashville: Abingdon Press, 1960), 175.

31. At least one scholar, Jürgen Weissbach, is convinced that this is in fact what Wesley did. See *Der neue Mensch im theologischen Denken* in *John Wesleys, Beiträge zur Geschichte des Methodismus*, No. 2 (Stuttgart: Christliches Verlaghaus, 1970), 218.

position as he understands it, he contends that human merit is *never* the basis for justification, whether initial or final; and against the Reformers, he argues that final justification is not apart from works. In terse form, this reduces to: we are not accepted for our works; and we are not saved apart from our works.[32]

If we bring to Wesley a Marxist understanding of the relation of work to human nature, however, we discover some intriguing parallels that may illuminate Wesley's underlying anthropology and in turn may clarify his notion of final justification.

The early Marx—the left-wing Hegelian humanist—has a special appeal for the advocates of liberation theology, in that he writes out of a deep compassion for the human plight. He wrestles to find categories not only to express that plight but to change it. During this early period he develops his basic understanding of human existence, as to both its nature and its implicit teleology.[33] For Marx, humans achieve their true being and come to self-consciousness through action.[34] Through our labor we take the empirical (*sinnlich*[35]) world outside ourselves and shape it into the authentic expression of our own being. In this process humans produce something that is objective and apart from themselves and that yet is their own product and the genuine expression of their own creativity, through which they find pleasure and a sense of fulfillment.[36] The artist is the paradigm of this process. The sculptor takes the empirical world of clay, stone, or metal and creates something that has an independent reality and is therefore "objective," but that also embodies the inner creativity and subjectivity of the artist.

We must add that what is expressed is not only individual but *social,* in the most profound sense. The sculptor is inextricably linked with the world that provides the material substance that interacts with

---

32. *Works* (Jackson), XII:399.

33. Cf. Joseph Petulla, *Christian Political Theology* (Maryknoll, N.Y.: Orbis Books, 1972), 12.

34. Karl Marx, *The Economic and Philosophic Manuscripts of 1844*, introduced by Dirk J. Struik (New York: International Publishers, 1964), 24.

35. The usual translation of *sinnlich* in Marxist literature is "sensuous," a term with misleading overtones for most English readers. *Sinnlich* refers to the empirical world known by the senses. Wesley's own term, "sensible world," would be a more felicitous translation were it not archaic English.

36. Note the parallel to the Hegelian notion of fulfillment through self-expression by positing the "other," a process that begins with God in creation.

subjectivity. The result is the product, not just of a single individual, but of the social, cultural, and natural context with which the individual interrelates and is in turn shaped. Thus "productive life is the life of the species. It is life-engendering life.... In creating a world of objects by his practical activity, in his work upon inorganic nature, man proves himself a conscious species being [*Gattungswesen*]," one whose product is the result of social interaction in community. "The object of labor is, therefore, the objectification of man's species life." (The term *Gattungswesen* carries overtones of linkage and interrelatedness, as well as of sexual creativity, that are missing in the English "species.") The human thus "duplicates himself not only in consciousness, intellectually, but also actively in reality."[37] This creation of the "other," which is at the same time the expression of the self in its interrelatedness, is the basic model of human fulfillment for Marx and describes humanity in its ideal state or, so to speak, before the Fall.

Marx introduces the term "alienation" *(Entfremdung)* to show how "the relationship of the worker to the objects of his production" has become distorted in industrialized, capitalist society. Industrialization produces more goods, but relegates workers to the condition of cogs in a machine. Work no longer can function as the creative objectivizing of the self; it becomes instead the constant loss and deprivation of the self as one's life is poured out. Not only is the *product* alien and no longer the authentic expression of the self, but the mode of production—the *labor expended* to produce it—is alienating. "In the very act of production (the worker] is estranging himself from himself." In his labor the worker "does not affirm himself but denies himself." The proof of this, according to Marx, is seen in the fact "that as soon as no physical or other compulsion exists, labor is shunned like the plague.... The worker therefore only feels himself outside his work, and in his work feels outside himself. He is at home when he is not working, and when he is working he is not at home." His labor is in effect forced labor. It does not fulfill the intended function of satisfying his humanity but "is merely a *means* to satisfy needs external to it." The worker is enslaved to the production process because he must have the necessities of life for himself and his family, but the way he spends most of his waking hours alienates him

---

37. Marx, *Economic and Philosophic Manuscripts*, 113–14.

from his essential humanity. Work ceases to be a means of genuine life and becomes a means of subsistance.[38]

Moreover, the loss is not just that of the individual. "In tearing away from man the object of production, [alienating] labor tears from him his species life"—his contribution as a social being whose interrelatedness must come to expression.[39] The products made by alienated workers give objective form to that alienation and to the system that produces it—a system with goals in contradiction to humanity as such.

Though one may quarrel with Marx's "romanticizing" of labor, his analysis of what happens when work is alienating cannot be ignored. For our purposes, however, this brief summary of Marx's notion of humanity as coming to expression through work is included for the light it may shed on the essential differences between Wesley and the Reformers in their understandings of the relation of work to salvation. It also may enable us to see more clearly the nature of the change that occurred in Wesley at Aldersgate—an issue of perennial interest and speculation.

WESLEY AND THE REFORMERS

The medieval preoccupation with the certainty of one's salvation was not substantially altered by the Reformation, although the way in which that certainty was provided did change. For both Luther and Calvin, the certainty of salvation was best guaranteed by lodging it with God. Divine mercy, in Luther, and divine election, in Calvin, functioned to ensure that human salvation would be accomplished in a way that could not be subject to institutional control or—equally important—to the foibles of the human will, the waverings of the human heart, or the inadequacies of human deeds. Only in this way could the Reformers spring free from the medieval church's monopoly on the means of grace and from the necessity of constantly examining the state of one's soul and one's works to determine whether one is indeed saved or not. With a single sweeping move they removed salvation from the realm of dependence on human action and placed it in the realm of divine promise and faithfulness. The Christian looks not to self or to an institution for assurance, but to divine steadfastness. God has elected us from eternity (Calvin) or declared himself for us in Christ Jesus (Luther). Therefore our salvation is where

---

38. Ibid., 109, 110, 111.
39. Ibid., 114.

God is—in eternity; or where the Son is—in heaven; and our fate cannot be determined by what we do or do not accomplish.

The price paid for this way of grounding security is a shift in the location of *essential* humanity, however. Our true being is to be found in God, in election by God, or in God's forensic declaration of our justification through Christ, rather than in our existence in this world. The result is the split to which Segundo refers—between the transcendent realm, in which our salvation is actually occurring, and this world, which is in effect bracketed out of salvation history.

Lest this be thought a peculiarly Catholic reading of the Reformation, Reformed theologian Otto Weber comments on these same developments in Protestant orthodoxy. He notes that a nonbiblical distinction was introduced. The "person" was separated from his or her "works." This distinction was first made in order to explain that sinners are justified, whereas their sinful deeds are not. But then, to guarantee that the justified would not rely on their good works, it was insisted that all good works must be attributed to the divine Spirit who instigates them. The work was "no longer a work of the person but an event independent of the person." The result was a kind of "pneumatological docetism," says Weber.[40] When action is no longer understood as the expression of the person who acts, it becomes difficult to show how the person is accountable for deeds that are extrinsic to him or her. Life in the world loses its cruciality and significance, leading historically to the twin reactions of antinomianism and otherworldliness. The Lutheran doctrine of "vocation" seeks to counteract these tendencies, but it cannot finally succeed if work must be viewed as extrinsic to the relationship that saves.

Although Wesley's early preoccupation with his own salvation and the certainty of heaven is reminiscent of Luther's search for a gracious God, when the assurance of divine love finally comes to Wesley, it is placed in the service of a grander scheme of the renewal of the world and the race.[41] Essential humanity becomes a *project,* to be realized not only in heaven but in this world. And the renewal of the race is an undertaking in which humans have their indispensable role; God enlists human

---

40. Otto Weber, *Grundlagen der Dogmatik* (Neukirchen-Moers: Neukirchener Verlag, 1962), vol. 2, 363.

41. This goal of the renewal of the race and of the cosmos is reiterated in a teleologically oriented series of sermons (*Works [Bicentennial]*, 2:422–510), as well as in Wesley's treatise on "Original Sin," *Works* [Jackson], IX:191–465).

beings in this redemptive process. They labor, knowing that God is at work in and through them, "to will and to do of his good pleasure." This is Wesley's model of synergism—human partnership with the divine. It is not that certain tasks in the process of salvation are parceled out to human initiative and free will while others require divine grace. On the contrary, all that humans say and do is to be inspired by the Spirit and, consistent with the nature of the Spirit, leads toward the perfecting of the individual and the restoration of the race.

"We know 'Without me ye can do nothing.' But, on the other hand, we know 'I can do all things through Christ that strengtheneth me.' . . . God has joined these together in the experience of every believer; and therefore we must take care, not to imagine they are ever to be put asunder." Because he works in us, we *must* work. "You must be 'workers together with him.' . . . Even St. Augustine, who is generally supposed to favour the contrary doctrine, makes that just remark, . . . 'He that made us without ourselves, will not save us without ourselves.'" The power of the kingdom, which has come near in the Spirit, provides both the goal and the motivation to those who in sanctification have been taken into partnership with the divine. "Say with our blessed Lord, though in a somewhat different sense, 'My Father worketh hitherto, and I work.'"[42] Even God's own being is seen in his work, which takes the form not of divine fiat in the counsels of heaven but of the creative intervention of divine love, intent to restore a lost creation.

We note in Wesley's anthropology, therefore, some strong formal parallels with Marx. Human life is seen fundamentally as activity; as work that is teleological, always directed toward some purpose—in Wesley's case, toward the service of God or the service of self in pride, vanity, gain, or whatever. This anthropology may be traceable in part to Jeremy Taylor, whose influence on the young Wesley was strategic, and whose *Rule and Exercises of Holy Living* enjoined upon the would-be disciple the most stringent accounting of time and activities:

> We must remember that the life of every man may be so ordered (and indeed must) that it may be a perpetual serving of God. . . . We have a great work to do, many enemies to conquer, many evils to prevent, much danger to run through, many difficulties to be mastered, many necessities to serve, and much good to do. . . . We must give account to the great Judge of men and angels. . . . We

---

42. *Works*, (Bicentennial), Sermon 85, 3:206.

must account for every idle word; not meaning that every word which is not designed to edification [is] . . . sin, but that the time which we spend in our idle talking and unprofitable discourses, that time which might and ought to have been employed to spiritual and useful purposes, that is to be accounted for."[43]

Because this theme of strenuous accountability is found in Wesley both before and after Aldersgate (e.g., his instructions to his preachers not only never to be unemployed, but never to be "triflingly employed"), and because they detect little modification in Wesley's basic anthropology and soteriology after 1738, Maximin Piette and others have concluded that the decisiveness of Aldersgate is more a matter of Methodist lore than historic fact.[44] As far as formal doctrine is concerned, they are correct. Wesley's *theory* of justification was already largely in place in his 1733 sermon, "The Circumcision of the Heart."[45] And formally, his anthropology does not change; work remains the expression of the committed person. But the foundation for that work, the spirit that informs it, and the nature of the goal toward which it is directed, are all decisively modified. The fastidious compulsiveness that drove the young Wesley is now more relaxed, though his intensity remains. His ministry breathes a freedom he previously had not known. And the agent of this transformation is the same Martin Luther from whom, up to this point, we have been attempting to distinguish Wesley.

Yet, in speaking of the role of Luther in Wesley's development, we have struck another of those perpetual puzzles in Wesley scholarship. How could the Luther whose "Preface to Romans" was the catalyst for Wesley's experience of justification be the object three years later of a broadside attack? After reading the Reformer's Galatians commentary, Wesley accuses him of being "muddy and confused. . . . How blasphemously does he speak of good works and of the law of God; constantly coupling the law with sin, death, hell, or the Devil! and teaching that Christ delivers us from them all alike."[46]

---

43. Jeremy Taylor, *The Rule and Exercises of Holy Living* (London: Ward, Lock & Co., n.d.), 3.

44. Maximin Piette, *John Wesley and the Evolution of Protestantism* (New York: Sheed & Ward, 1937), 306–7.

45. *Works*, Sermon 17, 1:401–14.

46. *The Journal of John Wesley*; hereafter cited as *Journal*, Nehemiah Curnock, ed., (London: Robert Culley, 1909), 2:467.

THE CHANGE AT ALDERSGATE

What many fail to notice is that Luther's "Preface to Romans," read that evening in May 1738, in the conventicle on Aldersgate Street, did not question the place of work in the Christian life. Quite the opposite. It explicitly and repeatedly linked faith and works in a way that was atypical for later Lutheran orthodoxy. The Luther of that preface is more holistic in relating person and work and—dare we say it?—makes instead the more Marxist distinction between works as the product of an alienated being and works as the expression of a reconciled being—and with this Luther put his finger on Wesley's problem:

> For even though you keep the law outwardly, with works, from fear of punishment or love of reward, nevertheless, you do all this without willingness, under compulsion; and you would rather do otherwise, if the law were not there. The conclusion is that at the bottom of your heart you hate the law.... To fulfill the law, however, is to do its works with pleasure and love, and to live a godly and good life of one's own accord, without the compulsion of the law.... Hence it comes that faith alone makes righteous and fulfills the law; out of Christ's merit, it brings the Spirit, and the Spirit makes the heart glad and free, as the law requires that it shall be. Thus good works come out of faith.... O, it is a living, busy, active, mighty thing, this faith; and so it is impossible for it not to do good works incessantly. It does not ask whether there are good works to do, but before the question arises, it has already done them, and is always at the doing of them. He who does not those works is a faithless man....
>
> [T]hus it is impossible to separate works from faith, quite as impossible as to separate heat and light from fire.[47]

In all likelihood that is the passage to which Wesley refers in his *Journal* as the word that overcame the alienation in his own life. "While he was describing the change which God works in the heart through faith in Christ, I felt my heart strangely warmed. I felt I did trust in Christ, Christ alone for salvation; and an assurance was given me that He had taken away *my* sins, even *mine*, and saved *me* from the law of sin and death."[48] The transformation that occurred at Aldersgate is not in Wesley's anthropology (the conviction that human life is fundamentally

---

47. Martin Luther, "Preface to Romans," *Luther's Works*, vol. 6 (Philadelphia: Muhlenberg Press, 1932), 451–52.

48. *Works*, 18:250.

purposive activity), but in the relational *foundation* that undergirds that activity. As Wesley looks upon his pre-Aldersgate existence, he sees that what Marx would call his "species" life was alienated. His good works did not flow out of freedom; they were not the expression of positive relations but emerged from the compulsive effort to fashion a life in which every thought and action would be well pleasing in God's sight and therefore worthy of salvation. "My chief motive, to which all the rest are subordinate, is the hope of saving my own soul," he had written to Dr. John Burton before setting sail for Georgia.[49] Toward this end he gave up all—"friends, reputation, ease, country; I have ... given my body to be devoured by the deep, parched up with heat, consumed by toil and weariness, or whatsoever God should please to bring upon me.[50] "But as he later recognized, all such efforts could bring no peace, for at their root was alienation. He could not serve freely the law he had imposed upon himself. Luther's words identified the basic difficulty: "At the bottom of your heart you hate the law." As Wesley later confessed, given this fundamental alienation, there was no way his works could be good, since they emerged as the expression of a species life that was basically distorted, in relation both to God and to his fellow creatures. All his efforts could not fulfill the law, because the foundation was wrong.

Into this vicious cycle of alienation came the good news of justification by faith—the new foundation laid by God in Christ Jesus, who is the outworking of God's redemptive intervention to release humanity from bondage. The Son does God's work in the world; he is the self-expression of the divine heart. His work alone provides the basis for reconciliation; it eliminates all human efforts toward self-justification because it makes them unnecessary. The new basis for relationship is his love that "has been poured into our hearts through the Holy Spirit which has been given to us" (Rom 5:5). The reception of this love overcomes estrangement and is marked by the sense of forgiveness and liberation.

Nothing may appear to have changed, in the sense that the same good works are done that were done before. Yet everything has changed, in that life is placed on a different foundation. In Marxist terms, the previous economic base with its alienated method of production has been replaced by a "substructure" that puts all relationships on a new footing. The actual job one does may be exactly the same after the revolution as

---

49. *Works*, 25:439.
50. *Journal*, 1:423.

it was before, but one's way of relating to the system has changed, and the result is a liberated worker whose work now expresses a free and co-responsible existence. Analogously for Wesley, the deeds may seem the same as before, but they issue forth from a new status and embody a fresh spirit. Nothing less than "new birth" will do to describe this change. It is the shift "from the faith of a *servant* to the faith of a *son;* from the spirit of bondage unto fear, to the spirit of childlike love . . . enabling [one]to testify, "The life that I now live in the flesh, I live 'by faith in the Son of God who loved me, and gave himself for me.'"[51] *Justification* describes this foundation and context within which life is now placed; *regeneration* describes the transformation in the person, made possible by the new mode of being related; and *sanctification* is the reordering and reconstituting of all interrelationships in conformity with the base.

The species character of this whole salvific process now becomes evident. New birth is a social event that brings divine love down into the human family to take effect here. The nature of Christ's love is that it turns us immediately and inevitably toward others. Love that is self-contained, or purely and simply between the soul and its God, is not "evangelical" love as Wesley understands it. It is not the intent of the love "which is shed abroad in our hearts" to draw human love to itself in the heavenly spheres but to spend itself in the world in outpoured service. It is, as it were, poured *through* our hearts into the world.

> In truth, whosoever loveth his brethren not in word only, but as Christ loved him, cannot but be zealous of good works. He feels in his soul a burning, restless desire of spending and being spent for them. . . . The Gospel of Christ knows of no religion, but social; no holiness, but social holiness. *Faith working by love* is the length and breadth and depth and height of Christian perfection.[52]

Sanctification—or Christian perfection—is not in the final analysis to be defined negatively, as the absence of sin, but positively, as the active presence of love expressed not only in word but in deed: from God to humanity, from humanity to God; from God through human beings, to their fellow human beings.[53] This is the power of the kingdom that be-

---

51. *Works,* Sermon 117, 4:36.

52. *The Poetical Works of John and Charles Wesley;* hereafter cited as *Poetical Works* (London: Wesleyan Methodist Conference Office, 1868), xxii.

53. This often-made point of the activity of love is given fresh interpretation by

gins to exercise its humanizing impact in the present age. Hence Wesley opposes the desire of some Christians to "separate themselves from sinners" in order to avoid commerce with the world as much as possible. Were they to withdraw, how could they fulfill their calling to be "the salt of the earth," he asks.[54] Sanctification is the enlisting of the individual in God's own work—the redemption of his creation.

Summarizing the effects of Aldersgate, we can say that (a) it did not change the anthropology of Wesley, insofar as both before and after the events of 1738 he understood genuine human existence as being brought to expression through work; but (b) it did expose the alienated nature of his previous works of self-justification; and (c) it did bring about a fundamental reconciliation with God and a genuine concern for others, growing out of the love introduced into Wesley's life by justification and the regenerative power of the Spirit; which in turn (d) placed a new foundation of grace under sanctification while linking justification to the continuing drive for the transformation of the individual and society.

Now we are in a position to see, in comparison with the Reformation, Wesley's unique understanding of the way justification and sanctification are united, and why he must insist both on "justification by faith without works" as the foundation, and on works as the condition for "final justification." He approvingly quotes Bishop Bull, who in his *Harmonica Apostolica*, "distinguishes our first from our final justification, and affirms both inward and outward good works to be the condition of the latter, though not the former."[55]

From the standpoint of the Reformers this notion of final justification seems to abandon the essential point of justification by faith, since it takes works into account. Even though he adds the proviso "Those fruits are only necessary *conditionally,* if there be time and opportunity for them,"[56] Wesley appears to undermine the security given with Calvin's understanding of divine election, and Luther's notion of the justification of the ungodly, putting the burden again on the creature to justify him- or herself by achievements in the world. The interpretations of Luther and Calvin offer security because justification by faith preempts final judgment by anticipating it in the present, facing its terror and invoking

---

Mildred Bangs Wynkoop, *A Theology of Love* (Kansas City: Beacon Hill Press, 1972).

54. *Works*, Sermon 24, 1:537.
55. *Letters*, 5:264.
56. *Works*, Sermon 43, 2:163.

the mercy of God manifested in the love of Christ, which covers the accused and guarantees divine acceptance and eternal life. The "faith that justifies" is so important because through it one grasps the indispensable condition of eternal life: reliance on divine mercy. For Luther, therefore, justification provides the substructure for heaven and our relationship with God—but not for life in this world, which is left to be dealt with on grounds other than faith. To suggest the possibility of a second justification would seem to question the sufficiency and certainty of the initial divine act.

Wesley disagrees. Like the Reformers, he insists on the sole sufficiency of divine mercy. Faith is the trust that allows God's own mercy in Christ to define and provide the basis of the relationship. This is the kind of trust the Spirit quickens within a heart that is confronted by the love of God in Christ. Reconciliation is therefore not without work. But the work is God's. *Our* works are excluded—not because they are of no value, but because, in strict adherence to the Reformation insight, at no point are they the source of our certainty or security, either initially or finally. When Wesley uses the term "final justification," therefore, he is not speaking of a justification on a basis different from the first. Justification by grace through faith remains the only foundation for the divine human relationship throughout the whole course of sanctification. What is new is a modification of the *telos*—the inherent goal and purpose of justification. No longer is it directed primarily toward heaven. This is not to say that Wesley does not have the traditional concern for heaven.[57] But the direction is reversed. Heaven is brought to earth—not in utopian, humanistic fashion, but in the way that justification provides the substructure for refashioning life in this world through sanctification. Typically, Protestants see justification, or conversion, as the decisive, revolutionary event. Wesley would agree. But then, just as typically, the revolution becomes the center around which the rest of life circles, rather than a bench mark that sets the course of the future that is to be built.

Accountability cannot end with justification, therefore. To eliminate further accountability is to make justification the equivalent of the eschaton and to collapse history into insignificance. But the process of sanctification is the purification of history, overcoming the elements of society and in the life of the individual that cannot stand at the latter day. Accountability must continue, for justification, though it is the

57. *Works*, Preface, 1:105.

revolution that provides a different base, does not mean that the struggle is over. An analogy may help to elucidate this: In Marxism the new economic substructure does not exist for its own sake but for the sake of the superstructure that is built upon it. The purpose of the revolution is not merely to defeat the sources of alienation in the previous system but to enable a new society and culture to be erected. Those revolutionaries who believe that everything has been completed when the revolution is successful constitute one of the main obstacles to further progress. The revolution, and the new economic base that it makes possible, are requisite to everything that follows. In that sense, the revolution never grows obsolete, since it is taken up and expressed in everything built upon it. But the foundation is laid in order that the superstructure might be built.

This analogy shows that Jürgen Weissbach is incorrect when he suggests that for Wesley justification is "only a temporary stage in the process of salvation"—a stage that is superseded.[58] On the contrary, justification is taken up and incorporated into everything that proceeds from it. The motto "the substructure is reflected in the superstructure" is as applicable to soteriology as it is to economics.

In evaluating a Marxist society, one would need to take into account not only the revolutionary efforts that brought it into existence but the extent to which the goals of the revolution were being effected. In the same way, justification does not stand by itself apart from the history it initiates. When the God who justifies has a stake in this history, it means, as Wesley knew, "A charge to keep I have." The fact that there is "a strict account to give,"[59] does not result in legalism or fear, however, because in final justification, one stands before the same God with whom one is reconciled in initial justification. Wesley's *doctrine of assurance* makes certain that the radical love of God that is encountered at the cross remains the experiential content of sanctification as well as of justification. His notion of final justification serves to preserve that accountability appropriate to the stewards of the good news of the kingdom.

Pursuing a line independent of the Reformation, Wesley is also conscious of the necessity to distinguish himself from a position on the other flank, which seeks to build the sanctified life on the old foundation, without benefit of justification and new birth. This is illustrated in his criticisms of his former spiritual guide, William Law, whom Wesley

58. Weissbach, *Der neue Mensch*, 217.
59. From Charles Wesley's hymn, "A Charge to Keep I Have."

accuses of having a "philosophical religion," which answers all questions within the web of its own speculations and "inner light."[60] Thus Law is not open to the renewing grace associated with judgment, repentance, and justification.

Consequently, we find Wesley battling two forms of *mysticism* that are opposed in many respects: the "Lutheran" mysticism of the Moravian quietists, with their exclusive emphasis upon forensic grace; and the "rationalistic" mysticism of Law, with his virtual neglect of community and the means of grace. Neither has a place for works. These are two fronts against which Wesley has to maintain his understanding of justification and sanctification. And this struggle provides us with a final comparison with Marx and Marx's criticism of Feuerbach's "mysticism."

WESLEY AND MARX VERSUS THE MYSTICS AND FEUERBACH

Wesley's controversy with the Moravians was really a dispute with Lutheran orthodoxy's forensic doctrine of sanctification and the quietist form of pietism that resulted from it. Advocates of "stillness" asserted that good works bring with them the temptation to trust in what one can do, rather than exclusively in Christ and the "alien righteousness" he bestows. In a conversation with Wesley, Moravian leader Count Nikolaus von Zinzendorf maintained, "From the moment one is justified he is entirely sanctified. . . . Till death he is neither more holy nor less holy." Zinzendorf understood both justification and sanctification to be entirely imputed, covering the saved person like a cloak of righteousness that God sees, rather than seeing the sinner beneath. Because righteousness is required for salvation, and because "the best of men are miserable sinners till death," the only righteousness that counts is that assigned to one from the merits of Christ. Zinzendorf continues, "I know of no such thing as inherent perfection in this life. This is the error of errors, I pursue it everywhere with fire and sword! . . . Christ is our only perfection. . . . Christian perfection is entirely imputed, not inherent. We are perfect in Christ; never perfect in ourselves."[61]

---

60. *Works* (Jackson), IX:466–509.

61. Albert Outler, ed. *John Wesley* (New York: Oxford University Press, 1964), 367–72.

While Wesley held no brief for the kind of inherent perfection Zinzendorf attacked, he did insist that righteousness is imparted as well as imputed. Christians are not just *declared* righteous, they are regenerated—endowed by the Spirit and nurtured through the means of grace actually to become what they are declared to be. According to the stillness doctrine, "one must *do nothing,* but quietly attend the voice of the Lord," avoiding reliance on any of the usual means of grace, such as the sacraments, prayer, and reading of the Scriptures, and one must not do any outward work, lest one be tempted to trust that which is of this world.[62] Wesley was no stranger to radical trust, but from his vantage point, the stillness doctrine could present only a truncated view of salvation. In effect, it collapsed sanctification into justification, though it did not understand the proper purpose of justification, and it left no room for the actualization of righteousness in the world and the fullness of salvation. For the quietists, justification sealed for heaven, sanctification purified for heaven, and both were accomplished extrinsically to the person, hence bracketing out actual existence in the world lest it contaminate the heavenly status of the saved soul. Wesley eventually withdrew from the Moravian influences at the Fetter Lane Society and formed a new society at the Foundery.[63]

The other mysticism with which Wesley broke was that of his onetime mentor, William Law, as Law came increasingly under the influence of the German mystic, Jacob Boehme. Law's *Christian Perfection* and *A Serious Call to a Devout and Holy Life* had made important contributions to Wesley's early development and, with Jeremy Taylor's theories, had formed him in the tradition of Anglican "practical mysticism." Now Law had come to espouse a withdrawal parallel to that of the quietists, reducing the Christian life to mystical devotion, and insisting that the mark of genuine faith can be tested by the following "infallible touchstone":

> Abstain from all conversation for a month. Neither write, nor read, nor debate anything with yourself. Stop all the former workings of your heart and mind, and stand all this month in prayer to God. If your heart cannot give itself up in this manner

---

62. See *Journal,* 2:499, for Wesley's description of this quietism.

63. Cf. John Simon, *John Wesley and the Methodist Societies,* 2nd ed. (London: Epworth Press, 1937), 9–15.

to prayer, be fully assured you are an infidel. . . . Be retired, silent, passive and humbly attentive to the inward light.⁶⁴

We may safely assume that this kind of mysticism held some attraction for Wesley, and certainly for his followers, for we find him writing,

> I think the rock on which I had nearest made shipwreck of the faith was the writings of the Mystics; under which term I comprehend all and only those who slight any of the means of grace.⁶⁵
>
> All the other enemies of Christianity are triflers; the Mystics are the most dangerous of its enemies. They stab it in the vitals, and its most serious professors are most likely to fall by them.⁶⁶

But he also grasped the essential inconsistency between these forms of piety and the understanding of Christian perfection he affirmed. The Moravians look to heaven; Law looks to the inner light; yet both fail to see that the existence given in faith is social and must therefore issue forth in action. A piety that does not result in works is alienated from its source in the redemptive activity of the God whose love toward all his creatures must be expressed.

> What is it to worship God, a Spirit, in spirit and truth? . . . To obey him . . . in thought, and word, and work . . . to glorify him, therefore, with our bodies, as well as with our spirits; to go through outward work with hearts lifted up to him; to make our daily employment a sacrifice to God; to buy and sell, to eat and drink, to his glory;—this is worshipping God in spirit and in truth, as much as praying to him in a wilderness.⁶⁷

This is why

> Christianity is essentially a social religion; . . . to turn it into a solitary one is to destroy it. . . . 'Ye are the light of the world: A city set upon a hill cannot be hid.' . . . Love cannot be hid any more than light; and least of all, when it shines forth in action, when ye exercise yourselves in the labour of love. . . . It is not only impossible to conceal true Christianity, but likewise absolutely contrary to the design of the great Author of it.⁶⁸

---

64. As quoted by Wesley, *Works* (Jackson), IX:502ff.
65. *Works* (Bicentennial), 25:487.
66. *Journal*, 1:420.
67. *Works*, Sermon 24, 1:543–44.
68. *Ibid.*, 1:533, 539.

When he calls Christianity a social religion, Wesley is of course not using the term in the full-blown, twentieth-century sense of the social gospel—that is, the application of the Christian message to social, political, and economic institutions and the structures of corporate life; he is arguing in his own eighteenth-century context, in opposition to Law and the quietists, whose views had infected the Methodist movement.

And he attacks those who "have advised us 'to cease from all outward action;' wholly to withdraw from the world; to leave the body behind us; to abstract ourselves from all sensible things."[69]

Wesley's differences with the mystics provide intriguing parallels to Marx's critique of Ludwig Feuerbach, parallels that reinforce my basic contention that the anthropology implicit in Marx's doctrine of alienated labor can provide a helpful perspective—in spite of the seeming contradictions—from which to view the anthropology implied in Wesley's doctrine of sanctification.

Feuerbach's critique of the alienating nature of religion provided the basic model, which Marx then applied to the alienation of labor; and Marx remained indebted to his fellow left-wing Hegelian for this insight. Feuerbach is essentially correct, says Marx, in describing religion as an alienating process in which humans reify their inner life by projecting it onto a cosmic screen, from whence it is reflected as an alien and oppressive judgment upon their existence. According to Feuerbach,

> Religion . . . is abstraction from the world; it is essentially inward. The religious man leads a life withdrawn from the world, hidden in God, still, void of worldly joy . . . But he thus separates himself only because God is a being separate from the world, an extra and supramundane being. . . . God, as an extramundane being, is however nothing else than nature of man withdrawn from the world and concentrated in itself, freed from all worldly ties and entanglements, transporting itself above the world and positing itself in this condition as a real objective being. . . . Religion is the disuniting of man from himself; he sets God before him as the antithesis of himself. God is not what man is—man is not what God is. . . . God is the absolutely positive, the sum of all realities; man the absolutely negative, comprehending all negations. . . . To enrich God, man must become poor; that God may be all, man must be nothing.[70]

---

69. *Ibid.*, 1:532.
70. Ludwig Feuerbach, *The Essence of Christianity*, Foreword by H. Richard Niebuhr

While agreeing with Feuerbach's analysis of religion as alienating, in his "Theses on Feuerbach," Marx claims that Feuerbach stops short of dealing with the real issue—Why do human beings engage in such self-deprecating projection?—because Feuerbach remains captive to his own kind of mysticism, even though he claims to be a materialist.

> [Feuerbach's] work consists in the dissolution of the religious world into its secular [substructure]. He overlooks the fact that after this work is completed the chief thing still remains to be done. For the fact that the secular foundation detaches itself from itself and establishes itself in the clouds as an independent realm is really only to be explained by the self-cleavage and self-contradictoriness of this secular basis. The latter must itself, therefore, first be understood in its contradiction, and then revolutionized in practice by the removal of the contradiction.[71]

Marx claims that Feuerbach, in spite of his avowed materialism, sees the contradictions primarily as wrong ideas in the mind. His materialism is still an idea, a system of thought, not praxis. The correct view of things will supposedly free human beings from the wrong notions that constitute their bondage. Feuerbach is still operating from a mentalism that does not realize that it is because humans are caught in economic deprivation that they engage in flights of fantasy and construct supernatural worlds of perfection, nor does he understand that a change in mental attitude is not enough. These material circumstances must be changed before alienation can be overcome effectively. The solution is to be found, therefore, at the level of *work*, not simply in the "contemplation" of material conditions (Theses 1, 5, and 9). Though an atheist, Feuerbach is still operating in an essentially pietistic framework. He has transposed the alienation from heaven to earth in order to "understand" it. But, as Marx adds in his familiar eleventh thesis, understanding and interpretation are insufficient. "The philosophers have only *interpreted* the world, in various ways; the point, however, is to *change* it." What is missing in Feuerbach is *praxis*, and without praxis, theory remains theory and never becomes incarnate; knowledge without practice is deficient and is not yet genuine knowledge. Genuine knowledge must

---

and Introduction by Karl Barth (New York: Harper & Brothers, 1957), 66, 33, 26.

71. Karl Marx and Friedrich Engels, *On Religion*, introduced by Reinhold Niebuhr (New York: Schocken Books, 1964), 69–72.

include human activity to change circumstances and therefore "can be conceived and rationally understood only as *revolutionizing practice*" (Thesis 3).[72]

I am suggesting that an important way to grasp what is involved in Wesley's doctrine of sanctification is to see it as "revolutionizing practice," which refuses to "abstract [itself] from all sensible things," but understands divine salvation to be working itself out in the relationships of this world. This is not to deny the deep divide between Wesley on one side, and Feuerbach and Marx on the other. But, given the fundamental differences, the fascinating parallels cannot be denied either. Like Feuerbach, Wesley accuses the Moravian quietists of projecting the work of God away from this world and into a doctrinal heaven, where it is abstracted from the "sensible world" and society—the very objects to be saved. But, like Marx, Wesley is not content with a description of an error in thinking; his concern is for actual transformation. Righteousness is not merely imputed; it is imparted in such a way as to bring about not only "a relative, but a real change" in the human condition.

Wesley was not unaware of the functions of ideology and the relations of theory to praxis. His impatience with the fine points of doctrinal dispute and his usual tolerance toward those with whom he had doctrinal differences "which do not reach to the marrow of Christian truth," was not because he was indifferent to the substance of doctrine, but because he knew that the substance can never be contained adequately in finite words, which are only the representation of the reality; the substance must be worked out in practice.[73] Therefore it was to the practice that he looked for the indication of adequacy of belief. Where he saw deficient practice—in the followers of Jacob Boehme, or in some of the Moravians, or in the antinomians within his own movement—his immediate concern was the doctrinal understanding that lay behind this deficiency. He would have found congenial the liberationist insistence that *orthopraxis* is a more reliable clue to faith than is *orthodoxy*.[74]

---

72. Ibid., 70.

73. Albert Outler, *John Wesley*, 28.

74. Cf. *Works*, 9, 513f. Wesley was also aware of the human tendency to project, and the inadequacy of those projections, e.g. Peter Brown's comments in Wesley's *Natural Philosophy*, "The multiplying and enlarging our own perfections in number or degree only, to the utmost stretch of our capacity, and attributing them so enlarged to God, is no more than raising up an unwieldy idol of our own imagination, without any foundation in nature" (434). Cf. Míguez Bonino, *Doing Theology in a Revolutionary Situation*, 81.

Wesley not only sides with Marx against Feuerbach's mentalism, he also turns Feuerbach's (and Marx's) notion of religion on its head. The God of Feuerbach absorbs all human labors and virtues into himself in heaven and dries them up on earth. According to Wesley, the reverse is the case: God pours himself into the world to renew the creature after God's image and the creation after God's will. The "design of the great Author" is that love "shine forth in action" until all things in the created order are restored to their glorious state.

> Suppose now the fulness of time to be come. . . . What a prospect is this! . . . Wars are ceased from the earth . . . no brother rising up against brother; no country or city divided against itself and tearing out its own bowels. . . . Here is no oppression to "make" even "the wise man mad"; no extortion to "grind the face of the poor"; no robbery or wrong; no rapine or injustice; for all are "content with such things as they possess." Thus "righteousness and peace have kissed each other"; . . . And with righteousness, or justice, mercy is also found. . . . And being filled with peace and joy in believing, and united in one body, by one Spirit, they all love as brethren, they are all of one heart, and of one soul. "Neither saith any of them, that aught of the things which he possesseth is his own." There is none among them that lacketh; for every man loveth his neighbour as himself.[75]

Hence, in contrast with the present order of things, Wesley envisions a society of economic justice, where, in striking anticipation of the Marxist formula, they "cannot suffer one among them to lack anything, but continually give to every man as he hath need."[76] Religion is not to be viewed, therefore, as alienated humanity's means of escape to a more tolerable, heavenly realm, but as participation in God's own redemptive enterprise, transforming alienated servants into liberated sons and daughters, whose works are at one and the same time the expression of their own life in the Spirit and the sign of the new age of justice and love that is to come.

This grand vision of the renewal of creation is the context within which Wesley's doctrine of Christian perfection, culminating in entire sanctification, must be understood. Unfortunately Wesley himself was responsible for much of the confusion surrounding this doctrine. His

---

75. *Works*, Sermon 4, 1:170f.
76. Ibid., 173.

definitive statement, "A Plain Account of Christian Perfection," is not a closely reasoned, comprehensive presentation, but a series of polemical, largely defensive arguments, assembled over many years in reply to attacks and published under one cover, in which Wesley spends most of his time attempting to convince his readers of the plausibility of perfection in this life.[77] To do so, he is forced to hedge "perfection" with casuistic distinctions, carefully calculated to claim neither too little nor too much. Too often in the past, sanctification has been considered only within the parameters of "A Plain Account." As a result the doctrine has not been seen in the context of Wesley's larger scheme of the divine renewal of fallen creatures and creation, with entire sanctification (which Wesley espoused because it seemed to be a scriptural promise and because he believed he had seen empirical evidence of it in the lives of others, though he never claimed it for himself) as an eschatological sign, a kind of first fruits of the age that is to come and an indication of what God through his Spirit can do in the world, "working among us that which is pleasing in his sight" (Heb 13:21).

Therefore, without denying Wesley's interest in the individual—which after all was the bright new discovery of Pietism and the Enlightenment in the eighteenth century—much of the foregoing would appear to argue against the common notion that Wesley's doctrine of sanctification is culture-bound to individualism and to his own time. This is not to say that Methodists have not interpreted it as such. What this chapter seeks to demonstrate, however, is that when Wesley is approached from the vantage point of liberation theologies, and especially from the perspective of the Marxist critique, his theology not only can be freed from the confines of pietistic individualism, it can counteract that individualism and offer resources for the responsible rethinking of theology in a time when both neo-Reformation and liberal models no longer suffice. Like Marx, Wesley reminds us that a theory must lead to a new praxis. Only a theology that is transformationist can do justice to the Christian doctrine of sanctification and to the quality of salvation which that doctrine seeks to express.

---

77. *Works* (Jackson), XI:366–446.

www.ingramcontent.com/pod-product-compliance
Lightning Source LLC
Chambersburg PA
CBHW051105230426
43667CB00013B/2448